THE STRUGGLE FOR THE ASHES II

The History of Anglo-Australian Test Matches

BY ROBERT GATE

ISBN 0 9511190 5 2

PUBLISHED BY
RE Gate
Mount Pleasant Cottage
Ripponden Bank
Ripponden
Sowerby Bridge
Yorkshire
HX6 4JL

Printed by Thornton & Pearson (Printers) Ltd., Bradford.
Typesetting by AJ Typesetting, Morley, Leeds.

ACKNOWLEDGEMENTS

Many people have provided valuable help in the compilation of "The Struggle For The Ashes II".

I am particularly grateful to Raymond Fletcher and Stuart Smith. Raymond has cast his expert eye over the statistical content and in so doing prevented a number of errors from appearing in print. His eye for detail is amazingly acute. Stuart was responsible for the striking artwork on the covers. Anyone wishing to commission Rugby League paintings would be well advised to make a bee-line for him before he becomes too famous!

The illustrative material has been culled from a variety of sources. Sometimes the exact origin of illustrations cannot be verified and if any copyrights have been infringed there has been no deliberate intent to do so. Special thanks go to the following for the provision of photographic and illustrative items: Andy Cole, Sam Coulter, Andrew Cudbertson, Charles Gate, Bob Holroyd, Les Hoole, David Howes, Andy Howard, Michael Inman, Curtis Johnstone, Sig Kasatkin and the *Rugby Leaguer* plus all those unknown photographers whose images have survived the ravages of time to grace this volume.

Thanks also are due to four Australian enthusiasts whose endeavours and favours down the years have been invaluable - Ian Collis, David Middleton, Michael Waring and John Wilkinson.

Finally I must express my appreciation of my wife, Myfanwy's, forbearance as the house becomes increasingly cluttered with piles of old photographs, crumbling newspaper clippings and unsold books. Ten years ago I dedicated the original "The Struggle For The Ashes" to her. All I can say is it doesn't seem anything like that length of time. Myfanwy must therefore be living proof of the expression that "time flies when you are enjoying yourself"!

NOTES ON THE TEXT

Although the terms Australia and Great Britain are used throughout the text for the sake of simplicity and consistency, it should be remembered that they did not always apply. Until the 1924 series the term Australasia was often used as New Zealanders found places in test teams and touring parties. Whilst Australia had found its proper title by 1924, Great Britain were not styled such until the 1948-49 home series, having first taken the title for the 1947 series against New Zealand. Previously they had been known as The Northern Union or simply as England, a usage which Australians still seem unwilling to discard notwithstanding the presence of Welshmen and Scots since the earliest tests.

In the strictest sense Australia should only be styled Kangaroos whilst on tour and Great Britain are properly only Lions whilst Down Under. Again, for the sake of simplicity, these conventions have occasionally been ignored in the text.

Where a player's name is accompanied by a (†) sign, it signifies that the player in question was making his test debut - not necessarily, however, in an Ashes test.

Readers may notice that distances throughout are recorded in yards rather than metres. This is because the author has been stricken by "Old Farts' Syndrome" but, fortunately, can live with it.

BACK TO THE FUTURE - ASHES OR FUNERAL PYRES?

Rugby League in the mid-1990s has become a maelstrom, a creature of chaos seething with anger, mistrust and confusion. The values which underpinned the game appear to have been swept away in a tidal wave of greed, self-interest and naked ambition.

Once upon a time fans talked about who they would be playing against next week, what a wally the referee was last week and wasn't it about time the directors and coach could see that what was needed to get their team moving up the table was a ball-playing forward and a bit of zip at half-back? Nowadays their conversations tend to be about sporting politics, media magnates, administrators who want to be more high-profile than the players and player contracts which beggar belief.

A great many people who have loved and supported the game have abandoned it in anger, grief or sheer bewilderment. The power brokers will shed no tears over such losses. They are actively seeking what they call "a new audience". They may or may not get it. Even if they do not get it their propaganda machine will claim that they have, for telling the big lie has become the stock-in-trade of the League media. "Be positive" has become the clarion call and forget what is really happening. The fact that the Rugby League trade press's letters pages are continually filled with anguished pleas for "justice" within the game does not cut any ice with the progressives who dictate official policy. The writers are dismissed as whingers or, even worse, traditionalists which has suddenly become a term of abuse encompassing anyone who does not share the new, seemingly compulsory, "vision".

In Australia hundreds of professional Rugby League players apparently experienced a communal vision around March-April 1995. They were all filled with a religious zeal for a new world order which was called Super League. The megabucks which the new order offered them had, of course, nothing to do with their embracing the holy vision. Verily they had seen the light. The big, bad Australian Rugby League (ARL) had never given them anything - if you ignore, that is, the fame and fortune they enjoyed purely as a result of being ARL players. It is hard to believe that zealots like the Super League visionaries would not tomorrow willingly embrace a different, even greater, vision if there happened to be a few more zeros in it.

The British Rugby League press has always been a bit of a pussy-cat. In many ways its relationship with the game has been cosy. Friction really had no place. There was usually nothing much to get worked up about, anyway. All that should have changed in the Spring of 1995. In some respects it did. For a couple of months all hell was let loose as Super League blundered and blustered about alienating a large proportion of the people it should have been wooing. The mergers fiasco should have been enough to force the principals involved to resign but they were too brass-faced to take the honourable path. To misquote that Rugby League icon, Tina Turner, *What's morality got to do with it?*

The Super Leaguers were, however, not brass-faced enough to reveal their true agenda which was clearly deemed to be too unpalatable to foist even onto all those silly old traditionalists. If they had had the guts to say what they really meant to do, they would have at least merited some respect for honesty as they contemplated selling useless parts of the League community down the river. What they should have been honest and bold enough to say was that their sainted vision involved big clubs playing in big stadia in big cities. When, seven months after the balloon went up, Maurice Lindsay said, on Radio Leeds on 6 November, 1995 at 1.08 pm, *You don't deny clubs like Featherstone Rovers, Keighley, Widnes, Salford (sic) and Hull Kingston Rovers the opportunity to play in Super League,* the cat was clearly still in the bag. The Super Leaguers should have said from the outset, *Thank you, Featherstone Rovers, Keighley, Widnes, Salford (sic), Hull KR and all you other piddling communities for serving the game so well for so long. Unfortunately, you don't fit the vision and you are therefore going to be the sacrifice necessary to get Super League to the very top of the sporting firmament. Thank you and good-bye.*

The merger furore and the prospect of satellite TV taking over sport in general occupied the Rugby League press for a while but the British Rugby League public were never properly appraised of what had actually transpired where it really mattered - in Australia. In some ways this was understandable. At the best of times British Rugby League pressmen on the nationals have enough trouble obtaining space for match reports and run-of-the-mill League news. Even those who are clued up enough or sufficiently interested in events on a wider scale would find it virtually impossible to screw space out of editors for whom Rugby League is at the bottom of their priorities. Even now it is unlikely that the vast majority British Rugby League fans have the faintest idea as to how the whole sorry Super League mess came about. The press, assisted, of course, by the power brokers, has failed to educate its readership as to the real issues involved.

Unless Rugby League followers had access to independent Australian newspapers they would not know about the conspiratorial nature of the campaign to dismantle the ARL, to discredit the new 20 team tournament launched in 1995, to take over control of the game itself. They have certainly not read the horrendously damning indictments of the individuals involved handed down by Justice Burchett. They have not been allowed to judge the facts for themselves as the British Rugby League press, with an honourable exception or two, has been unable or unwilling to deliver the messages. Sadly, personal experience has proved to the author that censorship is alive and thriving in the game.

The Super League war has claimed many casualties - old-fashioned, out-dated concepts such as truth, integrity, loyalty, tradition and democracy, to name but a few. There will doubtless be more before peace finally breaks out. One of the major casualties has been the Ashes series. As this is being written Great Britain are preparing for a tour Down-Under but with no Ashes series in the offing. Those involved will no doubt be upbeat about the enterprise but they will be unable to mask the fact that a tour Down-Under without an Ashes series can never be more than second-best. The unvarnished truth about international Rugby League, certainly as far as Britons are concerned, is that tests between Great Britain and Australia transcend everything else in the universe.

Moreover, until a rapprochement is made between the ARL and the Rugby Football League (or should that be Super League?) there can be no more Ashes tests for only teams picked by the legitimate national ruling bodies can properly be test teams. That is a crucial reason why the ARL should be supported by rational, right-minded Rugby League people. When the Super Leaguers bang on about spreading the game they conveniently omit to admit that they are wantonly trying to steal the ARL's clothes. The Fiji Nines are a poor imitation of the Sydney Sevens, the Oceania Cup (still a phantom as these notes are written) a mere attempt to mimic the long-established Pacific Cup and just who do the Super Leaguers think introduced the game to Fiji, Papua, Tonga, Western Samoa, Tokelau, American Samoa and the Cook Islands? It certainly was not Rupert Murdoch.

The unpalatable truth about significant international expansion in Rugby League is that, if it is to happen, history tells us that it should be left to the Australians. British Rugby League's record in this particular field is lamentable in the extreme. If it had been left to the British Australia, New Zealand and France would never have become League nations. The RFL was not a prime mover in the establishment of the game in any of those countries. BARLA's pioneering tours apart, the professional arm of Rugby League in Britain has failed to produce anything more meaningful in international expansion than a foothold in the former Soviet Union.

The fact that the British Rugby League authorities willingly allowed the British game to be used as the main tool to undermine the ARL has surely been sufficient cause for the ARL to take the measures it did to maintain its integrity and independence. Nothing the ARL has done since the Spring of 1995 can be viewed as unreasonable in the face of what its enemies have tried to do to it. In the circumstances bombs at Red Hall might have been justified. One of the most powerful weapons left to the ARL in the aftermath of the Super League cataclysm was its right to select its own test teams. Without that weapon the war may now have been over. The way the ARL has wielded its most potent weapon has proved just how important the Ashes are as a focal point for international Rugby League.

No one in their right mind believes the Ashes series will not be revived in the fullness of time. The damage that is being done to the game in the meantime, however, is incalculable. Many of us who have grown up with the game are fearful for its future. We have seen the very nature of the game so altered that it begins to resemble something we do not recognise as Rugby League. When the progressives scream that the modern game is better, faster, even sexier it leaves generations of followers cold. They know that a few short years ago the game was better than it is now. When many of those same traditionalists have also been shown in no uncertain terms that their clubs have been earmarked for merging (submerging would be a more accurate expression) it is little wonder that Cumbrians, Heavy Woollenites and folk from the Calder Triangle have left the game in droves.

Rugby League in Great Britain seems to have fallen for its own propaganda which trumpets that it is *the greatest game of all, the man's game for all the family.* It would be nice if it were true. The greatest game of all is demonstrably soccer. Some of us just happen to prefer Rugby League but we are and always will be a minority. Naturally we would like to become a bigger minority but if reality is faced the nature of our game will always militate against massive expansion, in Europe at least. Unfortunately, those in charge of the sport and its clubs seem to believe that Rugby League can operate in a soccer-type environment. League's own arch-rival Rugby Union, with whom our leaders seem to be on such sickeningly amicable terms after a century of shameless victimisation, has also fallen for the same self-deception. Rugby of neither code can hope to rival soccer as a popular sport.

Even with the Murdoch millions pouring into both codes it does not take a financial genius to work out that the sums will not add up. As well as being seen by many as undesirable, full-time professionalism in rugby will undoubtedly prove unsustainable. It would be a fool who would not have taken Mr. Murdoch's £87 million but surely League could have dictated the terms. SKY clearly needed League as much as League needed SKY. It has frequently been said over the past eighteen months that only Rugby League could have made the influx of such a fortune into such a public relations disaster. What have we had for our money so far? Precious little it appears from the vast majority of clubs' bleatings. Such a massive amount of money could have wiped out the entire debts of the RFL's clubs or gone a long way to the creation of a national stadium for the game, something conspicuously absent allowing for the passage of a mere century. Instead all the initial talk was about how many thousands of pounds player X could now command for a new contract and subsequently it seems that paying crazy contracts has remained the priority.

Rugby League's problem and beauty was that it was a game played and administered on a human scale. An old-time director could dip into his own pocket to find a hundred or two or a thousand or two for whatever needed doing. The scale of League's economy is now such that hundreds of thousands or even millions are required. We are in a different ball-park - the ball-park next to soccer's and we are literally out of our league.

There is one new crucial factor in this equation, one reason for trying to play in the wrong ball-park - the lure of Murdoch's millions. It has become the *sine qua non* and there will probably be no turning back. The stakes have become too high. Already it has become clear that a clique of top clubs is hell-bent on making sure that they get a larger and larger slice of any cakes that are going. The game as a whole can go hang. Spectators on the grounds will become secondary to faces in front of television screens. Doubtless when the five-year contract is up, another will follow. That will be the only saving grace - unless, heaven help us, there really is an agenda for a hybrid game.

The power brokers will say what they are providing is progress. They should remember that one man's progress is some other poor sod's perdition. The dissolution of the monasteries seemed like a good idea to Henry VIII. To the monks and nuns of sixteenth century England and Wales it looked like something entirely different. To the land speculators, mineral extractors, vote-grabbing politicians, ambitious military leaders and settlers of nineteenth century America the taming of the West seemed like a mighty fine idea. To the Plains Indians it spelled death and degradation.

At the moment a few over-influential, unyielding power brokers hold the game's future in their hands. They are playing with fire. Let us hope that the only Ashes Rugby League ends up with are those that for three-quarters of a century have represented a celebration of the game at its most sublime level.

Robert Gate
Ripponden
27 August, 1996

Note - The author is acutely aware that by the time this appears in print towards the end of October, 1996 the Super League appeal decision(s) should have been made. The game may at that point have developed a clearer sense of where it is heading.

Great Britain skipper Jonty Parkin displays the Ashes Cup with his 1928 Lions. The trophy was donated by the Sydney City Tattersall's club in 1928 and is still the symbol of Ashes supremacy despite interloping sponsors' attempts to replace it with their company-branded trophies.

SOMEONE ONCE SAID

"These (Ashes) matches are apart from any other games ..... These tests have been, and still are, the life-blood of the Rugby League game. May they always keep up the standard of the past, and may they still continue to cement that happy feeling between England and Australia." Harold Wagstaff, 1937

"The finest attraction sport can offer - a Rugby League test match between Australia and Great Britain with the Ashes hanging in the balance." Rugby League News, 1954

"Of all the great international sporting classics which thrill Australian crowds none has greater appeal than the Rugby League test series between Australia and Great Britain. It has been this way since the (Ashes) series came here way back in 1910. It will always be thus." Rugby League News, 1954

"To represent your country in an England v Australia test match is the greatest honour any League player can achieve." Gus Risman, 1962

"The visit of an English team to Australia is the king-hit of Rugby League. It surpasses in importance all other football." Clive Churchill, 1962

"Rugby League football reaches its highest pitch of skill and excitement in tests between Great Britain and Australia." Gough Whitlam, Prime Minister of Australia, 1974

"Nineteen thousand kilometres separates the test men of Australia and Britain but after an international they can share the mutual satisfaction of having taken part in one of the greatest sporting events of them all." Big League, 1979

"The Ashes - Rugby League's greatest prize and for more than three-quarters of a century the real symbol of world supremacy." Big League, 1984

"If we can beat the British and bring home the (Ashes) Test Trophy again, then I'll hang up my boots a happy man." Mal Meninga, 1994

"Great Britain have always been the traditional enemy and wearing the green and gold against them is the ultimate in Rugby League." Bob Fulton, 1994

"At the end of the day I'm going to be judged as an international coach on my record against Australia ..... so I want to pit myself against the very best, as do our players." Phil Larder, 1996

"I've never agreed with it being called the Ashes, anyway. The Ashes are in cricket." Maurice Lindsay, 1995

"REALLY, OLD MAN — THIS ISN'T CRICKET!"

Sunday Telegraph (Sydney) Souvenir 1946.
Maybe Maurice is right after all.

KANGAROOS, LIONS, TESTS AND ASHES

Every fourth autumn a strange, seemingly natural, phenomenon used to occur. Rather like the annual sighting of the first swallow or the hearing of the first cuckoo, the first indignant letter of the retired Brigadier Blink of Chipping Sodbury or the former Rear-Admiral Blank of Newton Abbot would suddenly appear in *The Times* or *The Daily Telegraph*. Apparently it is a biological imperative of nature that ex-public school, establishment-bound, retired military or naval gentlemen feel bound to take to task some unfortunate Rugby League hack or broadcaster who has had sufficient temerity or bad taste to refer to "tests", "Lions" and "Ashes" in relation to the first clash of a series between Australia and Great Britain.

Blink and Blank are invariably beside themselves with indignation. The thrust of their argument is that Ashes and tests can only relate to cricket and that Rugby Union is the only proper connotation for Lions. They are adamant. How dare those Rugby League types misappropriate the language of their sports?

Oddly enough no one ever queries the use of the term Kangaroos for the Australian test team. Thankfully in 1908-09 at the same time that Dinny Lutge's pioneering Australian Rugby League team was facing the rigours of a terrible winter tour of the Northern Union, their Rugby Union counterparts were also touring England and Wales for the first time. They chose to dub themselves Wallabies and the distinction between them and the Rugby League Kangaroos has been unambiguous ever since.

When it comes to calling the Great Britain Rugby League XIII Lions, however, some Rugby Unionists develop paranoia. According to them, the only true Lions are the British Isles Rugby Union teams which have toured South Africa or Australasia. Union historians generally attribute the official adoption of the title Lions to the 1930 tour of New Zealand and Australia, although unofficially some claim the distinction for the 1924 tourists to South Africa.

Annoyingly Rugby League history is not so clear cut. From the earliest Northern Union tours until the last tour before the Second World War the Australian press invariably referred to British teams as England. For variety they tended to refer to the British as bulldogs or John Bulls. However, when it came to depicting them in cartoons or other artwork, it was almost always as lions mauling or being knocked about by kangaroos that they were portrayed. The Lions tradition in Rugby League is therefore a longstanding one, whatever the pedants believe. Moreover since 1945 there has been in existence a properly constituted Lions Association. Ironically enough the prime mover of the organisation was Harry Sunderland, an Australian to the core. Its inaugural chairman was James Lomas, captain of the 1910 Australasian tourists, whilst its first secretary was Frank Williams, one of the injured parties in the epic Rorke's Drift Test of 1914. Ever since 1945 the committee of The British Rugby League Lions Association has been composed of players and officials who have toured Australasia. The Blinks and Blanks of this world should try telling those men that they cannot call themselves Lions!

The term test or test match was undoubtedly derived from cricket and has been applied in Rugby League from the very first series played - that of 1908 between The Northern Union and New Zealand. In passing it is interesting to recall that the term test match had been used prior to 1908 in relation to Rugby League although there had been no connotation with international rugby. As far back as 1898 Northern Unionists had used the expression to denote a play-off for inclusion in the Lancashire Senior Competition between Morecambe and Barrow played at Lancaster (7 May, 1898). Moreover, the term test match, relating to similar play-offs, went back even further in both Rugby Union and Association Football.

Of course, anyone with even the remotest interest in sport knows that The Ashes originated in cricket and are the symbol of supremacy between Australia and England in that game. It has been thus since 1883 when a group of Australian ladies burnt a stump and presented the ashes to the Hon. Ivo Bligh, later Lord Darnley, the English captain. The urn which contains those ashes resides permanently at Lord's. It must have seemed entirely natural and appropriate, albeit plagiaristic, for the Edwardian rugby authorities, press and spectators to adapt a similar, admittedly mythical, trophy in 1908 when the two nations met in a three match series under the laws of Northern Union Rugby Football. From the very beginning everyone referred to The Ashes as the prize for winning an Anglo-Australian test series. It could hardly be otherwise, for whenever England or Great Britain meet Australia in any sport, from bowls to speedway, symbolically the Ashes are at stake, whatever Blink and Blank may think.

In point of fact Rugby League has had its own Ashes trophy since 1928. It was in that year that the City Tattersall's Club of Sydney presented a gold cup for presentation to the Ashes-winning team. British skipper Jonty Parkin was the first recipient of the trophy. Although the trophy went temporarily missing in the 1930s, until recently it remained the embodiment of the struggle for the Ashes. In an echo of 1883 the President of the New South Wales Rugby Football League, Harry Flegg announced in 1932 that he would make sure the City Tattersall's Ashes Cup would contain some *dinkum Ashes* for he would burn a football for the purpose if Australia lost that season's series against the Mother Country. Australia did lose but whether Mr. Flegg set fire to a ball is not recorded.

Somewhere out there in the blue yonder there is a relic even more venerable than the Ashes Cup. In 1914 following the titanic victory of Harold Wagstaff's John Bulls in the "Rorke's Drift Test", tour manager Joe Houghton cut out a piece of turf from the centre of the Sydney Cricket Ground. It was placed in a neat cut glass case topped by a silver lid and presented to the President of the Northern Union, Mr. JH (Jack) Smith, on the tourists' return to Britain. In 1956 Jack Smith's son was reported to have offered the Rugby Football League the case and its contents to perpetuate his father's memory (*The Liverpool Echo*, 25 August, 1956). Whether his offer was accepted is unknown to the author.

The 1990s saw commercial imperatives undermining the status of the Ashes Cup. In 1990 British Coal presented a beautiful but colossally heavy coal sculpture trophy for competition and subsequent series have produced other sponsored trophies as Ashes prizes. In 1995 at the height of the Super League shambles the British Chief Executive, Maurice Lindsay, was reported to have declared that the Ashes Cup was defunct and that it was not wanted for the new Anglo-Australian Super League series. He was reported to have said, *I've never agreed with it being called the Ashes anyway. The Ashes are in cricket. We'll be quite happy to get another trophy*. (*Rugby League Weekend*, 10 November, 1995). It may have been a throw-away line for a throw-away society but it was doubtless manna to the Blinks and Blanks.

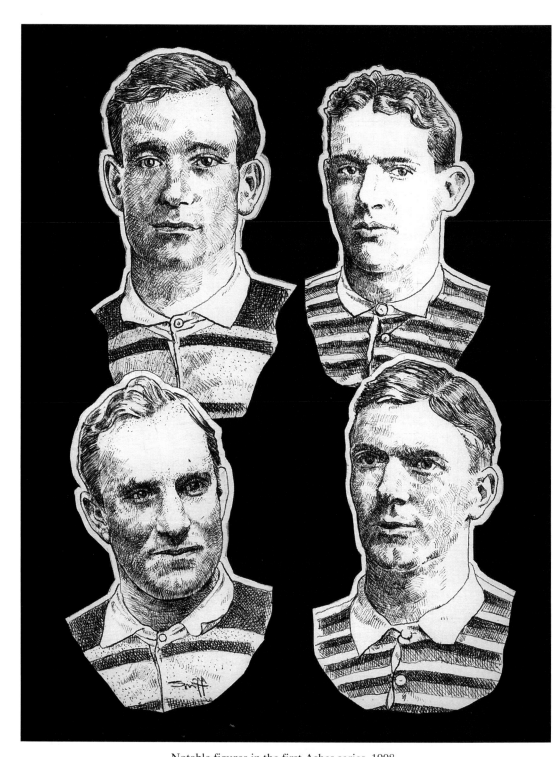

Notable figures in the first Ashes series, 1908.
Top left: Jim Devereux, scorer of the first try hat-trick in Ashes tests.
Top right: Bert Jenkins, captain of Great Britain's first Ashes team.
Bottom left: Dally Messenger, Australia's first captain who also kicked off in the first Ashes test and scored the first Ashes points.
Bottom right: Johnny Thomas, scorer of the first try in Ashes football.

TEST MATCH 1

AT PARK ROYAL, LONDON – 12 December, 1908
GREAT BRITAIN 22 AUSTRALIA 22 (HT 14-5)

†H Gifford (Barrow)	†M Bolewski (East End Natives, Bundaberg)
G Tyson (Oldham) T	†WG Heidke (Bundaberg)
†G Dickenson (Warrington)	†SP Deane (Norths)
TB Jenkins (Wigan) capt	J Devereux (Norths) 3T
W Batten (Hunslet) 2T	HH Messenger (Easts) capt 5G
†E Brooks (Warrington) T,2G	A Halloway (Easts)
J Thomas (Wigan) T	†A Butler (Souths) T
A Robinson (Halifax)	†PB Walsh (Newcastle)
A Smith (Oldham)	†EJ Courtney (Newtown)
†WH Longworth (Oldham)	SC Pearce (Easts)
†W Jukes (Hunslet) T	†A Burdon (Glebe)
†JW Higson (Hunslet)	†J Abercrombie (Wests)
†A Mann (Bradford N)	L O'Malley (Easts)

Referee - JH Smith (Widnes)   Crowd - 2,000   Gate - £70
Scoring - 0-2 3-2 6-2 6-5 11-5 14-5 17-5 17-10 17-15 20-15 20-20 20-22 22-22

Administratively the Northern Union management blundered in taking the first Anglo-Australian test to London. They had obviously been swayed by their success ten months previously when 15,000 curious southerners had attended the second test against New Zealand at Chelsea. Unfortunately, the counter attractions of the Varsity Rugby Union match at Kensington and an important soccer match between Chelsea and Newcastle United kept the crowd down to a paltry 2,000 for this historic occasion. An added disincentive to spectators was the poor transport service to Park Royal, home of Queens Park Rangers.

The game, however, was all for which Northern Union officials had hoped and set a standard which came to be the hallmark of Anglo-Australian encounters. A reporter wrote,

No better sporting match could have been offered for the attraction of the Metropolitan public. It was fast, open and interesting throughout, abounding in points of individual and collective excellence, and fought out on the whole in a good, healthy sporting spirit.

The general feeling was that the British were much the better side and at one stage looked to be coasting home but the Kangaroos, displaying the greater fitness, a sphere in which they have always excelled, and possessing a supreme individualist in Dally Messenger, came back from the dead only to have victory snatched away at the very last gasp.

It was Messenger who kicked off in this first ever test between the game's most deadly rivals and it was the sublime Dally who inevitably put the first points on the board by landing a penalty. Britain, however, began to assume the upper hand and half-back Johnny Thomas snapped up a loose ball before dashing over for the first try which was soon followed by another from Billy Batten after some fine passing. The riposte was a try from Jim Devereux after an equally fine movement. With the home forwards dominant, particularly Mann, Jukes and Smith, the Kangaroos were forced to concede tries to Brooks and Batten before the interval and when Tyson dashed over on the right shortly after the break to make it 17-5, Australia were facing disaster.

As the last quarter approached the Kangaroo reserves of stamina began to tell and within three minutes tries were scored by Devereux and Butler, both converted by Messenger. Britain reasserted themselves and a movement initiated by Harry Gifford, the star turn at full-back, and continued by Jenkins, Brooks and Batten led to the finest try of the match being scored by Jukes.

The last five minutes simply throbbed. Messenger intercepted on his own "25" and shattered the defence before serving Devereux a pass which the centre had to pick off his boots before romping away for the first hat-trick in test football. Dally converted and then proceeded to kick a penalty to put the Aussies into the lead. The British, who hardly deserved to lose, were offered a last minute life-line when a hotly disputed penalty for obstruction was awarded and Ernie Brooks, not a noted kicker and off target most of the game, stepped up to kick the most crucial goal of his career and ensure a fitting end to the first of many epic encounters between these two warring Rugby League nations.

TEST MATCH 2

AT ST. JAMES' PARK, NEWCASTLE – 23 January, 1909
GREAT BRITAIN 15 AUSTRALIA 5 (HT 8-0)

H Gifford (Barrow)	M Bolewski (East End Natives, Bundaberg)
G Tyson (Oldham) T	†D Frawley (Easts)
†J Lomas (Salford) capt T,3G	HH Messenger (Easts) capt T,G
TB Jenkins (Wigan)	†AD Morton (Norths)
W Batten (Hunslet)	AA Rosenfeld (Easts)
E Brooks (Warrington)	†A Conlon (Glebe)
J Thomas (Wigan) T	A Butler (Souths)
†R Silcock (Wigan)	L O'Malley (Easts)
A Robinson (Halifax)	J Abercrombie (Wests)
A Smith (Oldham)	†TJ McCabe (Glebe)
WH Longworth (Oldham)	SC Pearce (Easts)
W Jukes (Hunslet)	PB Walsh (Newcastle)
JW Higson (Hunslet)	EJ Courtney (Newtown)

Referee - WM McCutcheon (Oldham)   Crowd - 22,000   Gate - £568
Scoring - 5-0 8-0 10-0 10-5 13-5 15-5

Australia, lacking Deane, Devereux and Halloway, and faced with Jim Lomas, the Northern Union's antidote to Messenger, spent most of the match on the defensive and by all accounts were fortunate to escape a bigger defeat. Apart from the magnificent Messenger the Kangaroos were desperately short of attacking ideas and were often penalised for obstruction, off-side and feet-up, which just goes to show that things were ever thus!

From a financial and promotional point of view the Northern Union was vindicated in its decision to take the test to another association football ground in virgin territory but the match itself did not measure up to the previous test. There were complaints that the space between the goal and dead-lines was *almost dangerously narrow* and the game, being so far north, ended in darkness.

The first incident of note was a superb tackle by the diminutive Rosenfeld to prevent the barnstorming Batten from crossing. Eventually, however, a barrage by the British resulted in a five yard scrum after Frawley had dragged Batten off the ball as he was about to score. From the set-piece Brooks served Thomas who scooted over without an Aussie finger being laid on him. Lomas kicked the easy goal.

Courtney and O'Malley were impressive in the Australian pack but the nearest the Kangaroos came to scoring was an abortive drop at goal from 50 yards by Messenger. The Australian three-quarters were hard pressed and only last ditch tackles by Rosenfeld on Jenkins and Bolewski on Batten kept the line intact. Two minutes before the break Brooks at last broke the defensive cordon to find the ubiquitous Lomas in support and screaming for the ball. Brooks slung out an atrocious pass but Lomas somehow scooped the ball up and scored in the corner, hitting the post with his attempt to convert.

A Lomas penalty made it 10-0 early in the second half and when McCabe was compelled to retire the Australians were in dire straits. Typically Messenger was the man to raise the siege. Taking the ball around half-way Dally began to dance his way past hypnotised defenders until he found a clear course for the line, whereupon he left everyone in his wake to score a try which brought the house down. His conversion brought the Aussies to within five points of the British. It was to be the Kangaroos' only score, however, for the British forwards took control and began to dribble instead of heel. The culmination of one of these dribbling manoeuvres was a try to winger George Tyson and the *coup de grâce* was delivered shortly afterwards when Lomas smartly landed the first drop-goal in Ashes history.

First blood to Britain!

Some of the first Kangaroos as seen by the cartoonist of *The Athletic News*. Featured in this collage from games against Rochdale Hornets and Warrington are Tedda Courtney, Tom Anderson, Bill Bailey, Dan Frawley, Dally Messenger, Andy Morton and Charlie Hedley.

TEST MATCH 3

AT VILLA PARK, BIRMINGHAM – 15 February, 1909
GREAT BRITAIN 6 AUSTRALIA 5 (HT 3-0)

† FH Young (Leeds)	C Hedley (Glebe)
G Tyson (Oldham) T	D Frawley (Easts) T
J Lomas (Salford) capt	WG Heidke (Bundaberg)
TB Jenkins (Wigan)	J Devereux (Norths) G
W Batten (Hunslet)	M Bolewski (East End Natives, Bundaberg)
E Brooks (Warrington)	SP Deane (Norths)
J Thomas (Wigan) T	† AE Anlezark (North Rivers)
W Jukes (Hunslet)	L O'Malley (Easts)
† R Padbury (Runcorn)	RH Graves (Balmain)
A Smith (Oldham)	A Burdon (Glebe) capt
WH Longworth (Oldham)	SC Pearce (Easts)
A Mann (Bradford N)	EJ Courtney (Newtown)
† F Boylen (Hull)	PB Walsh (Newcastle)

Referee - EH Smirk (Wigan)   Crowd - 9,000   Gate - £227
Scoring - 3-0 3-2 3-5 6-5

Note - Some English sources report that Deane was captain of the Australian team. Australian sources attribute the captaincy to Burdon.

In taking the deciding test to a "soccer city" in the Midlands on a Monday afternoon in the deepest English winter, the Northern Union were nothing if not optimists. *The Yorkshire Post* commented that *the measures taken to bring the event to the notice of the Birmingham public appeared to be lacking in efficiency, yet the attendance was good.* Fortunately the weather held fine but a heavy, greasy pitch militated against open rugby. Sadly for the tourists Messenger was ruled out injured and the feeling was that had he played the Kangaroos would have tied the series for his goal-kicking alone would have won the test.

The Yorkshire Post reported that *to the majority present the Northern Union game was novel. No such form of football had been played in Birmingham before, and the genuine Rugby game (i.e. Rugby Union) has in the city but a limited constituency. Much of the play obviously created amusement, for Socker followers cannot understand why players should be brought down bodily when making quick tracks for goal.*

Whilst it was not an outstanding game much was made of the tremendous tackling of both sides. As has become the test tradition no quarter was asked nor given yet there was no undue roughness. The catching and kicking of the backs was exemplary but the passing left something to be desired whilst it was reported that the Northern Union forwards were good to a man with Frank "Patsy" Boylen the most conspicuous. Boylen was the first ex-England Rugby Union cap to earn test status in the new code. The Australian pack lost nothing in comparison with Alec Burdon, the *cause célèbre* of the code Down Under, and "Jersey" O'Malley being the pick. The Kangaroos were decidedly unlucky to have a try disallowed early on from a forward rush and *O'Malley might have gone through had he not shown the usual Colonial weakness of looking round for someone to pass to,* wrote one critic.

The only score of the first half came after 25 minutes when Brooks broke through the Australian defence at half-way, took Hedley's tackle and put his half-back partner Thomas under the posts. Lomas surprised everyone by fluffing the kick.

In the second half the Kangaroos gained the upper hand and, after Devereux had landed a penalty following Bert Jenkins' off-side, they took the lead when a poor kick by full-back Frank Young let in the speedy Frawley for an unconverted try. Clinging desperately to a 5-3 lead, the Australians suffered injuries to Deane and Heidke and finally buckled when Brooks, Thomas and Lomas combined to send Tyson over for a late match-winning try to secure the Ashes for the representatives of the Northern Union.

For the first time British players were awarded caps as well as jerseys.

By the time the series was decided the tourists had been in Britain for six months and injuries had ravaged the party. A load of 45 matches had taken a heavy toll, for of the 34 tourists fourteen played in fewer than ten games whilst the tour captain Dinny Lutge was restricted to a mere five appearances and missed all the tests.

TEST MATCH 4

AT THE ROYAL AGRICULTURAL SHOWGROUND, SYDNEY – 18 June, 1910
AUSTRALIA 20 GREAT BRITAIN 27 (HT 12-11)

† CJ Russell (Newtown)	† J Sharrock (Wigan)
C Woodhead (Norths, Brisbane) T	J Leytham (Wigan) 2T
† JJ Hickey (Glebe) T	TB Jenkins (Wigan)
HH Messenger (Easts) capt T,4G	J Lomas (Salford) capt 3G
A Broomham (Norths)	W Batten (Hunslet) T
† W Farnsworth (Newtown)	J Thomas (Wigan) T
† CH McKivat (Glebe)	† TH Newbould (Wakefield T)
WS Noble (Newtown)	† AE Avery (Oldham)
† JT Barnett (Newtown) T	† R Ramsdale (Wigan)
† C Sullivan (Norths)	† E Curzon (Salford)
† W Spence (Souths)	W Jukes (Hunslet) 3T
† RR Craig (Balmain)	† F Webster (Leeds)
EJ Courtney (Norths)	† W Ward (Leeds)

Referee - T McMahon (NSW)   Crowd - 42,000   Gate - £1,550

Scoring - 5-0 5-3 7-3 12-3 12-8 12-11 12-14 12-19 12-24 12-27 17-27 20-27

Note - Some sources give the British goal-scorers as Leytham, Lomas and Thomas.

The first Ashes test in Australia provided a game worthy of the occasion. The largest crowd yet to assemble at a Northern Union match in either hemisphere was treated to *a perfect exhibition of Northern Union rules, brilliant combination, beautiful dribbling, judicious kicking and hard tackling.* The game in Australia never looked back after Lomas and his Lions, like Caesar and his legions, came, saw and conquered.

Before the match the two greatest men of their nations, Dally Messenger and James Lomas, took part in a goal-kicking contest in which the Australian champion bowed to the British. If it was to be an omen for the serious contest it proved to be a false one, at least in the initial stages, for it was Australia, well marshalled by two of her finest half-backs, both making their test debuts, who set the pace. Chris McKivat and Billy Farnsworth set the standards by which all subsequent Australian half-backs have been judged.

Australia took the lead when Farnsworth thwarted Johnny Thomas' attempt to kick clear, raced away and put "Darb" Hickey over for Messenger to convert. The British won a succession of scrums and after considerable pressure the Lions' forwards dribbled 50 yards for Leytham to score an unimproved try. Messenger replied with a penalty before Jim Sharrock was stretchered off and Bert Avery was compelled to fill in at full-back. Worse followed for the Lions as Farnsworth, McKivat and Craig engineered a try for Messenger which he converted himself. Down to twelve men and 12-3 in arrears, Britain's response was immediate. From a scrum Newbould served Thomas who shot over for a try, completely flat-footing the Australians. Lomas' conversion made it 8-12 and on the stroke of half-time a dazzling bout of passing ended in Jim Leytham taking Broomham and Russell limpet-like over the line as he touched down.

The second half was still young when amazingly the Lions took the lead. Seven men handled before Billy Jukes snapped a try from the ruck. A reporter wrote, *the game was now wonderfully vigorous and the crowd in one continuous roar of excitement.* Sharrock, though heavily concussed, returned to the fray in time to see a great forward rush scatter the Kangaroos. The home "25" was reached, Ward gathered the ball and Jukes forced his way over for Lomas to convert. The great Dally then made a magical mystery tour through the British ranks but his pass went astray. Newbould gathered and released Batten who sped from one "25" to the other and there was Jukes racing away like a thoroughbred for the first hat-trick by a forward in Ashes conflict. Lomas goaled. Ramsdale and the omnipresent Jukes then led another dribble before Lomas picked up, shrugged off several defenders and sent Batten dashing to the line to give Britain a commanding 27-12 lead, the Lions having scored the last 24 points.

With ten minutes to go Lomas just failed to score on one wing before Australia took the ball to the other for McKivat to scamper to the Lions' "25". "Towser" Barnett supported and raced off "like a draught horse" to the posts. Messenger added the goal before embarking on a brilliant dash to the "25" where all the three-quarters handled to enable Woodhead to record the final points of a momentous test.

THE FIRST LIONS, 1910
Back: Helm, Ruddick, Shugars, Ramsdale, Curzon, Leytham, Winstanley.
Standing: Boylen, Thomas, Kershaw, Smith, Lomas (capt), Newbould, Jukes, Bartholomew, Ward.
Seated: Dell (visitor), Webster, Batten, B Jenkins, Houghton (manager), Clifford (manager), Avery, Riley, Davies, Murray (trainer).
Front: Sharrock, Young, T Jenkins, Farrar

TEST MATCH 5

AT THE EXHIBITION GROUND, BRISBANE – 2 July, 1910
AUSTRALIA 17 GREAT BRITAIN 22 (HT 11-10)

D McGregor (Bundaberg)	J Sharrock (Wigan)
C Woodhead (Norths, Brisbane)	J Leytham (Wigan) 4T
JJ Hickey (Glebe) G	† JG Riley (Halifax)
HH Messenger (Easts) T	J Lomas (Salford) capt 2G
WG Heidke (Bundaberg) capt	W Batten (Hunslet)
W Farnsworth (Newtown)	J Thomas (Wigan) T
CH McKivat (Glebe) T	† F Smith (Hunslet)
R Tubman (Ipswich) T	F Webster (Leeds)
H Brackenreg (Norths, Brisbane)	† W Winstanley (Leigh)
JT Barnett (Newtown) T	† H Kershaw (Wakefield T) T
† E Buckley (Valleys, Brisbane)	R Ramsdale (Wigan)
H Nicholson (Souths, Brisbane)	W Jukes (Hunslet)
RR Craig (Balmain) T	G Ruddick (Broughton R)

Referee - J Fihelly (Queensland)   Crowd - 18,000   Gate - £650
Scoring - 3-0 6-0 11-0 11-5 11-10 11-13 11-16 11-19 11-22 14-22 17-22

Great Britain retained the Ashes after a game which seemed lost on the quarter-hour, when Australia led by eleven clear points, was turned on its head by a Herculean forward effort which left the blue and maroons nonplussed - Australia did not adopt the green and gold until 1928. Scoring 22 points in the second and third quarters without reply, the British pack - well over a stone per man heavier than their opponents - established a stranglehold which Australia could not break until too late into the game. Behind such a dominant pack the British halves, Johnny Thomas and Fred Smith, had a field day whilst "Gentleman Jim" Leytham, a winger of rare pace and resource, helped himself to four tries, a record yet to be equalled in Ashes tests.

Australia began at a cracking pace. Messenger, full of cheek born of confidence, dropped at goal from just inside his own half with only seconds of the game gone but the ball passed narrowly wide. Three minutes had elapsed when a scrum went down on the Lions' "25". McKivat had the ball quickly away to Farnsworth who sent Woodhead surging for the flag. On being nailed the winger turned the ball inside to Barnett who opened the scoring. Messenger failed with the kick but it was all Australia and within four minutes Dally was seen streaking for a try at the corner after Lomas had failed to gather a pass as Britain raided. On the quarter-hour Australia extended their lead to 11-0 when Farnsworth made a dash from the ruck to send McKivat under the bar for Hickey to land a simple conversion.

Play was fast and open and despite Australia's whirlwind start it was noticeable that their forwards were beginning to wilt. It was Lomas who initiated the recovery for Britain when he made a buffalo-like charge to send Leytham over. Lomas goaled and with the pack constantly winning possession Australia had no answer when Thomas zipped through and exchanged passes with Webster before touching down to maintain a remarkable sequence of scoring a try in each of the five Ashes tests so far played. Lomas' goal brought Britain to within a point of the lead as the sides turned round.

Messenger made one of his labyrinthine runs to beat half-a-dozen defenders but hurt himself after kicking ahead and crashing into Ramsdale. Whilst he was being attended to Britain took the lead for the first time as Thomas created a try for Kershaw. When Messenger returned to the fray the correspondent of *The Referee* remarked laconically that *the Master was without dash*. Johnny Thomas was certainly not without dash for a break down the blind-side soon had Leytham sprinting away for another try. The referee, Jack Fihelly, a 1908 Kangaroo, ruled that Thomas' conversion missed but the Lions pointed out that one of the "goal umpires" had raised his flag, whereupon they were penalised for wasting time. Shortly afterwards he disallowed a British try and to cap everything sent off George Ruddick for allegedly striking Hickey. The dismissal, unwarranted as the referee later admitted, seemed to spur Britain to greater efforts as Leytham raced over for two more tries after text-book bouts of passing. During the last fifteen minutes the depleted Lions felt the pressure and conceded tries to Craig and Tubman but with both Messenger and Brackenreg missing the conversions their advantage was not seriously threatened.

TEST MATCH 6

AT ST. JAMES' PARK, NEWCASTLE – 8 November, 1911
GREAT BRITAIN 10 AUSTRALIA 19 (HT 7-19)

J Sharrock (Wigan)	† C Fraser (Balmain)
† J Miller (Wigan)	A Broomham (Norths)
† H Wagstaff (Huddersfield)	† H Gilbert (Souths)
TB Jenkins (Wigan)	† H Hallett (Souths) T
† WT Davies (Halifax) 2T	CJ Russell (Newtown)
J Thomas (Wigan) capt 2G	† V Farnsworth (Newtown) 2T
F Smith (Hunslet)	CH McKivat (Glebe) capt
† F Harrison (Leeds)	† ARH Francis (NZ) T,2G
† O Burgham (Halifax)	† PA McCue (Newtown)
JL Clampitt (Broughton R)	WA Cann (Souths) T
† B Gronow (Huddersfield)	EJ Courtney (Wests)
W Winstanley (Wigan)	† R Williams (Easts)
AE Avery (Oldham)	RR Craig (Balmain)

Referee - B Ennion (Wigan)   Crowd - 6,500   Gate - £338

Scoring - 5-0 5-3 7-3 7-6 7-11 7-16 7-19 10-19

At last! Victory over the mother country in a test! After five unsuccessful attempts Australia had triumphed. Led by ex-Wallaby Chris McKivat, the Kangaroos ran out emphatic winners having reduced the British defence to tatters before the interval. In the run-up to the test series the Kangaroos had looked likely winners in losing only once in thirteen matches during which 59 tries were scored and only 22 conceded.

On both sides there were notable test debutants. The British fielded for the first time Harold Wagstaff, the "Prince of Centres", who was to be such a thorn in the Aussies' side in years to come but not on this occasion. His Fartown team-mate, the mighty Ben Gronow was also appearing in his first test and would in later years give Australia plenty to rue. Bert Gilbert, soon to become an idol at Hull, Howard Hallett, Chook Fraser and Viv Farnsworth made happier starts to great test careers than the Huddersfield pair, however.

Early indications were that the British would succeed for after only five minutes their half-backs opened out play and fine passing amongst the three-quarters led to a stunning try to Will Davies at the corner. Thomas added a superb conversion but soon afterwards was taken from the field badly shaken although he did return to the fray later. The Kangaroos struck back when a smart piece of play by "Bolla" Francis, a former All Black, led to a try by Farnsworth. No conversion was forthcoming and when Thomas kicked a penalty for the home team to make it 7-3 Australia looked far from confident.

The final fifteen minutes of the half, however, saw the crucial phase of the match and it was the Australians who established complete dominance. With their forwards ruling the tight play the Australian halves and centres were able to paralyse the home middle backs and four tries were plundered in quick succession to put the issue beyond doubt. First McKivat sparked a move involving Farnsworth and Craig to put Francis over. Then Wagstaff uncharacteristically lost the ball in a tackle for Hallett to swoop in and release Farnsworth for his second try, converted by Francis. Up 11-7, the Kangaroos pressed hard and Francis gained possession, ignored the defence and sent Cann over for a try which the New Zealander converted. A final try by Hallett on the stroke of half-time gave Australia an irretrievable 19-7 cushion.

The second half saw Britain tighten their game and for half an hour there was no real threat to either line. Then the Kangaroos faltered and the British halves managed to find a little space for Davies on the wing. The Welshman was dumped into touch-in-goal but not before he had registered his sixth touchdown in three representative games against the tourists. It was the only score of the second period.

There was no doubting the merit of Australia's triumph for they were the better team in all respects and the home press was scathing in its treatment of Britain. The forwards were said to *have lost all notion of effective tackling* but the backs were even poorer with one critic reporting that *worse defensive tactics than those at half-back and at centre-three-quarter have rarely been seen in representative football.*

TEST MATCH 7

AT TYNECASTLE PARK, EDINBURGH – 16 December, 1911
GREAT BRITAIN 11 AUSTRALIA 11 (HT 11-3)

† AE Wood (Oldham) G	H Hallett (Souths)
† A Jenkinson (Hunslet)	CJ Russell (Newtown) T
H Wagstaff (Huddersfield) 2T	V Farnsworth (Newtown)
J Lomas (Oldham) capt T	H Gilbert (Souths)
W Batten (Hunslet)	D Frawley (Easts) T
† J Davies (Huddersfield)	W Farnsworth (Newtown)
F Smith (Hunslet)	CH McKivat (Glebe) capt T
R Ramsdale (Wigan)	ARH Francis (NZ) G
W Winstanley (Wigan)	PA McCue (Newtown)
B Gronow (Huddersfield)	WA Cann (Souths)
† D Clark (Huddersfield)	EJ Courtney (Wests)
† T Woods (Rochdale H)	WS Noble (Newtown)
F Harrison (Leeds)	RR Craig (Balmain)

Referee - F Renton (Hunslet)   Crowd - 6,000   Gate - £336
Scoring - 3-0 3-3 6-3 11-3 11-8 11-11

Just how keen the rivalry between the two great sporting nations had already become was clearly echoed by the correspondent of *The Yorkshire Post* who opined, *in comparison with success in the tests, even gate money is a secondary consideration.* That was just as well for the Northern Union's persistence in playing tests on soccer grounds beyond the game's northern confines was certainly not economically viable even if the evangelising aspect was meritorious.

That the Scots enjoyed the match was clear as one contemporary account related, *the match was well received by the majority of those who saw it, and we know that eminent Ruggerites in Edinburgh passed compliments alike upon the game and the spirit in which it is played.*

After only three minutes Britain hit the lead when Wagstaff capitalised on fielding errors by Billy Farnsworth and Hallett but Wood's conversion failed. Undismayed, Australia were level two minutes later as Billy Farnsworth shot away up the left flank with the ball at his feet. Frantic British covering was of no avail as Dan Frawley, one of the fastest players of his generation, supported Farnsworth to streak away for the try.

Gradually Britain began to wear down their opponents who were forced to employ off-side and spotting tactics to negate the clever home backs. The British pack was well on top and the Australians were constantly being forced into passing erratically and from one such wild pass Batten was able to start a movement which led to Davies creating a try for Lomas. As the panic spread through the Kangaroos Hallett miscalculated his covering of a kick to touch and before he realised what was afoot Wagstaff was in possession to trot unhindered to the posts. Wood converted. Remarkably, the two tries Wagstaff recorded were the only scores he made in his entire test career.

Australia came nearest to scoring when a great run by Gilbert was ruined by a final pass that was *wild and useless,* whilst a long-range penalty from Francis caused some controversy as the Australian touch-judge's view that a goal was scored was not shared by the home touch-judge and the referee.

The fiftieth minute of the match proved to be the turning point for until then the British clearly held the whip hand. At that juncture, however, Alf Wood received a kick on his thigh in bravely stopping a Kangaroo forward rush and took no further part in the game. With Gronow pulled out of the pack to full-back the British forwards fought manfully but, from a dribble by Craig, the ubiquitous McKivat was able to pick up and score for Francis to convert and reduce the deficit to three points. With ten minutes remaining Australia created an overlap for Russell to race in for the equalising try. Even so it was the depleted British who nearly snatched victory in the closing minutes as Lomas almost had Batten over and Jenkinson could have given Wagstaff his hat-trick but failed to pass at the critical time.

Just as injuries had contributed significantly to Australia's demise in the 1908-09 series, so they were contributing to her triumph in the series of 1911-12 for this somewhat fortuitous draw meant that Britain could not win the series.

T. BERECRY

C.H. McKIVAT

D. FRAWLEY

P.A. McCUE

Four double-try scorers for Australia in their Ashes-winning victory at Birmingham in 1912 – Tom Berecry, Chris McKivat, Dan Frawley and Paddy McCue.

TEST MATCH 8

AT VILLA PARK, BIRMINGHAM – 1 January, 1912
GREAT BRITAIN 8 AUSTRALIA 33 (HT 8-11)

AE Wood (Oldham) G	H Hallett (Souths)
A Jenkinson (Hunslet)	†T Berecry (Norths) 2T
TB Jenkins (Wigan)	V Farnsworth (Newtown) T
J Lomas (Oldham) capt T	H Gilbert (Souths) G
W Batten (Hunslet)	D Frawley (Easts) 2T,2G
J Davies (Huddersfield)	W Farnsworth (Newtown)
F Smith (Hunslet)	CH McKivat (Glebe) capt 2T
F Harrison (Leeds)	C Sullivan (Norths)
T Woods (Rochdale H)	R Williams (Easts)
R Ramsdale (Wigan)	WS Noble (Newtown)
AE Avery (Oldham)	RR Craig (Balmain)
W Winstanley (Wigan)	PA McCue (Newtown) 2T
D Clark (Huddersfield) T	WA Cann (Souths)

Referee - R Robinson (Bradford)   Crowd - 4,000   Gate - £213/17/3

Scoring - 5-0 8-0 8-3 8-6 8-11 8-16 8-19 8-22 8-25 8-30 8-33

For Australia a joyous and historic occasion as her representatives won the mythical but coveted Ashes for the first time and rattled up the highest score in the history of the tests thus far, a score which was not to be surpassed until the first test in Sydney in 1954. McKivat's Kangaroos were to be the last Australian team to win the Ashes in Britain for over half a century and it was not until 1979 that another Australian combination went through a series undefeated.

For the British there was only disappointment and another wickedly cruel trick of the demon, Injury. In the very first minute Wigan's Dick Ramsdale, following up a drop-out from the home "25", charged into Dan Frawley and sprained his knee so badly that he took no further part in the match. Worse was to follow for before the first half was over Lomas too was crocked but gamely played on and late in the game Jenkinson was led from the field with a jaw injury.

Even so, during the first quarter the British were inspired and there were hopes that they might yet square the series. After five minutes the inspirational Lomas was touching down at the corner following a superb build-up by Smith, Davies, Harrison and Jenkinson. A fine conversion from Wood ensued and ten minutes later a tremendous dribble by Douglas Clark, possibly the strongest forward to have played the game, produced a stunning try and the Kangaroos were eight points down. It was to be the home side's last fling, however, as Australia began to make their numerical supremacy count.

McKivat, as ever the catalyst, broke away and enabled Frawley and Craig to put Viv Farnsworth over for the first of nine tries. It was not long before Berecry, a revelation in his only test, shook off Batten, mesmerised two more defenders and sent in McKivat. McCue finally edged the Kangaroos into the lead with a try converted by Frawley. The second half soon became *deplorably one-sided* and with Lomas reduced to a passenger the British tackling simply stopped. A procession of tries to McCue, converted by Frawley, Berecry, Frawley, McKivat, Frawley again and Berecry again took the score to its record proportions. It would have been worse had any of the Aussies had their kicking boots on for there was only a conversion by Gilbert to Frawley's second try. It had been the best of the Australian scores, initiated by the wily Billy Farnsworth deep in his own quarters and ending with Frawley sprinting from half-way.

Once in control, the Kangaroos proved their mettle. One report ran,

They controlled the packs, and made unlimited play for McKivat and W. Farnsworth, who in turn gave the three-quarters any amount of scope to show their running and passing abilities .... in which the Farnsworths, Gilbert, Frawley and Berecry were conspicuous .... Many spectators did not understand the game, but they appreciated the individual efforts of the Colonials, and after the match one could hear expressions of admiration for the play of the 'outside-left' and 'outside-right'.

Eleven Lions backs, tour manager, Joe Houghton (standing, extreme left) and trainer, Dave Murray (standing, extreme right) form an unusual grouping in 1914. *Standing:* G. Thomas, O'Garra, Williams *Seated:* Robinson, Wood, W.A. Davies, Jenkins, Hall *Front:* Smith, Francis, Prosser

TEST MATCH 9

AT THE ROYAL AGRICULTURAL GROUND, SYDNEY – 27 June, 1914
AUSTRALIA 5 GREAT BRITAIN 23 (HT 0-5)

H Hallett (Souths)	† W Jarman (Leeds)
† H Horder (Souths)	† JE Robinson (Rochdale H) T,2G
† W Kelly (Balmain)	TB Jenkins (Wigan)
SP Deane (Norths) capt	H Wagstaff (Huddersfield) capt
† H Bolewski (Bundaberg) G	† S Moorhouse (Huddersfield) 2T
† R Norman (Souths) T	† W Hall (Oldham)
A Halloway (Easts)	F Smith (Hunslet)
C Sullivan (Norths)	† D Holland (Oldham) T
PA McCue (Newtown)	† AP Coldrick (Wigan)
† F Burge (Glebe)	R Ramsdale (Wigan)
EJ Courtney (Wests)	† F Longstaff (Huddersfield) 2G
SC Pearce (Easts)	† J Chilcott (Huddersfield)
† J Watkins (Easts)	D Clark (Huddersfield) T

Referee - T McMahon (NSW)   Crowd - 40,000   Gate - £1,775

Scoring - 0-2 0-5 0-10 0-12 0-15 0-20 0-23 5-23

Cynic, writing in *The Referee,* had this to say of Australia's humiliation,
Not the glimmer of excuse can be put forward for the home team, who were outclassed in general forward play, in general combination, in defence among backs, in tackling, in pace, in stamina, and in their physical strength. The palm goes to the Englishmen (sic), who so excelled the home team, beating them at their own game - open and spectacular football.

Rarely has an Australian pack, "Bluey" Watkins excepted, shown so little spirit and dash whilst the British forwards - *girthy as well-fed cobs* - frolicked up and down the field like another set of backs. Not that the British backs, manipulated masterfully by Wagstaff, needed much help as they threw the ball from flank to flank in brilliant combined movements on a slippery surface which seemed to trouble only the home players. Britain led almost from the start when Longstaff landed a penalty from the centre-line and only a fine piece of covering by Watkins prevented Moorhouse from scoring at the posts. A score was not long coming, however, as Australia were *shaping like a football rabble - the Englishmen like a machine.* A scrum formed wide on the half-way line and the ball was whisked via Smith, Hall and Jenkins to Wagstaff who cleverly lobbed the leather over Kelly and Horder to Moorhouse who fairly flew down the left wing. Watkins was there to challenge the winger who threw inside to Bert Jenkins. Jenkins made tracks for the flag but fell to Hallett's tackle and popped the ball into Moorhouse's path for the winger to sweep over and race behind the posts. Amazingly Jarman, usually a forward but full-back today, was entrusted with the simple kick and made a hash of it. In all other respects, however, the novice full-back was a revelation.

By the beginning of the second half the Lions were so confident that they did not baulk from passing the ball from wing to wing along their own goal-line. One such movement produced a magnificent try as Moorhouse tore down the left wing and as the hapless defence disintegrated there was Wagstaff to receive an inside pass from which he put over that mighty forward Douglas Clark, who had backed up from his own line. Robinson potted the simple conversion and then Longstaff, the long-range expert, booted a stupendous goal from eight yards inside the home half and almost on the touch-line to give his side a 12-0 lead. That soon became 15-0 when Harold Horder, having a nightmare test baptism, unaccountably failed to gather a stationary ball about 35 yards from his goal allowing Robinson to dribble forward, gather and outrun Hallett to the flag. Australia's torment continued as Wagstaff rounded off a bewildering passing bout by whipping the ball out to Moorhouse who ran almost to the line before presenting a try to Holland near the sticks. Robinson goaled and another bewitching movement soon followed which unleashed the deadly Moorhouse. The winger was halted by Hallett's tackle at the corner but in the process Hallett hit the flag and was laid out allowing Moorhouse to wriggle over. Australia at last replied shortly before time when from a scrum near the Lions' 25" Halloway served Norman who short-punted over the defence and, as the ball settled in the in-goal, dived for the touchdown. Bolewski converted but it had been a bad day for Australia and heads would roll.

TEST MATCH 10

AT SYDNEY CRICKET GROUND – 29 June, 1914
AUSTRALIA 12 GREAT BRITAIN 7 (HT 7-7)

H Hallett (Souths)	† GW Thomas (Wigan)
D Frawley (Easts)	JE Robinson (Rochdale H)
SP Deane (Norths) capt	W Hall (Oldham)
† W Messenger (Easts) 3G	H Wagstaff (Huddersfield) capt
† R Tidyman (Easts)	† F Williams (Halifax)
C Fraser (Balmain) T	† JH Rogers (Huddersfield) 2G
A Halloway (Easts)	F Smith (Hunslet)
C Sullivan (Norths)	D Holland (Oldham)
WA Cann (Souths)	AP Coldrick (Wigan) T
F Burge (Glebe) T	R Ramsdale (Wigan)
EJ Courtney (Wests)	W Jarman (Leeds)
SC Pearce (Easts)	J Chilcott (Huddersfield)
RR Craig (Balmain)	D Clark (Huddersfield)

Referee - T McMahon (NSW)   Crowd - 55,000   Gate - £2,647
Scoring - 0-2 0-4 0-7 2-7 7-7 12-7

For the first time Sydney Cricket Ground became the scene of an Anglo-Australian test and was blessed with a benign day and a record crowd. In the intervening years the venerable ground has housed over 30 such clashes which have been witnessed by over one-and-a-half million people. Few games could have given Australians more pleasure than this splendid affair which constituted the Lions' first test defeat in the colony. Australia were unrecognisable from the side which was humbled only two days previously in the first test. Whilst Britain again played admirable, adventurous rugby and exhibited better combination in the back-line, this time they were met by a resolute Australian defence which refused to buckle. "Tedda" Courtney and Frank Burge magnificently marshalled a rearguard action which effectively stifled all save one of Britain's powerful thrusts, wiped out a seven points deficit and finished the stronger of two teams of titans.

Great Britain had the opportunities to have established a winning lead by half-time as their flank to flank passing stretched the home defence to its limits but somehow Australia kept the Lions out. With "Chook" Fraser clearly uncomfortable at stand-off, passing when kicking was required, it was not too surprising when Britain ran into a seven points lead. The first points came from a well-struck penalty by Johnny Rogers from near touch on the "25". Australia responded with a scintillating move when one of Fraser's long passes at last came off releasing Tidyman who shot down the wing before cross-kicking on the British "25" only to see Deane crashed to earth in front of the posts.

Britain raised the siege and Rogers potted another goal when Australia handled in the scrum. Play now whizzed from end to end but Australia lost a golden chance when Tidyman surged 50 yards up-field and served Deane whose try-scoring pass to Frawley was dropped. Britain did not shun the next try-scoring opportunity as Hall intercepted a pass within his own "25" to set up a sweeping movement between Rogers, Wagstaff and Williams. Hallett fielded at half-way but in trying to kick was blocked by the onrushing Williams who deftly picked up and sent Coldrick charging over from 35 yards.

Australia redoubled their efforts and were rewarded with a penalty-goal from Wally Messenger when the Lions obstructed. A tremendous barrage on the British line ensued with Hallett losing the ball at one corner and Messenger being stopped at the other. At last the British line broke when Halloway fed Fraser from a scrum and, instead of passing to Deane, the stand-off suddenly veered diagonally, grubber-kicked to the posts and dived for the try. Messenger converted and at half-time the scores were 7-7.

Australia began where they had left off and Gwyn Thomas performed miracles in preventing Courtney and then Tidyman from scoring. Disaster struck the Lions when Robinson fell and fractured his collar-bone leaving Britain to face a rejuvenated home XIII for the best part of the second half a man short. Australia began to come *with the sting of winners* and valorously though Wagstaff's men strove they eventually capitulated when the Australian pack came with a foot-rush from the centre. Burge and Sullivan dribbled toward the corner and, when challenged by Thomas, Burge kicked the ball in-field almost along the goal-line where it came to rest behind the posts. Burge pounced in triumph and Messenger's goal wrapped up Australia's first home victory against the Lions.

TEST MATCH 11

AT SYDNEY CRICKET GROUND – 4 July, 1914
AUSTRALIA 6 GREAT BRITAIN 14 (HT 0-9)

H Hallett (Souths)	AE Wood (Oldham) 4G
D Frawley (Easts)	F Williams (Halifax)
SP Deane (Norths) capt T	W Hall (Oldham)
R Tidyman (Easts)	H Wagstaff (Huddersfield) capt
W Messenger (Easts) T	† WA Davies (Leeds) T
C Fraser (Balmain)	† WS Prosser (Halifax)
A Halloway (Easts)	F Smith (Hunslet)
C Sullivan (Norths)	D Holland (Oldham)
WA Cann (Souths)	AP Coldrick (Wigan)
F Burge (Glebe)	R Ramsdale (Wigan)
EJ Courtney (Wests)	† A Johnson (Widnes) T
SC Pearce (Easts)	J Chilcott (Huddersfield)
RR Craig (Balmain)	D Clark (Huddersfield)

Referee - T McMahon (NSW)   Crowd - 34,420   Gate - £1,721
Scoring - 0-2 0-7 0-9 0-14 3-14 6-14

Enshrined in Rugby League folklore as "The Rorke's Drift Test", the third and deciding match of the 1914 series remains quite simply the most famous match in test history. Wagstaff's Lions overcame the most disheartening odds to wrest back the Ashes and earn for themselves a piece of sporting immortality. Playing under protest - the whole series was completed in the space of a week - Britain entered the test minus half-a-dozen key players against an unchanged Australian team buoyed up by their victory five days earlier.

Within minutes of the start winger Frank Williams was crocked by a knee injury necessitating the withdrawal of Albert Johnson from the pack to help on the flank. Williams hobbled around as a passenger until a further wrenching forced him off for good in the early stages of the second half. Douglas Clark broke a thumb during the first half, had it strapped and played on until he fell trying to avoid "Pony" Halloway's tackle midway through the second half and dislocated his collar-bone. Ten minutes from time Billy Hall was concussed and retired from the fray leaving Great Britain with only ten men to hold an increasingly desperate and frustrated home XIII. The tenacity with which this set of British bulldogs held on to their hard-won lead was surely the very essence of sporting heroism.

Apart from the mishap to Williams, Britain got off to a good start on a soft and heavy pitch to establish an advantage which they were able to defend in the true spirit of John Bull. After a series of Australian offences Britain secured a position from which Alf Wood landed a simple penalty. Australia came back hard and camped for fully five minutes on the British line until Holland dribbled clear. Still the Aussies attacked incessantly and Courtney claimed a try but Frawley had knocked on. Burge was then ruled off-side as he strode towards the posts after collecting Messenger's cross-kick and following a great run by Tidyman Messenger was brought to ground at the corner. Billy Cann broke beautifully to the centre but the ball went loose and Prosser, Hall, Wagstaff and Avon Davies swiftly worked the ball down the left wing where Davies kicked infield past Hallett, toed on again and raced shoulder to shoulder for the touchdown with Tidyman who made the first contact but failed to ground properly. Davies did not make the same mistake and Wood converted. Soon afterwards the full-back kicked his third goal when Fraser went off-side.

As things began to look blacker for the depleted Lions mid-way into the second period a stunning and totally unexpected score came to their aid. A scrum went down far to the right on the centre-line and the ball came to make-shift winger Johnson who began a dribble. Halloway seemed rooted to the spot and made no challenge. Messenger found himself outwitted on the ground and Johnson proceeded to hoof the ball past Hallett before regaining possession. Cann tried to tackle Johnson but was met by a mighty fend and Johnson fell over the line for a glorious try to which Wood added the goal. Even with a 14-0 lead Britain dared not miss a solitary tackle. Cann and Halloway at last pierced the British line to get Messenger over at the flag but the British simply would not give in even when for a few minutes they were actually down to nine men as Prosser was badly winded. Australia's tactics could certainly have been better but blunder followed blunder, the worst being when Courtney lost the ball in the act of scoring and by the time Deane scored at the posts from a scrum four yards out it was too late to deny Wagstaff's men everlasting glory.

MY GREATEST TEST MATCH.

Ten Englishmen Triumph in Historic "Rorke's Drift" Struggle.

"I never have seen the bulldog tenacity, the courage and heroic skill of the Englishmen that afternoon surpassed on the football field. That day Wagstaff, the English captain, played with inspiration that left upon my memory that it was the most wonderful game any man has ever played in the face of colossal odds.

"Wagstaff, always a great player, that day became *the ubiquitous*, and the King of the game. . . . Here, there and everywhere, all the time he was doing the work of half-a-dozen men, inspiring his valiant band, dominated by misfortune, to transform themselves each one into two men. Wagstaff the Great."

This is what J. C. Davis, the Editor of "The Sydney Referee," wrote about the "Rorke's Drift" match, the deciding Test between England and Australia in 1914, played on the Sydney Cricket ground.

In the following article, the last in a series which has aroused interest wherever Rugby League football is played, Harold Wagstaff tells his own story of the greatest Test match in which he played.

By HAROLD WAGSTAFF
(concluding the story of his football career).

THE 1914 TOUR, the opening of which I told about last week, had a disastrous start. We lost the first two matches, and our football was poor because we were not fit. The newspapers were exceedingly rude about our work—talked about our football being like that of a lot of schoolgirls—and we had to be quick to do some-

just think of it, three Tests in eight days for a tour team crippled with injury. When Mr. Clifford returned from the Blue Mountains to hear of what had happened he was wild with indignation.

Anyway, Alf Wood decided to take the full-back position, though his nose was far from right, and we turned out with this side:—

Wood: Frank Williams, Hall, Wagstaff, W. A. Davies; Smith, Prosser; Holland, Coldrick, Ramsdale, Johnson, Clark, Chiliott.

The Australian side was:

Hallett; Frawley, Deane, Tidyman, W. Messenger; Halloway, Frazer; Pearce, Sullivan, Cann, Craig, Courtney, Burge.

My first memory of the day on which that match which came to be known as the "Rorke's Drift" match, was played—if you look in the records in the Rugby League handbook you will see that while the other Test matches are numbered, this one is distinguished by having (R.D.) alongside it—has to do with the fighting speech that was made to us by Mr. J. Clifford, who was so upset about the way in which the arrangements for the match had been rushed through behind his back.

Words of Fire.

He called the men who were playing that afternoon—the 13 of us—into a room in the hotel, and he outlined the whole story of the revision of the fixture. Then he said that he expected everyone of us to play as we had never played before.

"You are playing in a game of football this afternoon," he said, "but more, than that, you are playing for England, and more, even, than that, you are playing for Right versus Wrong. You will win BECAUSE YOU HAVE TO WIN. Don't forget that message from home: England expects every one of you to do his duty.

Mr. John Clifford.

he tapped the ball over the line, and dived for the touch.

Alf. Wood kicked the goal, and there we were 14-3. Billy Hall recovered and came back for the last ten minutes to help us in a defence that was successful, until, in the last few minutes, Sid Deane scored the second Australian try.

But the victory was ours, and the Australian crowd gave us full credit for it. They swung round to our side in the second half, and they were with us to the end, cheering us on in inspiring fashion. When

I was called into conference by the managers, and my suggestion was that we should straightaway get down to it —that we should go to the ground every morning, have lunch sent there to us, and continue training in the afternoon until we had felt we had had enough.

Everyone in the side tackled the business keenly, and we made a quick and entirely satisfactory revival. It was a revival so satisfactory, at all events, that when the first Test was played on the Agricultural Ground, Sydney, we were able to win comfortably.

Yet we took the field in that match without a regular full back. Alf. Wood had broken his nose and Gwyn Thomas had a fractured rib, and we had to play "Bill" Jarman, the Leeds forward, at full back.

We went out that day determined to show the people of Sydney that we were not what they thought we were. A goal kicked by Longstaff from inside our half—the crowd jeered when he placed the ball, for they thought he had no chance—gave us a quick lead. We got 23 points and they did not get a point until the last five minutes.

23-5 was good enough.

Toll of Injuries.

The second Test was played the following Monday—it was the King's Holiday—and, because Jarman, Longstaff, Moorhouse and Bert Jenkins were injured, we were hard put to it to get a team.

Gwyn Thomas and Wood the full-backs, was not fit, Francis, another of the backs, was out of the reckoning because of injury, and it was more or less a scratch side that we were compelled to field.

We were beaten 12-7, in a game in which we had our first experience of the substitution rule that was worked in Australia in those days, and so the position in the battle for the "Ashes" stood one each. The arrangement was that the final Test should be played at Melbourne when we returned from our trip to New Zealand.

An England v. New South Wales match had been fixed for Sydney the following Saturday, and on the Wednesday morning Mr. J. Clifford, one of our managers, took a team up to Bathurst in the Blue Mountains. Then the Australians began an agitation for the third Test to be played at Sydney in place of the England v. New South Wales game on the Saturday.

Mr. Clifford was away and could not be consulted, and, in the end, the Australian authorities cabled to England to ask the Northern Union Council to agree to the third Test being played as the Australians desired.

The Message from England.

A special meeting of the Northern Union Council was called in England, they agreed to the Australians' demand, and they sent this cable to the English party in Australia:

Play match as Australians desire; England expects that every man will do his duty.

So it came about that the third Test was played on the Saturday following the first—impressed and smiled as never swore or since by a speech. You could see our fellows clenching their fists as Mr. Clifford spoke, and I know that when we left the room none spoke.

We were prepared to go all out when we went on to that field at Sydney; but before there had been a scrummage in the match Frank Williams, on the wing, had twisted his leg. We took "Chick" Johnson out of the pack to help Williams on that wing.

We managed to lead at half-time by 9-3. Percy Coldrick had scored a try, and Alf Wood had kicked three goals.

Immediately we started the second half, Douglas Clark smashed his collar-bone. He had broken a thumb in the first half and it had been bandaged tightly so that he could carry on.

In the early stages of the second half, Clark got a pass and went racing clear of all, it seemed, for the line. But "Pony" Halloway challenged him.

Douglas put out his hand to push Halloway off and then remembered the broken thumb. He withdrew his hand and went in to Halloway to give him his shoulder, but Halloway stalled. Clark, unable to recover his balance fell on his shoulder and the collar bone went.

Douglas Clark in Tears.

He had it strapped and twice he made an effort to return to the game; but in the end he had to decide that it was impossible for him to carry on. There were tears in his eyes when he left the field for the last time.

Frank Williams hurt his leg again, and he had to go off and there we were left with 11 men. Then Billy Hall, of Oldham, was carried off with concussion—he received his injury when he went down for the ball—and we had ten men to face thirteen.

Ten men and thirty minutes to go!

But never had I such nine men with me on a football field as I had that day. We were in our own half all the time, and for most of the time we seemed to be on our line; but we stuck at it. Our forwards gave their all.

In the scrummages, the remnant of the pack that was left did its job, and, in the loose, the men who had been brought out tackled as fiercely and as finely as the backs did. "Chick" Johnson was on one wing, and Percy Coldrick was on the other wing, and Willie Davies was in the centre with me.

As often happens in such circumstances, we continued to get the ball from the scrummages, Holland, Ramsdale and Chilcott were heroes.

There were twenty minutes left when I managed to make a cut through after taking the ball from Fred Smith and Prosser. I went to the wing on which was Johnson, and when I gave "Chick" the ball there was only the full back in front of him.

"Chick" went away with it; but then none of us dreamt that we were to witness the scoring of as wonderful a try as Test football ever will produce.

A few yards from Hallett, the Australian full back, "Chick" put the ball on the ground and began a dribble.

He had half the length of the field to go; but he went every inch of the distance. And the ball never left his toes. It might have been tied to his feet—a ball on the end of a piece of string—so perfectly did he control it.

Played to a Standstill.

No international Association player could have dribbled a ball better than Johnson did that afternoon on the Sydney cricket ground. Man after man he beat, until finally had gone to the last gasp, and were just about finished

Some friends from Huddersfield had come to see us play, and when the victory was won, they produced some champagne, and never was champagne more welcome. I know that most of us stayed in our red and white jerseys and blue pants, content to sit resting thankfully for at least an hour after the match. We were simply too tired to make the move to the brake that was there to carry us back to our hotel.

We lost no more than three matches on that tour—the first two and the second Test —and when we returned from New Zealand we had to play New South Wales at Melbourne. Now that match at Melbourne was supposed to be an exhibition affair—a game to help the code in Melbourne, where there was little or no Rugby League football.

But there were, I am afraid, old scores to be paid on both sides, and the result was that the Melbourne match was the roughest in which I have played.

An "All In" Match.

I shall never forget the sight of the two parks standing up to each other in some real all in stuff, with a tremendous crowd cheering like mad because they thought it was all in the game they were seeing for the first time. An exhibition game!

It was, however, the last of the bad matches. In those days, for some reason or other, we never seemed to get to know the fellows on the other side.

When you passed an Australian player in the street, neither of you thought about stopping for a chat. You just growled and walked on.

After the war, things improved enormously. The men on both sides mixed, became friends and learned to appreciate each other. Frank Burge that great Australian forward, who played in the Melbourne match, always used to mention it when I saw him, and whenever he writes to me now he touches upon it, but he never fails to point out that, though we played in that match in which neither side squealed, we learned to become great friends, and great friends we still are.

I could go on for a long time writing about these Australian Test matches, and about the international matches in which it has been my fortune and pleasure to play since first I represented England at Huddersfield on January 1, 1909. That season I played for England v. Wales at Coventry. I played first in Test football in 1911-12, turning out at Newcastle and Edinburgh—that was the match in which Frank Renton overruled a touch-judge regarding a goal.

I played first in Test football in Australia in 1914, and I I played in two of three Tests in Australia when I captained the 1920 Tour team.

Then, in 1921, I played in two of the three Tests when the Australian side, which included Duncan Thompson, Blinkhorn, Caples, Craig, Horder, Fraser, Burge, Pearce and the others, were over here.

I was in the side when at Salford in 1921 we regained the "Ashes" we have held ever since, and I claim that I hold the "Ashes."

After that match at Salford in 1921, the Australians made me a present of a silver cigarette case to commemorate England's victory in the "Ashes," and when they gave it to me they placed in it, as a joke, of course, the ash from the cigarettes they then were smoking.

I have many souvenirs of my football career. There are none I treasure more than that cigarette case and the football with which we played in the "Rorke's Drift" Test at Sydney in 1914.

TEST MATCH 12

AT THE EXHIBITION GROUND, BRISBANE – 26 June, 1920
AUSTRALIA 8 GREAT BRITAIN 4 (HT 3-4)

† H Fewin (Carltons, Brisbane)
† N Broadfoot (Grammars, Brisbane)
V Farnsworth (Wests)
R Vest (Wests)
HN Horder (Norths) G
C Fraser (Balmain) T
A Johnston (Newtown) capt
† N Potter (Wests, Brisbane)
SC Pearce (Easts)
W Schultz (Balmain)
F Burge (Glebe) T
† W Richards (Wests, Brisbane)
† A Gray (Glebe)

GW Thomas (Huddersfield)
† JA Bacon (Leeds)
H Wagstaff (Huddersfield) capt
† D Hurcombe (Wigan)
† WJ Stone (Hull)
JH Rogers (Huddersfield)
† J Parkin (Wakefield T)
B Gronow (Huddersfield) 2G
† A Milnes (Halifax)
A Johnson (Widnes)
† H Hilton (Oldham)
† F Gallagher (Dewsbury)
D Clark (Huddersfield)

Referee - LH Kearney (Queensland)   Crowd - 28,000   Gate - £2,532
Scoring - 0-2 0-4 3-4 8-4

An Australian team cast very much in the role of underdogs won a test match at Brisbane for the first time by virtue of an impenetrable and uncompromising defence. Whilst there was no doubt as to the worthiness of Australia's victory, the struggle was protracted with the winners not taking the lead until the final quarter. Upto that point it had seemed that the prodigious goal-kicking of Ben Gronow would decide the honours.

As a spectacle the game was disappointing, hard and fierce in the extreme but punctuated by bad temper and no fewer than 39 penalties (20 to Australia). One newsman railed,

The contest was not characterised by anything striking in sportsmanship: that is, the striking things done were with the fists or boots. The spirit of neither side was what it should have been, and for that reason the game fell below football excellence associated with International struggles, especially one in which the Ashes are the prize. This hard spirit has been prevalent for too long in fights between England and Australia, and it is time players were taught a salutary lesson.

Australia should have taken the lead in the first few minutes when Johnston worked the blind-side of a scrum to send Farnsworth prancing down to the British "25". Farnsworth threw inside to the supporting Potter who would certainly have scored had he not spilled the pass. After seven minutes the crowd gaped in disbelief as Gronow teed up a penalty ten yards inside the Australian half but almost on the right touch-line. They were even more astounded when the ball sailed through the posts just clearing the bar.

Britain were sorely pressed, however, to keep Australia out and were fortunate when Farnsworth in leaping over a prostrate player near the posts dropped Johnston's pass. It was the unfortunate Farnsworth who conceded a penalty at a play-the-ball from which Gronow struck a second monster goal from just inside the Australian half at the centre to give the Lions an advantage of four points.

Australia's luck seemed to be out as Horder, normally such a lethal finisher, twice made a hash of good openings and Burge missed a sitter of a penalty. It seemed inevitable that the British forwards - *big, powerful chaps with backs like shire horses and feet like racers* - would subdue their lighter opponents but Australia refused to be cowed and after a series of scrums near the British line Johnston secured twelve yards out and served Fraser on the open-side. Quick as a flash the five-eighth wheeled and skirted the blind-side completely bamboozling the defence to score a remarkable try at the corner. Half-time arrived with the Lions clinging to a lead of a solitary point.

Australia were unlucky when from a scrum orthodox passing between halves and centres saw Broadfoot thrown into touch at the flag and then an angled penalty by Fraser was declared no goal when the touch-judges gave a split decision. Broadfoot was equally crestfallen after crashing into the post when attempting to score from a high Farnsworth cross-kick and another chance went begging when Fraser pulled wide an easy penalty. Just when it seemed they would never get in front, Australia's luck turned in the 65th minute as Johnston broke down the blind-side of a scrum near half-way. Horder galloped away and cross-kicked at the "25" for Burge to plunge over for the decisive score as a defender failed to hold the falling ball. Horder's conversion completed the scoring.

TEST MATCH 13

AT SYDNEY CRICKET GROUND – 3 July, 1920
AUSTRALIA 21 GREAT BRITAIN 8 (HT 8-8)

C Fraser (Balmain) G
R Vest (Wests) T
V Farnsworth (Wests) T
H Gilbert (Wests) capt T
HN Horder (Norths) T,G
A Johnston (Newtown)
DF Thompson (Norths)
W Schultz (Balmain)
SC Pearce (Easts)
N Potter (Wests, Brisbane) T
A Gray (Glebe)
W Richards (Wests, Brisbane)
F Burge (Glebe) G

GW Thomas (Huddersfield)
JA Bacon (Leeds)
H Wagstaff (Huddersfield) capt
D Hurcombe (Wigan)
WJ Stone (Hull)
JH Rogers (Huddersfield)
† RA Lloyd (Halifax)
B Gronow (Huddersfield) G
A Milnes (Halifax)
A Johnson (Widnes) T
D Clark (Huddersfield)
H Hilton (Oldham)
F Gallagher (Dewsbury) T

Referee - T McMahon (NSW)   Crowd - 40,000   Gate - £2,826
Scoring - 0-2 2-2 5-2 5-5 8-5 8-8 13-8 16-8 21-8

The second test was the perfect antidote to the first. Gone were the rancour and spite, the spoiling and off-side tactics. In their place unfolded a match brimful of exciting, imaginative and audacious movements despite some deadly tackling. In the end Australia won with plenty to spare to regain the Ashes although no one could have foreseen that it would be another 30 years before they again performed the feat. More importantly the game itself recovered some of the honour it had lost at Brisbane for as *The Cynic* wrote in *The Referee,*
Australia have won against a valiant foe who fought with characteristic national grit, and has taken the whacking with characteristic sportsmanship .... Football is no parlor game. Men have to give and take knocks, and it was good to see them given and taken in this contest without any semblance of bitterness or venom.
From the start the pace was furious and it was against the run of play when in the seventh minute Gronow edged Britain into the lead with a fine penalty. The home team exerted almost continuous pressure throughout the first quarter but epic deeds by the defenders prevented Australia from scoring until the twentieth minute when Stone found himself in dire straits at the corner and punted the ball straight to Fraser near the "25". The full-back steadied himself and calmly dropped a gem of a goal to level the match. Australia took the lead with a splendid try when Thompson broke down the short-side from a scrum before linking with the flying Horder who made good ground before turning the ball into his supporting forwards for Burge and Schultz to send Potter in at the corner. Britain came back to pen Australia on their line where risky passing amongst the home backs broke down allowing Britain to kick over the line where Johnson dived for an opportunist try.
Australia soon regained the lead, however, when Farnsworth capitalised on a mistake by Bacon to shoot down the left wing and touch down at the corner. Twice they could have extended their lead but on both occasions Burge had tries disallowed for forward passes. Just on half-time Britain equalised with a breathtaking try. Lloyd, Rogers, Wagstaff and Hurcombe released Bacon on the wing. Horder gave chase but as he collared his quarry Bacon passed inside to Hurcombe. Rogers and Wagstaff took up the running to sweep cross-field to the left wing where Clark gave the final pass to Gallagher. The teams turned round level.
The second half was mostly a case of Australia hammering at the British line. The try which gave them the lead was one of the classic tries of test history and developed from a scrum on the right wing in centre-field. The ball was kept alive by at least a dozen passes amongst the backs, Johnston handling three times, before a bemused British defence saw Horder finish the move under the posts. He also converted and Australia had a firm grip. Burge had a third try disallowed, this time for off-side, before Thompson, breaking craftily down the blind-side, drew Gwyn Thomas to send Vest scorching over for an unimproved try. Shortly before time Thompson and Johnston, as good a pair of halves as ever played for Australia, opened up the right flank before Johnston threw inside to Farnsworth whose judicious pass sent Herb Gilbert on a 50 yards sprint to the line. Burge's conversion hardly made up for his hat-trick of disallowed tries!
Gilbert's try meant that all the Australian three-quarters had touched down - an unprecedented occurrence in Ashes tests.

TEST MATCH 14

AT THE ROYAL AGRICULTURAL GROUND, SYDNEY – 10 July, 1920
AUSTRALIA 13 GREAT BRITAIN 23 (HT 8-6)

C Fraser (Balmain)	GW Thomas (Huddersfield) capt
R Vest (Wests)	JH Rogers (Huddersfield) 3G
V Farnsworth (Wests) T	WJ Stone (Hull) 2T,G
H Gilbert (Wests) capt	JA Bacon (Leeds) T
HN Horder (Norths)	†S Stockwell (Leeds)
A Johnston (Newtown)	†EW Jones (Rochdale H)
DF Thompson (Norths) T	J Parkin (Wakefield T)
W Schultz (Balmain)	†W Cunliffe (Warrington)
SC Pearce (Easts)	†J Cartwright (Leigh)
N Potter (Wests, Brisbane)	†GA Skelhorne (Warrington)
A Gray (Glebe)	D Clark (Huddersfield)
W Richards (Wests, Brisbane)	H Hilton (Oldham) 2T
F Burge (Glebe) T,2G	F Gallagher (Dewsbury)
SUB J Robinson (Balmain) for Horder	

Referee - T McMahon (NSW)   Crowd - 32,000   Gate - £1,908
Scoring - 0-3 0-6 2-6 5-6 8-6 10-6 10-11 10-16 13-16 13-21 13-23

The omens for Great Britain appeared inauspicious facing a team cock-a-hoop from clinching the Ashes in the first two tests. They were without their master tactician Wagstaff, Gronow the Boot and Danny Hurcombe, their most versatile back. They had five new caps, including the entire front row. This latter aspect, in view of the result, must have given the selection committee a nasty attack of hindsight for in the previous two tests Britain had taken the misguided risk of playing without any specialist props and paid the penalty.

As a match the encounter was a disappointment. It had none of the sparkle of the second test nor the ferocity of the first. Conditions were perfect but the play, particularly of the home team, was riddled with errors. For a test match it meandered along remarkably aimiably and it was a real surprise when towards the close the Australian forward, Bill Richards, a notably fair player, was sent off for tripping Squire Stockwell as he (Richards) was flat on his back at a ruck. Richards thus became the first Australian to be sent off in an Ashes test.

Britain quickly impressed as the likelier victors but the first real chance fell to Australia when Horder brilliantly gathered a cross-kick from Vest to cross under the bar only for Mr. McMahon to rule off-side. By the 25th minute Britain had collected two unconverted tries. The first followed a determined piece of play from Bacon who had received Parkin's long pass from a scrum, quickly beat a man on the inside, broke through Vest's low tackle and shrugged off a high tackle from Gilbert to score wide out. The second followed a comedy of errors as a whole succession of players seemed incapable of holding on to the leather until at last Hilton managed to retain it and drove forcefully over near the posts only for Jones to miss the simple kick.

Burge reduced the lead with a fine touch-line penalty shortly before Horder retired from the fray with an injured shoulder. To everyone's surprise Australia took the lead before the interval when two pieces of magic by Duncan Thompson produced two tries. For the first Thompson foxed the defence by kicking over it from twenty yards out when all expected a pass. Gray was first to the ball to send Farnsworth scampering over at the flag and then from a "25" scrum Thompson scorched round the blind-side to score a fine individualist try at the corner.

Soon after the interval Burge extended the home lead to 10–6 with a penalty goal and the great mystery was how Australia had managed to lead having played so poorly. The advantage was soon lost, however, when Fraser threw a reckless pass to Gilbert twenty yards from his own line. The captain dropped the ball and Hilton scooped it up, exchanged passes with a colleague, bumped off two defenders in a touch-line run, crossed at the corner and ran behind the posts for Johnny Rogers to land a simple goal. Another bad pass from Fraser was snapped up by Billy Stone 80 yards out for the winger to sprint unmolested for a runaway try, again converted by Rogers. A brief rally brought a dubious try to Burge after an apparent knock-on but this was negated when good play by Bacon prised an opening for Stone to waltz over for Rogers to pot a third simple conversion. The scoring was completed when Stone landed a fine goal following Richards' dismissal. Australia's misery was complete when Gilbert lost the ball in the act of scoring.

Australian squad prior to the Brisbane Test of 1920.
Back: V Farnsworth, O'Donnell, Schultz, Gray, Horder
Standing: Sunderland, Ryan, Richards, Potter, Pearce, Broadfoot
Seated: Fraser, Burge, Flegg, Johnston, Burdon, Connaghan, Vest

Four Lions principals, 1920.
John Wilson (tour manager), Harold Wagstaff (captain), Sydney Foster (tour manager),
Gwyn Thomas (vice-captain).

TEST MATCH 15

AT HEADINGLEY, LEEDS – 1 October, 1921
GREAT BRITAIN 6 AUSTRALIA 5 (HT 3-5)

WG Thomas (Huddersfield)	C Fraser (Balmain) capt
WJ Stone (Hull) T	HN Horder (Norths)
H Wagstaff (Huddersfield) capt	R Vest (Wests)
JA Bacon (Leeds)	† JH Craig (Balmain) G
S Stockwell (Leeds) T	CR Blinkhorn (Norths) T
J Parkin (Wakefield T)	A Johnston (St. George)
JH Rogers (Huddersfield)	DF Thompson (Norths)
W Cunliffe (Warrington)	F Ryan (Newtown)
J Cartwright (Leigh)	SC Pearce (Easts)
GA Skelhorne (Warrington)	CW Prentice (Wests)
† JR Beames (Halifax)	A Gray (Glebe)
† DE Morgan (Hull)	J Watkins (Easts)
† J Price (Broughton R)	F Burge (Glebe)

Referee - F Renton (Hunslet)   Crowd - 32,000   Gate - £3,959
Scoring - 3-0 3-5 6-5

The Kaiser's War had broken out whilst the 1914 Lions were completing the second tour of Australasia and almost ten years had elapsed since a test match had been staged in England. The fact that Britain ached to regain the Ashes lost Down Under in 1920 coupled with the startling performances of Les Cubitt's 1921-22 Kangaroos in the lead-up to the test series was sufficient to draw a huge crowd to Headingley and yield bigger receipts than had ever been taken in a Northern Union fixture. Cubitt unfortunately suffered injury and missed all the tests. The Kangaroos had tremendous popular appeal possessing two real flying-machines in wingers Harold Horder and Cec Blinkhorn, an outrageously prolific try-scoring forward in Frank Burge and a masterly scrum-half in Duncan Thompson.

In pure footballing terms the game was not one of the greatest tests ever played but it was thrilling to a degree with never more than three points between the sides and some desperately close shaves. Although the three tries were all scored by wingers it was amongst the forwards that the match was decided. Both packs were decidedly good but the British ultimately proved the better with the front row scrummaging magnificently to deny the Australian backs possession whilst the back three, all debutants, ran and tackled demonically. Most conspicuous of all was Edgar Morgan, an ex-Welsh Union cap from Llanelli, who had only a couple of months professional experience to his credit. Of the Australian pack *The Yorkshire Observer* remarked, *their forwards, prominent among whom were Burge, Watkins and Pearce, were a fine, hefty lot, not too good in the scrummage, but exceptionally fast in the open. In this department they used their hands better than their feet, and were not so good as the English forwards in controlling the ball.*

Britain could have won the test on goals alone but almost paid heavily for not fielding a recognised goal-kicker. At least nine shots at goal were missed by Stockwell, Stone, Price, Rogers and Thomas. After ruining several chances to take the lead Britain nosed in front with a try which owed much to good fortune. Johnston tried to clear his line by kicking only for Parkin to charge the ball down. Blinkhorn failed to secure the rebound and Billy Stone needed no second invitation to touch down an unconverted try. The lead was short-lived, however, as a clever, incisive move between Thompson, Burge and Vest had Blinkhorn crossing for a try superbly converted by Craig. At this point the Kangaroos were rampant and would surely have sealed the game had Burge not knocked on with the line at his mercy and Blinkhorn committed the same sin within minutes of the first.

Even so the Kangaroos seemed likely to hold on and it was not until the 77th minute that their citadel fell. Jack Beames initiated a passing bout which culminated in Fraser being tackled over his own line. From the resulting scrum Rogers, Parkin and Bacon whipped the ball out to Squire Stockwell who, with seemingly no room to manoeuvre, somehow managed to double inside the redoubtable Horder and score at the corner. A point up and two minutes to go, the delirium of the crowd turned to palpitations as Horder, so well shackled previously, left Bacon and Stockwell for dead and sped like a hare for the line and victory. Only Gwyn Thomas barred his way as Wagstaff and Stone vainly sought to cut him off. Thomas was left behind as Horder elected to kick and chase and it developed into a sprint between Horder and Stone which tantalisingly neither won as the ball crossed the dead-line. Thirty-two thousand Britons breathed again.

TEST MATCH 16

AT THE BOULEVARD, HULL – 5 November, 1921
GREAT BRITAIN 2 AUSTRALIA 16 (HT 2-2)

WG Thomas (Huddersfield)	C Fraser (Balmain) capt
WJ Stone (Hull)	HN Horder (Norths) T
W Batten (Hull)	†G Carstairs (St. George)
JA Bacon (Leeds)	R Vest (Wests) T
S Stockwell (Leeds)	CR Blinkhorn (Norths) 2T
J Parkin (Wakefield T) capt	†H Caples (Easts)
JH Rogers (Huddersfield) G	DF Thompson (Norths) 2G
W Cunliffe (Warrington)	W Schultz (Balmain)
J Cartwright (Leigh)	SC Pearce (Easts)
GA Skelhorne (Warrington)	CW Prentice (Wests)
JR Beames (Halifax)	†RA Latta (Balmain)
DE Morgan (Hull)	J Watkins (Easts)
J Price (Broughton R)	F Burge (Glebe)

Referee - R Robinson (Bradford)   Crowd - 21,504   Gate - £2,924/8/-

Scoring - 0-2 2-2 2-5 2-10 2-13 2-16

In the preceding test Britain had triumphed largely because the Australian three-quarters had been denied freedom to run but on this occasion the British forwards were depleted for almost the whole game as Price had to go into the three-quarters to cover for the injured Stockwell. Consequently Britain's five packmen were hard pressed to contain the Kangaroo six let alone stifle the sizzling Aussie back-line. All the Australian three-quarters performed brilliantly with Carstairs and Horder particularly sharp.

Despite the disadvantage caused by Stockwell's injury the British forwards held their opponents well during the first half and half-backs Parkin and Rogers were the equals of Caples and Thompson, whilst at full-back Gwyn Thomas could not be faulted. The first quarter seemed to indicate that Australia would run away with the game but remarkably they were unable to score and it was not until the 25th minute when Thompson kicked a penalty that the Kangaroos finally took the lead. For the last fifteen minutes of the half Britain rallied strongly with Johnny Rogers twice going close to a try and it was only justice when Rogers equalised with a goal kicked from a mark after Stone had made a fair catch.

The second half was no contest as the Australian three-quarters cut loose. First Vest intercepted a British passing movement and shot down the touch-line to score. Britain retaliated briefly and there could have been tries for both Stone and Batten had the pace or support been sufficient. Carstairs, however, dashed British hopes by instigating a fine try for Horder who cut diagonally through a somewhat reluctant defence to score at the posts. Thompson improved and at 10-2 Australia were never again in danger. Two tries to the deadly Blinkhorn were merely salt in the home team's wounds. The first was due to the winger's resolute running but the second was a gift as Stone dropped a pass and seemed content to observe as Blinkhorn raced away.

In the second half the British, with the exception of Bacon and Batten, had simply given up tackling. *The Yorkshire Post* made no bones about it: *the general defence was not worthy of a third-rate side. The way Horder was allowed to sprint straight through for his try was enough to make an old Rugby man weep but the culminating display of feebleness was that given by Stone, who after dropping a reasonably accurate pass, stood still and watched Blinkhorn run over the line.*

For Jonty Parkin it was an unhappy first captaincy of his country in a test - on his 27th birthday. For two other truly great players it was their swansong in test match rugby. Billy Batten and Syd "Sandy" Pearce had both played in the first Anglo-Australian test match at Park Royal back in 1908. Remarkably each fathered a son who played in subsequent Ashes series, each in the position graced by their fathers.

FOUR STAR MEN FROM OVERSEAS

BUT WE
SHALL
HOLD 'EM !

Harold Horder (N. Sydney).—The most dangerous man in the Australian three-quarter line.

J. Craig.—The Balmain centre-three-quarter. A star in his own domain; very elusive.

Duncan Thompson.—The brilliant N. Sydney half-back. Has a pair of hands like a safe deposit.

J. (Bluey) Watkins.—Star of the Eastern Suburbs Club. Most brilliant all-round forward in the Sydney Rugby League.

A quartet of star Kangaroos of the 1921–2 tour

TEST MATCH 17

AT WEASTE, SALFORD – 14 January, 1922
GREAT BRITAIN 6 AUSTRALIA 0 (HT 3-0)

WG Thomas (Huddersfield)	C Fraser (Balmain) capt
D Hurcombe (Wigan)	HN Horder (Norths)
H Wagstaff (Huddersfield) capt	G Carstairs (St. George)
JA Bacon (Leeds)	R Vest (Wests)
†J Owen (St. Helens Recs)	CR Blinkhorn (Norths)
†J Greenall (St. Helens Recs)	H Caples (Easts)
JH Rogers (Huddersfield)	DF Thompson (Norths)
W Cunliffe (Warrington)	W Schultz (Balmain)
J Cartwright (Leigh)	CW Prentice (Wests)
GA Skelhorne (Warrington)	F Ryan (Newtown)
†R Taylor (Hull)	RA Latta (Balmain)
H Hilton (Oldham) T	W Richards (Wests, Brisbane)
F Gallagher (Dewsbury) T	F Burge (Glebe)

Referee - R Jones (Widnes)   Crowd - 21,000   Gate - £2,450
Scoring - 3-0 6-0

Five of the finest players international rugby has known adorned the test arena for the last time in this gruelling altercation in the deep mid-winter of Weaste. Frank Burge and "Chook" Fraser finished as losers but for the Holy Trinity of Huddersfield, Harold Wagstaff, Gwyn Thomas and little Johnny Rogers, it was joy unconfined as Britain regained the Ashes which they were not to surrender until 1950.

For the rival captains the contrast could hardly have been greater as they left the international scene. For "Waggie" the ecstasy as he was borne aloft by an enraptured crowd and carried in triumph from the field of glory, his white Northern Union shirt torn to shreds by adoring relic hunters. For "Chook" the agony, the Ashes lost and his right leg broken five minutes before the interval as he fell awkwardly in a tackle by Danny Hurcombe.

The match had originally been scheduled somewhat vaguely to be played *in Manchester* with Old Trafford, Maine Road or the Broughton Rangers' ground, The Cliff, all being mooted. In the event the test was allotted to Salford where 2,000 tons of cinders had to be laid for banking purposes to accommodate the crowd. The match only went ahead because ten tons of straw had protected the pitch from snow. The conditions therefore prejudiced the issue against the Australians - it was reported that only Fraser had ever before seen snow. The whole of the British back three was changed and one critic remarked pointedly that *the reconstructed forward division might have been designed specially for such a day.* Old Ebor (AW Pullin) of *The Yorkshire Evening Post* wrote, *it was certainly a cheerless and watery appearance which the enclosure presented. It is not exactly a sylvan retreat at the best of times, and today it had a very gloomy and uninviting aspect.*
Under the circumstances the game was tremendous. One journalist, *The Veteran* wrote,
As a test of real Northern Union football the match exceeded all expectations, for notwithstanding a treacherous surface it was fought at a terrific pace, and though hard enough in all conscience it was never rough, although there were just one or two trifling incidents that might have been done without. Bob Jones kept a firm hand on them, and, after all, the Rugby game at its best is one to be battled by men.
Only two scores were registered. The first, after 20 minutes, followed an unsuccessful penalty by Rogers which failed to reach touch. Fraser fielded the ball but Hilton and Taylor were on to him like the hounds of Hell forcing him to hurriedly pass to Carstairs. Owen intercepted and gave to Skelhorne who short passed to Cunliffe. Horder checked the prop but he parted to Taylor, who, falling to Fraser, somehow contrived to conjure the final pass to Hermon Hilton who took two Kangaroos over the line for a fine try. The game was settled in the 68th minute when a scrum formed in the Australian "25". Although Thompson gained possession he was so forcefully tackled by Gallagher that he spilled the ball which Gallagher dribbled to the line for the touchdown. Australia, gallant losers, became the first team in test history to be nilled and for the first time too a test match was completed without a goal being kicked, only four being landed in the entire series.
Britain won because they adopted the correct policy of constant foot rushes whilst the Aussies tried to play dry weather football. The twin threat of Horder and Blinkhorn was throttled at source by Hurcombe and Owen who clung to them like grim death.

TEST MATCH 18

AT SYDNEY CRICKET GROUND – 23 June, 1924
AUSTRALIA 3 GREAT BRITAIN 22 (HT 3-4)

† E Frauenfelder (Ipswich)	† J Sullivan (Wigan) 5G
† CJM Aynsley (Wests, Brisbane) T	† S Rix (Oldham) T
HN Horder (Souths)	† CW Carr (Barrow)
† T Gorman (Toowoomba)	† T Howley (Wigan)
CR Blinkhorn (Souths)	† J Ring (Wigan)
† AL Blair (Souths)	D Hurcombe (Wigan)
JH Craig (Ipswich) capt	J Parkin (Wakefield T) capt 2T
N Potter (Ipswich)	W Cunliffe (Warrington)
† H Watt (Balmain)	† Jack Bennett (Rochdale H)
A Oxford (Easts)	† W Burgess (Barrow)
† Jim Bennett (Toowoomba)	† J Darwell (Leigh)
† A O'Connor (Souths)	J Price (Wigan) T
RA Latta (Balmain)	F Gallagher (Batley)

Referee - T McMahon (NSW)　　　　Crowd - 50,005　　Gate - £4,715
Scoring - 0-2 0-4 3-4 3-6 3-11 3-16 3-19 3-22

Two of the greatest figures in the pageant of Anglo-Australian conflict made their test debuts in this hard fought contest. Tom Gorman, a stylish centre from Queensland, was to play in ten consecutive Ashes tests and become one of his country's most notable captains. On the British side for the first time was the prodigious Jim Sullivan, finest of all goal-kickers and a match winner *par excellence.*

Sullivan's first act in test rugby was sensational and a dire warning to the Aussies of the mayhem he would cause them for the next decade. The Governor-General of Australia kicked off and, as is the custom under such circumstances, a scrum was ordered at the centre. Australia were penalised and Sullivan was told by his captain to kick at goal. To do so he had to retire several yards inside his own half. The kick was his first in test rugby and fully 55 yards. The crowd was stunned when the mighty Sullivan sent the ball unerringly between the sticks. Two minutes later Jack Bennett was tripped and Sullivan booted another towering penalty. Australia, through Oxford and Horder, proceeded to throw points away as three penalties were missed but it was the Kangaroos who were clearly on top throughout the first half.

Only heroic defence kept Australia out but after 35 minutes the Kangaroos were rewarded when a scrum went down near half-way on the right wing. Jimmy Craig broke away down the blind-side, passed to O'Connor and was there for the return pass. Taking Sullivan's tackle, Craig popped out the ball to Aynsley who streaked 25 yards to the touchdown. Oxford missed the conversion.

The forward exchanges were becoming heated and Burgess was cautioned whilst Potter and Darwell seemed to be conducting a running feud. Still the Aussies pressed and for the first twenty minutes of the second half were well in command but unable to gain anything tangible from several brilliant movements and fell further behind to another fine Sullivan goal. The forward battle finally erupted when Potter was sent off on the hour for striking Darwell.

From then on the British pack gained the ascendancy and with Jonty Parkin in constant possession the Kangaroos' defence disintegrated. From a scrum near the left centre Parkin darted down the field and released Howley who quickly made ground before sending Price hurtling over between the posts. Sullivan's goal was a formality. Soon afterwards Parkin was at it again. Breaking from a scrum he used Ring as a foil and Craig's tackle was too late to prevent the try at the corner. Sullivan converted off the touch-line. At 16-3 Australia were shattered. Parkin was not finished yet, however, and coming through his own pack was hauled down a foot from the line and clearly grounded. The crowd was incensed when Jonty was awarded a try after a blatant double movement. Just before the close Gallagher punctured the defence and sent Rix away on a fine run, the winger handing off Horder and Blinkhorn before scoring wide out.

Great Britain had triumphed by virtue of forward power and Sullivan's boot. As to the violence *The Sydney Sportsman* opined, *it was never anticipated that the game would be played with kid gloves but more of the players were lucky not to get marching orders. Both sides were to blame, but England did most of the nasty bits.* Mr McMahon was clearly not flavour of the month in Sydney.

TEST MATCH 19

AT SYDNEY CRICKET GROUND – 28 June, 1924
AUSTRALIA 3 GREAT BRITAIN 5 (HT 3-0)

E Frauenfelder (Ipswich)	J Sullivan (Wigan) G
HN Horder (Souths)	S Rix (Oldham)
JH Craig (Ipswich) capt	CW Carr (Barrow)
T Gorman (Toowoomba)	T Howley (Wigan)
CJM Aynsley (Wests, Brisbane) T	†F Evans (Swinton)
†J Hunt (Ipswich)	F Gallagher (Batley)
DF Thompson (Toowoomba Valleys)	J Parkin (Wakefield T) capt T
N Potter (Ipswich)	W Cunliffe (Warrington)
H Watt (Balmain)	Jack Bennett (Rochdale H)
Jim Bennett (Toowoomba)	W Burgess (Barrow)
†LV Armbruster (Toowoomba Valleys)	†JF Thompson (Leeds)
A O'Connor (Souths)	J Darwell (Leigh)
RA Latta (Balmain)	†A Brough (Oldham)
†SUB JC Ives (Norths) for O'Connor	

Referee - T McMahon (NSW)   Crowd - 33,842   Gate - £2,831
Scoring - 3-0 3-5

Thirty-six hours of torrential rain considerably helped the British cause by preventing the Australians from effectively using their greater speed which on a dry day would surely have found out a British side hard hit by injuries and boldly gambling by playing their roly-poly octopus of a loose-forward Frank Gallagher at stand-off. Ironically when the game ended the Australians had lost the Ashes but in both games had been, if anything, the better team. *Cynic,* reporting in *The Sydney Referee* wrote, *if you overlook goal-kicking Australia was a trifle the better side on the day* but wisely he added, *you cannot overlook it.* Any side overlooking this crucial factor when opposed to a team including Sullivan did so at its own peril. Australia missed several shots at goal and in the end were only defeated by Sullivan's late, late conversion, the only goal of the match.

A crowd of exceptional proportions under the circumstances saw Craig win the toss and give Australia first use of a strong breeze. The game began at a furious pace as Australia, intent upon playing as if the going was firm, tossed the ball about almost with abandon. Craig missed a penalty when Burgess was ruled off-side but after eight minutes a wonderful piece of open play yielded three points to the Kangaroos. The forwards secured a position in the Lions' "25" on the right flank and Duncan Thompson whipped the ball out to Hunt who parted to Craig. The Australian captain drove forward in a diagonal run, committed a tackler and served Gorman, the outstanding three-quarter of the series, who cleverly veered out to the left wing, drew Rix into the tackle and passed out to Aynsley who planted the ball just inside the corner flag as a flying British tackler slithered yards past him in a vain attempt to prevent the score.

Australia continued to dominate but for all Thompson's varied tactics there was no breaching of the Lions' defence as Parkin and Gallagher snuffed out Australian attempts to spread the play. The British were spoiling desperately, going off-side at scrums and during foot rushes and moved *Cynic* to say that *some of them in these things show no conscience.* Even so, it was almost half-time before the British took play as far as the home "25".

In the second half Britain used the wind to much better effect than had their opponents but with the mud foiling all and sundry it began to look as if Aynsley's try would decide the test. With ten minutes remaining, however, the game was snatched from Australia's grasp. For once Parkin slipped the defence from a scrum 35 yards out. Instead of passing to Gallagher, the Lions' skipper grubber kicked past the inside backs. Frauenfelder misfielded and Parkin was on to the ball to kick through again. The ball stuck fast in the mire as Horder rocketed back and lunged for it but slithered erratically and missed it altogether as the persistent Parkin toed it yet again, the ball coming to rest a dozen yards from the posts in the in-goal area. A mud-spattered defender desperately raced Parkin for the touchdown but there was no stopping the little Englishman. Normally the kick would hardly have caused Sullivan a moment's worry but under the circumstances, with the Ashes at stake, it was no formality. A deathly silence fell with all Australia praying for a miracle but Sully's nerve never faltered, the goal was kicked and prayer discredited.

TEST MATCH 20

AT THE EXHIBITION GROUND, BRISBANE – 12 July, 1924
AUSTRALIA 21 GREAT BRITAIN 11 (HT 4-5)

E Frauenfelder (Ipswich)
CJM Aynsley (Wests, Brisbane) 2G
JH Craig (Ipswich) capt G
T Gorman (Toowoomba)
W Paten (Ipswich) T
J Hunt (Ipswich)
DF Thompson (Toowoomba Valleys) 2G
N Potter (Ipswich)
H Watt (Balmain)
Jim Bennett (Toowoomba)
A O'Connor (Souths)
LV Armbruster (Toowoomba Valleys) T
RA Latta (Balmain)
SUB A Oxford (Easts) T,G for O'Connor

J Sullivan (Wigan) G
S Rix (Oldham)
T Howley (Wigan)
JA Bacon (Leeds)
F Evans (Swinton) 2T
D Hurcombe (Wigan)
J Parkin (Wakefield T) capt T
W Cunliffe (Warrington)
Jack Bennett (Rochdale H)
W Burgess (Barrow)
J Price (Wigan)
J Darwell (Leigh)
F Gallagher (Batley)

Referee - J Roche (Queensland)   Crowd - 36,000   Gate - £3,315
Scoring - 0-2 2-2 2-5 4-5 9-5 14-5 19-5 21-5 21-8 21-11

For the only time in the history of Ashes football, apart from 1992, Brisbane housed a third test - traditionally it has staged the second test of a series. The experiment was hugely successful from Australia's stand-point - an ultimately comfortable victory and the ground full three hours before the kick-off. The game itself, however, was no classic. *Traveller,* the Brisbane correspondent for *The Sydney Referee,* wrote, *as a spectacle, the game was not particularly satisfactory. It was fierce at times, almost beyond football description, and players on both sides had to put up with what was - well, let us say it was not football, and leave it at that.*

The ferocity of the forward confrontation culminated in the dismissal of Jim Bennett and Frank Gallagher and the game was riddled with penalties with the Lions the worse offenders especially in the sphere of "shepherding".

Despite the score-line many critics wondered how the Lions managed to lose the test as for the greater part they had been the better team with the forwards ruling the scrums and Parkin playing all over Thompson. In the final analysis it was the greater overall pace of the Kangaroos which decided the game plus a little luck and a rare off-day for Sullivan's goal-kicking.

It was Sullivan, however, who drew first blood with a towering drop goal from the half-way mark in the early minutes. Aynsley levelled with a well-struck penalty but the Lions dominated the half. Only dreadnought defence by the home defence with Hunt, Craig, Gorman and Paten excelling prevented the Lions from establishing a winning position. Their meagre reward was a delightful try by Frank Evans engineered by the wily Parkin but Craig's penalty goal kept Australia well in contention despite the pounding received.

The game was turned on its head in the second half when Evans fumbled a kick and in a twinkling Gorman was sending Paten over for a try. Minutes later it was Gorman again racing down the touch-line before cross-kicking to the centre where Armbruster beat Sullivan to the touchdown. The Lions claimed the second-rower was at least eight yards off-side and they were equally sure that from a similar move a few minutes later Oxford was off-side in scoring from Aynsley's cross-kick. The three tries were converted, two by Thompson and one by Oxford, and within a short period Australia had leapt from a one point deficit to a fourteen points lead. Aynsley added a further penalty goal before Britain staged a late rally. Evans scored his second try forcing his way determinedly past Paten but Parkin had the last word by completely fooling the defence with a blind-side dash. Parkin thus scored a try in each test to emulate Johnny Thomas' feat in the 1908-09 series.

Bill Paten had been the pick of the Australian backs whilst Danny Hurcombe had proved the most dangerous of the British rear division but it was "Whip" Latta who was awarded a silver cup as the game's outstanding player. Jonty Parkin had been heartily barracked during the match and a section of the crowd made a demonstration against him at the close but having changed into an Australian jersey he was not molested.

TEST MATCH 21

AT THE EXHIBITION GROUND, BRISBANE – 23 June, 1928
AUSTRALIA 12 GREAT BRITAIN 15 (HT 7-13)

JH Craig (Ipswich) G	J Sullivan (Wigan) capt 3G
†J Freestone (Tumut) G	†TC Askin (Featherstone R)
T Gorman (Brothers,Brisbane) capt	†J Oliver (Batley)
†N Hardy (Easts)	†JW Brough (Leeds)
CJM Aynsley (Wests, Brisbane) T,G	†A Ellaby (St. Helens) T
†FC Laws (Toowoomba Town)	LS Fairclough (St. Helens) T
†AEG Edwards (Valleys, Brisbane)	W Rees (Swinton)
†H Steinohrt (Toowoomba Valley)	W Burgess (Barrow)
†A Justice (St. George)	†N Bentham (Wigan Highfield)
†DV Dempsey (Ipswich)	H Bowman (Hull)
†AG Treweek (Souths)	†W Horton (Wakefield T) T
†C York (Queanbeyan)	R Sloman (Oldham)
LV Armbruster (Grammars, Brisbane) T	AE Fildes (St. Helens Recs)

Referee - C Broadfoot (Queensland)   Crowd - 39,200   Gate - £4,366

Scoring - 0-2 0-5 2-5 2-10 5-10 7-10 7-13 10-13 12-13 12-15

For the first time Australia donned their famous livery of green and gold - previously they had worn blue and maroon, or plain blue - but the change proved to be no good luck charm. Despite the closeness of the scores there was never much doubt that John Bull's boys would take the laurels. Australia fielded no fewer than nine men new to the test arena, the most notable of whom were Herb Steinohrt, Dan Dempsey and George Treweek, three forwards to rank alongside the greatest of Australian packmen. Britain, lacking skipper Jonty Parkin, likewise threw caution to the wind and brought in six test debutants including such luminaries as Alf Ellaby, Jim Brough, Joe Oliver and Bill Horton.

Britain's supremacy was founded on the performance of a dominant pack belligerently led by Bob Sloman and a bewitching display by half-backs Les Fairclough and Billo Rees. As a result the home halves were completely subdued and Hardy and Gorman, the main dangers, were rarely allowed to display their talents. Sullivan failed with a penalty shot from 60 yards very early in the proceedings but had soon landed another long-range opportunity to set the Lions on the winning path. Within two minutes the lead was increased as from a scrum near half-way the hare-quick Fairclough latched on to Rees' pass to link with Askin in a blind-side move. The winger made a lot of ground before tossing inside to Fairclough who went round Craig as if he were not there to score a superbly executed try at the corner. Craig pulled back two points with a well-stuck penalty but Britain delivered another hammer blow after 24 minutes. This time it was Rees, a tiny terror, who did the damage by somehow persuading all the Australian inside backs to converge on Fairclough as Britain heeled at a scrum. Rees had no intention of passing to his partner and was through a huge gap before the home team knew what was happening. As he approached the line he was met by Craig's challenge but turned the ball to the supporting Horton who just beat Freestone to the line. Sullivan's goal pushed Britain's lead to 10-2.

Australia replied with a smartly worked try as Edwards, departing from his normal route, dashed down the short side of a scrum and found his forwards so quick to support that Treweek, York and Armbruster were the last three men to handle before the latter touched down. There was no goal from Freestone, Craig and Aynsley already having failed with half-a-dozen shots at goal which cost Australia dear. Eventually Freestone did find the target with a difficult penalty but on the stroke of half-time Britain conjured a magical try. A scrum went down 40 yards out and Rees served Fairclough who ducked below Laws' flailing arms and, falling, passed to Askin careering infield from the wing. A long pass to Brough, a short one to Oliver and thence to Ellaby at full throttle for the winger to race past Craig to the corner.

Australia raised hopes of victory in the second half when for a change the ball reached Gorman from a scrum at the Lions' "25". Faced with a phalanx of defenders, Gorman veered back toward the breaking scrum and punted over it. Sullivan was strangely casual as the ball entered the in-goal and Aynsley profited to register a soft try. Four minutes from time Ellaby streaked 70 yards for a disallowed try emanating from an obstruction on Gorman. The penalty was potted by Aynsley and Australia trailed by a solitary point. Gorman almost won the game after intercepting near half-way but was hauled to the ground by the shirt-collar by a desperate Fairclough and Britain drove to the other end where Sullivan settled the affair with a fine goal on the stroke of time.

Sydney, second test, 1928.
British skipper Jonty Parkin
kicks away from a muddy ruck.

TEST MATCH 22

AT SYDNEY CRICKET GROUND – 14 July, 1928
AUSTRALIA 0 GREAT BRITAIN 8 (HT 0-5)

N Hardy (Easts)	J Sullivan (Wigan) G
† H Byrne (Easts)	TC Askin (Featherstone R)
T Gorman (Brothers, Brisbane) capt	J Oliver (Batley)
JH Craig (Ipswich)	JW Brough (Leeds)
† P Maher (Souths)	A Ellaby (St. Helens) T
† E Weissel (Temora)	W Rees (Swinton)
† J Busch (Easts)	J Parkin (Wakefield T) capt T
H Steinohrt (Toowoomba Valley)	W Burgess (Barrow)
A Justice (St. George)	N Bentham (Wigan Highfield)
DV Dempsey (Ipswich)	JF Thompson (Leeds)
AG Treweek (Souths)	R Sloman (Oldham)
C York (Queanbeyan)	AE Fildes (St. Helens Recs)
LV Armbruster (Grammars, Brisbane)	W Horton (Wakefield T)

Referee - L Deane (NSW)   Crowd - 44,548   Gate - £4,298
Scoring - 0-5 0-8

Persistent heavy rain and the customary plethora of curtain-raisers conspired to render the SCG a quagmire. Despite the conditions the game offered more entertainment than could have been expected and Britain had to fight hard to clinch the Ashes from a tenacious Australian XIII. The decisive factor proved to be the marvellously skilful footwork and dribbling of the British forwards whose tactics were made for such a morass. Aided by a masterful display of field kicking by Jim Sullivan and Nat Bentham's 34-28 pull in the tight, Britain always looked the likelier winners but were hard pressed to break the home defence.

Within minutes of the start most of the players had acquired a thick coating of the Cricket Ground's notorious "Bulli" mud and were unrecognisable. The first chance fell to the Lions when "Snowy" - a misnomer on this day if ever there was one - Justice upended Sullivan after he had cleared his line. With the ball still relatively dry Sullivan essayed a mighty kick at goal but narrowly missed. Australia mounted a good deal of pressure as Parkin constantly gave away penalties for feeding. Oliver had to go down in the shadow of his own posts to stop an Australian foot-rush and Ellaby was obliged to scramble the ball out of play near the corner. Craig failed at goal from an impossible distance before Sullivan thwarted a clever dribble by Weissel.

Eventually Britain began to gain the ascendancy and after a wonderful piece of dribbling by Joe Thompson a passing movement developed which seemed certain to produce a try until the inevitable knock-on occurred. Five minutes before half-time, however, the Australian citadel fell as a scrum formed in home territory. Justice heeled and Busch elected to clear his lines by kicking only to be blocked by Parkin who was on to the ricochet in a trice. Hardy got to grips with the scrum-half but Parkin's impetus carried them both over the line and the try was given about a dozen yards from the flag. Sullivan blasted the heavy ball out of the mud for a crucial conversion and Britain had a lead they would not yield.

The first fifteen minutes of the second half saw Australia's most dangerous period as Treweek, Craig and Gorman led a succession of forays which Britain repulsed with some difficulty but Australia gained no tangible rewards for their pains and gradually the sting was drawn from their play. Brough was unfortunate in dropping the ball in a scoring position and Parkin suffered a fractured thumb but stayed on to do a captain's duty. Australia barely survived a kick and rush by Ellaby before being saved by Weissel's brave dive on his goal-line and, as a mist began to obscure the play even more, Britain sealed the match and the Ashes with a superb try on the hour. The forwards had driven to the half-way line when the ball was kicked to the pavilion corner where Hardy fielded and kicked back into the centre-field. Joe Oliver gathered and began a passing bout which took play from right to left and Brough and Rees made light of the muddy ball to send Ellaby past a helpless cover to touch down next to the flag. There was no hope of even the redoubtable Sullivan landing the conversion but the eight point cushion was more than enough to keep a tiring Australia at bay.

Australia was thus rendered pointless for the first time on home soil.

The dribbling of the British forwards, amongst whom Thompson, Sloman and Horton were outstanding, had been a wonder to behold and more than one good judge deemed it the best display of the art to have been seen in Australia in League or Union.

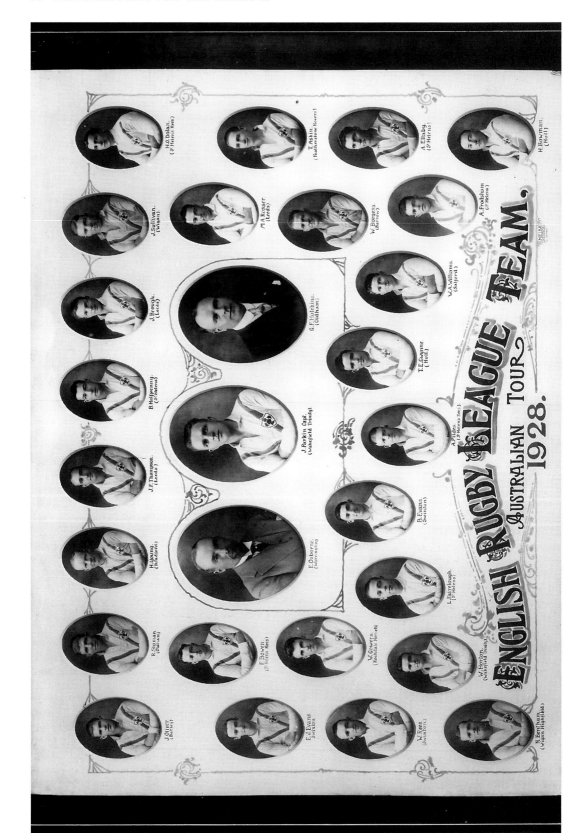

TEST MATCH 23

AT SYDNEY CRICKET GROUND – 21 July, 1928
AUSTRALIA 21 GREAT BRITAIN 14 (HT 9-7)

N Hardy (Easts)

†B Wearing (Souths) 2T,3G

T Gorman (Brothers, Brisbane) capt

JH Craig (Ipswich) 3G

†CG Pearce (Wests) T

E Weissel (Temora)

J Busch (Easts)

H Steinohrt (Toowoomba Valley)

A Justice (St. George)

DV Dempsey (Ipswich)

AG Treweek (Souths)

†J Kingston (Young)

LV Armbruster (Grammars, Brisbane)

J Sullivan (Wigan) capt 4G

†TE Gwynne (Hull)

TC Askin (Featherstone R)

J Oliver (Batley)

A Ellaby (St. Helens)

LS Fairclough (St. Helens) 2T

W Rees (Swinton)

W Burgess (Barrow)

N Bentham (Wigan Highfield)

H Bowman (Hull)

R Sloman (Oldham)

AE Fildes (St. Helens Recs)

W Horton (Wakefield T)

Referee - L Deane (NSW)   Crowd - 37,380   Gate - £3,118

Scoring - 2-0 4-0 4-5 6-5 9-5 9-7 9-9 11-9 13-9 13-14 16-14 21-14

With the series already conceded Australia surprised the pundits with a spectacular triumph in a game which throbbed with excitement from start to finish. In contrast to the previous week the SCG provided an ideal pitch for fast, open football on a perfect day. One critic remarked that it was *no game for a weakling to be mixed in* and Bill Horton, the British back-rower, was sent off near the end. For all that, the game was conducted in a fine, sporting spirit with the crowd at fever pitch as the scores fluctuated furiously. In the final analysis Australia should have had a superior winning margin and scored more than three tries but were denied by an inordinately stubborn defence.

Australia were quickly on the score-board when Jimmy Craig, on his last test appearance, kicked a touch-line penalty and for a time it looked as if Britain would be overrun. Hardy made a beautiful break and should have created a try but wily Jim Sullivan fooled him into running away from his supports. The pressure told, however, and Craig was able to land a simple ten yard penalty before Benny Wearing brought the crowd to their feet following superb passing between Busch, Weissel, Craig and Gorman. Wearing shot clear at half-way, punted over Sullivan at the "25" and won the race to the ball in-goal but nudged it forward before touching down.

Two minutes later Britain made Australia pay as Fairclough intercepted Busch's transfer to Weissel at a scrum on the home "25" to race to the posts. Sullivan's conversion gave Britain the lead but they held it only briefly as Craig potted a straight penalty from 27 yards. A disputed Australian try followed as Armbruster dummied through on the Lions' "25" before sending Treweek, the game's outstanding forward, on a surge towards the posts. Treweek was hauled down but managed to sling out a long lofted pass to the wing where Wearing was able to dash over having mishandled the ball. Britain claimed a knock-on but the referee allowed the score. Just before the interval Sullivan reduced Australia's lead to 9-7 with a fine touch-line penalty.

Within a minute of the restart Sullivan had repeated the dose to level the match and play swung merrily from end to end. Wearing, playing the game of his life, was smothered at the corner in one valiant effort to score but had the satisfaction of nosing Australia ahead with penalty-goals in the 50th and 60th minutes. As the game entered its final quarter Britain sneaked in front when Fairclough, receiving from Rees at a scrum near half-way, sliced clean through for a magnificent solo try near the posts. Sullivan's goal gave the Lions a 14-13 lead. The Australian response was stunning. Busch secured from a mid-field scrum and fed Weissel on the blind-side. Weissel sent Wearing away and the winger punted over the "25". Gwynne knocked Wearing off balance but he stumbled forward, regained balance, kicked on again past Sullivan and dived for a spectacular touchdown. Shortly after this Kingston was seen to be flat out, Horton was sent off on the intervention of a touch-judge and a depleted Lions XIII could not prevent Gorman from creating a delightful try for Pearce. Wearing converted to equal Jim Leytham's record of twelve points in an Ashes test and beat the old Australian record of eleven points set by Dally Messenger back in 1910. Remarkably Wearing made only this solitary appearance in test rugby, yet, as one noted critic observed, *men like Wearing give us the champagne of Rugger.*

TEST MATCH 24

AT CRAVEN PARK, HULL – 5 October, 1929
GREAT BRITAIN 8 AUSTRALIA 31 (HT 2-18)

† TE Rees (Oldham)	† F McMillan (Wests)
TE Gwynne (Hull)	† W Spencer (Bundaberg) T
† RM Kinnear (Wigan)	T Gorman (Brothers, Brisbane) capt
† W Dingsdale (Warrington)	† CR Fifield (Wests)
A Frodsham (St. Helens)	† WJ Shankland (Easts) 2T
LS Fairclough (St. Helens) capt	E Weissel (Temora) T,5G
W Rees (Swinton)	J Busch (Easts)
H Bowman (Hull)	† W Brogan (Wests)
N Bentham (Halifax)	† G Bishop (Balmain) T
JF Thompson (Leeds) G	† P Madsen (Toowoomba)
† A Middleton (Salford) T	AG Treweek (Souths) T
W Horton (Wakefield T)	LV Armbruster (Valleys, Brisbane)
† J Feetham (Hull KR) T	† WJ Prigg (Newcastle) T

Referee - R Robinson (Bradford)   Crowd - 20,000   Gate - £2,065
Scoring - 0-5 0-8 2-8 2-13 2-18 5-18 5-23 5-26 8-26 8-31

Herbert Campbell wrote in *The Leeds Mercury* that *the crowd was thrilled, amazed and generously appreciative of the wonderful pace and resource of the Australians, but they were frankly disappointed by the limitations of the English team.*

The home performance was all the more woeful when viewed in the light of the British pack's 5-1 monopoly of possession from the tight. The fact that Australia ran the British ragged to register seven tries on such meagre rations was a terrible indictment of Britain's back play. Australia won most of their possession from tremendously quick and skilful heeling at the play-the-balls.

Britain trailed from the seventh minute when rapid passing from a scrum near the home "25" between Busch, Spencer and Armbruster put Treweek over for a try converted by Weissel. A few minutes later Busch came away from a scrum and fed Shankland who combined swerve and speed brilliantly in a dazzling run before carrying Tommy Rees over the line with him for a try at the flag. Britain pulled back a couple of points after nineteen minutes when Thompson blasted over a long-range penalty and for quarter of an hour it appeared that Australia might be contained.

The last five minutes of the half proved otherwise as the game swung irretrievably away from Britain. Shankland paved the way for a try as he made a fine dodging run before being grassed by Gwynne, the best of the home backs. His effort had stretched the defence to breaking point and from the play-the-ball Busch dashed on before turning the ball inside to Prigg for a debut try to which Weissel added the goal. Within minutes Australia had crossed for another try following exquisite passing between Gorman and Shankland which totally bemused the defenders and allowed George Bishop to touch down under the bar. Bishop thus became the first hooker to score an Ashes test try. Weissel landed the goal and there was still time for Britain to respond, Horton crossing but being recalled because Billo Rees had knocked on earlier in the movement.

The initial stages of the second half held some hope for a home recovery as Gwynne displayed fine opportunism to create a try for Middleton. Thompson's wide-angled conversion struck the post and bounced out and to all intents and purposes Britain's bolt was shot. Shankland was soon to be seen cantering for a try at the posts and Weissel's conversion lifted Australia's lead to 23-5. Prigg and Gorman then opened up the British defence with magical passing to send Spencer careering over before Britain spluttered back to life with a try from Feetham, again engineered by Gwynne. The final score deservedly went to Australian stand-off Eric Weissel who shot under the posts and then converted to set up a record individual total of thirteen points. His fifth goal of the match also equalled the match record jointly held by the immortals, Dally Messenger and Jim Sullivan.

For several of the home side, most notably Fairclough and Bowman, there would be no more tests but Australia had unearthed some rare gems in debutants Frank McMillan, Bill Shankland, "Mick" Madsen and the great Wally Prigg, whilst Tom Gorman's performance had been a minor masterpiece. The game itself had been a delightful exhibition of football without the slightest hint of the unsavoury element that sometimes mars test rugby but so one-sided that it had hardly seemed like a test. The only consolation to which Britain clung was the knowledge that they could hardly play as badly again.

TEST MATCH 25

AT HEADLEY, LEEDS – 9 November, 1929
GREAT BRITAIN 9 AUSTRALIA 3 (HT 7-3)

J Sullivan (Wigan) 3G	F McMillan (Wests)
A Ellaby (St. Helens)	W Spencer (Bundaberg)
†A Atkinson (Castleford) T	T Gorman (Brothers, Brisbane) capt
W Dingsdale (Warrington)	CR Fifield (Wests)
†S Smith (Wakefield T)	WJ Shankland (Easts) T
W Rees (Swinton)	E Weissel (Temora)
J Parkin (Wakefield T) capt	J Busch (Easts)
W Burgess (Barrow)	P Madsen (Toowoomba)
N Bentham (Halifax)	G Bishop (Balmain)
†DM Jenkins (Hunslet)	H Steinohrt (Toowoomba Valley)
†M Hodgson (Swinton)	DV Dempsey (Ipswich)
AE Fildes (St. Helens Recs)	AG Treweek (Souths)
†FA Butters (Swinton)	WJ Prigg (Newcastle)

Referee - R Robinson (Bradford)   Crowd - 31,402   Gate - £3,902

Scoring - 2-0 2-3 4-3 7-3 9-3

After the debacle of the first test Great Britain retained only three members of the side so humiliated at Hull. Of the five debutants loose-forward Fred Butters was the best man in either pack on the day, whilst Arthur Atkinson, Stanley Smith and Martin Hodgson went on to become some of the greatest players to grace the test arena. For Dai Jenkins, a Welsh Rugby Union cap, it was to be his first and last test.

The first test had indicated that the Kangaroos could not be matched in the pack for speed and handling ability and the home side was picked to contain rather than entertain. One critic wrote, *not being able, successfully, to play the Australians' game, England played their own, and put the others off theirs, and put them off it most effectively. It was good tactics, but was it good propaganda?*

The Yorkshire weather joined the conspiracy against Australia for *a villainous rain storm* erupted at 1 o'clock and within half an hour rendered the pitch *tricky, heavy and treacherous.* It was not to be the Australians' day.

There were not too many scoring chances during the match but the general feeling was that Australia should have been buried by half-time. Britain had the benefit of a stiff breeze but had to settle for a four point interval lead. Within minutes of the start Albert Fildes dribbled expertly into Australian territory only for the flying Stanley Smith to miss the touch-down by inches. Britain edged in front after six minutes, however, when Sullivan landed a penalty goal. Australia began to exert their own pressure when Gorman sent the speedy Bill Spencer on a run from half-way. Spencer slipped Smith and managed to circumvent Sullivan but was grounded three yards from the line by Smith, whose lightning recovery was something to behold. There were more close shaves on both wings for the home side as Shankland and Spencer were stopped at vital moments. At the other end there was a scare for the Kangaroos when Atkinson dropped a pass which would certainly have brought a try under the bar.

Atkinson must have wished the ground would swallow him when a few minutes later he sent a sloppy pass out to Ellaby. Shankland pounced for the interception and streaked away from the pursuing Rees and Sullivan to score too far out for Weissel to improve. The Kangaroos held the lead for only seven minutes for in the 34th minute Sullivan kicked a stupendous goal off the touch-line from almost 50 yards. How the Australians wished he had stayed in Wales!

Just before half-time Britain struck a killer blow. Parkin, as usual, was the instigator, Atkinson the executioner. A scrum went down and Parkin passed to Rees, who returned the favour. A moment's indecision in the Australian three-quarter line and Parkin slung the ball wide to Atkinson who ran straight and hard but was felled a yard short but not held. Scrambling to his feet the big centre threw himself over the line to redeem his previous sins. For a change Sullivan missed the conversion but in the 57th minute scored the only other points of the match with a long penalty struck low and accurately into the wind. Australia never looked capable of scoring in the second half save for one occasion when Gorman escaped the defence only to flounder on the rock that was Jim Sullivan. Britain's solitary opportunity to score a try dissipated when Butters failed to provide Ellaby with the ball when he must have scored.

This was no game for the purists but one which at least restored shaken British confidence.

TEST MATCH 26

AT STATION ROAD, SWINTON – 4 January, 1930
GREAT BRITAIN 0 AUSTRALIA 0 (HT 0-0)

J Sullivan (Wigan)	F McMillan (Wests)
A Ellaby (St. Helens)	W Spencer (Bundaberg)
A Atkinson (Castleford)	T Gorman (Brothers, Brisbane) capt
† H Halsall (Swinton)	CR Fifield (Wests)
S Smith (Leeds)	WJ Shankland (Easts)
† J Oster (Oldham)	E Weissel (Temora)
J Parkin (Wakefield T) capt	J Busch (Easts)
W Burgess (Barrow)	H Steinohrt (Toowoomba Valley)
N Bentham (Warrington)	A Justice (St. George)
† AG Thomas (Leeds)	W Brogan (Wests)
AE Fildes (St. Helens Recs)	AG Treweek (Souths)
M Hodgson (Swinton)	LV Armbruster (Valleys, Brisbane)
FA Butters (Swinton)	J Kingston (Cootamundra)

Referee - R Robinson (Bradford)   Crowd - 34,709   Gate - £4,186/11/-

In the entire history of Rugby League test football there has been a solitary scoreless draw. The record books show that it took place at Swinton in 1930 but to Australians there was no doubting that Gorman's Kangaroos were robbed blind of the victory they had earned and of the Ashes they had deserved.

For fully three-quarters of the match Australia held total command and with two minutes remaining the score which had eluded them seemed to have finally materialised. A scrum was formed around the home "25" on the Kangaroos' right flank. Pint-sized hooker "Snowy" Justice struck quicker than Nat Bentham and the ball was out on the Australian side. "Chimpy" Busch, the combative Kangaroo scrum-half, picked up, looked to pass but in a flash had wheeled and was going hell-for-leather down the blind-side, brushing off the attentions of Stanley Smith. A final lung-bursting surge and Busch was flying over at the corner, the ball planted safely over the line. However, in the very act of his Ashes-winning dive he was hit by a desperate tackle by loose-forward Fred Butters and, amid a welter of wildly flailing arms and legs, the corner flag toppled. It did not matter that the referee, Bob Robinson, thought the try a fair one and reportedly told the Australians that it was a legitimate score. Simply, he could not overrule the touch-judge and he deemed that Busch had taken the flag before grounding the ball. No try - whether it was or not!

Amid the gathering gloom Butters was led from the field, blood pumping from an evil gash on his ear. Australians said he sustained the wound hitting the flag, others that he caught Busch's boot. As the drama died and the dusk fell no one noticed that the Australian full-back Frank McMillan had been laid out in the final rush and was left motionless in the mud as the teams retired. Some of the crowd took pity on him and carried him in.

The Yorkshire Post summarised the match thus:

From first to last it was a grim struggle between two strong physical forces, who fought for every inch of ground and countered every attempt at running by stern and relentless tackling. Science, as understood in football, was seldom or never given a chance of asserting itself. To call it a game is a misnomer. War is a more appropriate term. Yet, with all its fierceness, it was not a match that could be called either unfair or unpleasant. Possibly the natural combativeness of the average man gave enjoyment in it to the onlookers. Certainly the crowd experienced 80 minutes of bursting excitement. The result was an anti-climax. All the fuss and fury had produced was a blank score sheet.

Lord Derby was present to hand over the Ashes Cup to the victors but the trophy was returned to its case and no presentation was made although in theory Britain, by virtue of not losing the series, had already retained the Ashes.

So tight a grip had Australia exerted in the first half that Britain were restricted to only two serious attacks. Gorman schemed beautifully and McMillan outshone Sullivan as the Kangaroos laid siege to the British line but for no tangible result. In the second half Sullivan almost snatched the match with a colossal drop at goal which passed just outside the post. It would have been scant justice had the ball bisected the sticks.

Jonty Parkin had announced previously that the game would be his last test and though a fourth test was arranged his word was his bond. It was also the last test for that great Barrow scrummager, Bill Burgess.

A scene at the Swinton Ground when the record gate of over £4000 for a test match between England and Australia was taken, and the match ended in a draw—nil all. Note the straw piled up on the side touchline and the patches of soft soil, as well as the players in white marked with mud. The grounds are also oblong, with the spectators close up, and not oval cricket fields as in Australia.

Two echoes of the only scoreless Ashes test at Swinton in 1930.
Above: A faded photograph from *The Rugby League News* (Sydney, 19 July, 1930) with its original caption.
Below: A wry cartoonist's view.

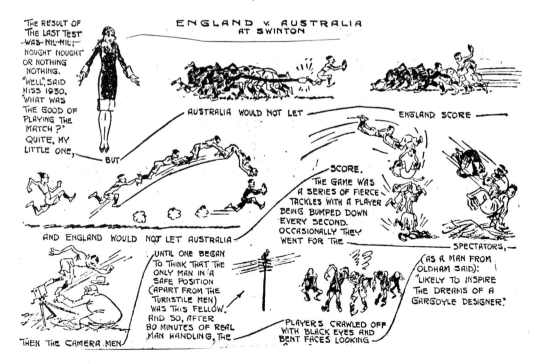

TEST MATCH 27

AT THE ATHLETIC GROUNDS, ROCHDALE – 15 January, 1930
GREAT BRITAIN 3 AUSTRALIA 0 (HT 0-0)

J Sullivan (Wigan) capt	F McMillan (Wests)
† T Blinkhorn (Warrington)	W Spencer (Bundaberg)
† S Brogden (Huddersfield)	T Gorman (Brothers, Brisbane) capt
A Atkinson (Castleford)	CR Fifield (Wests)
S Smith (Leeds) T	WJ Shankland (Easts)
W Rees (Swinton)	FC Laws (Toowoomba Town)
B Evans (Swinton)	J Busch (Easts)
† WA Williams (Salford)	H Steinohrt (Toowoomba Valley)
N Bentham (Warrington)	A Justice (St. George)
AG Thomas (Leeds)	W Brogan (Wests)
AE Fildes (St. Helens Recs)	AG Treweek (Souths)
† H Crowther (Hunslet)	LV Armbruster (Valleys, Brisbane)
† HD Young (Huddersfield)	J Kingston (Cootamundra)

Referee - R Robinson (Bradford)   Crowd - 16,743   Gate - £2,056
Scoring - 3-0

With the series drawn pressure uniquely brought about a deciding fourth test, largely because the Australian management felt it would be good business. As far as the home country was concerned the Ashes were not for contention although the public could not quite swallow that.

The relative performances of the sides in the series can be gauged from the telling statistic that Australia awarded caps to eight new men - all in the first test - whereas Great Britain, fortunate indeed to win the series, had to blood no fewer than seventeen into test rugby. However, at the fourth time of asking the home team were at last truly deserving victors, having the upper hand for a good two-thirds of the match, which was a far more entertaining affair in footballing terms than those at Leeds and Swinton.

Once again the defences were razor-sharp but there was also an incisiveness to both sides' offensive play which warranted more than the single try yielded by the relentless tacklers.

Whilst Britain were deserving winners Australia, obdurate as ever, could count themselves unlucky to lose having weathered the British barrage until the 74th minute. It is a moot point whether their line would have fallen had their gritty centre Cec Fifield not suffered a broken ankle in the 65th minute. The additional pressure thereafter surely counted for something as Jack Kingston was withdrawn from the forward struggle to bolster the three-quarters.

Hector Crowther had narrowly failed to score in chasing a ball almost to the dead-line a few minutes before the decisive moment of the match and the tension was unbearable amongst the players and spectators alike as a scrum formed inside the Kangaroos' territory. Bryn Evans secured the ball and dashed sharply away before serving Stan Brogden. Brogden's pace was sufficient to stretch the Australian defence to breaking point and his final pass to Stan Smith was precision itself. Smith, transferred a fortnight earlier from Wakefield to Leeds for a record £1,075, demonstrated just why he was worth the fee, with a blistering surge to the line, crossing too far out for Sullivan to convert.

Great Britain owed their victory to the excellence of their pack which was described as *strenuous in scrummaging, fearless in rushing, and mighty in tackling* with Crowther and Fildes outstanding. The Swinton half-back pairing of Billo Rees, playing his farewell test, and Bryn Evans combined beautifully and were too clever for their opposites. The Australians clearly missed their outstanding stand-off Eric Weissel and their most dangerous back once more was the scheming Gorman but it was a day when the jet-propelled Kangaroo backs were mastered by determined defensive tactics. Amongst the hard-working, hard-pressed Australian forwards none was superior to Bill Brogan.

Only one match remained for Gorman's 1929-30 Kangaroos, perhaps the most unlucky of all touring teams. Three days later they bowed out in style after whacking Wales 26-10 at Wembley. Four of the test team returned to play for English clubs - Armbruster to Rochdale Hornets, Fifield to Hull, Busch to Leeds and Shankland to Warrington.

TEST MATCH 28

AT SYDNEY CRICKET GROUND – 6 June, 1932
AUSTRALIA 6 GREAT BRITAIN 8 (HT 6-8)

F McMillan (Wests)	J Sullivan (Wigan) capt G
†J Wilson (Ipswich)	A Ellaby (St. Helens) T
FC Laws (Toowoomba Town)	A Atkinson (Castleford) T
E Weissel (Temora) 3G	S Brogden (Huddersfield)
CG Pearce (Wests)	S Smith (Leeds)
†EJ Norman (Easts)	†E Pollard (Wakefield T)
†H Gee (Ipswich)	B Evans (Swinton)
H Steinohrt(Toowoomba Valley)capt	†N Silcock (Widnes)
†J Little (Valleys, Brisbane)	†LL White (Hunslet)
P Madsen (Toowoomba Brothers)	JF Thompson (Leeds)
DV Dempsey (Ipswich)	M Hodgson (Swinton)
†SHW Pearce (Easts)	W Horton (Wakefield T)
WJ Prigg (Central Newcastle)	J Feetham (Salford)

Referee - W Neill (NSW)   Crowd - 70,204   Gate - £6,513

Scoring - 0-3 2-3 4-3 4-8 6-8

Following the first test of the 1932 series *The Referee's* leader column ran: *England is one up in the Rugby League ladder. In the hottest, hardest, and most desperate Rugby game ever seen between first-class teams in Australia, England in scoring 8 points to 6 was the merest shade the finer combination.*

The match was a marvel from beginning to pulsating end and was witnessed by a record crowd of over 70,000. Thousands more were locked out and some desperate fans even climbed the tower of the grandstand at the neighbouring Agricultural Ground to sneak a glimpse of the great match.

Australians had feared a hiding before the game for the 1932 Lions were regarded by many as the finest Rugby team to have visited the southern hemisphere. The forwards were truly formidable but the team's crowning glory was to be found in its brilliantly gifted and swift three-quarters. In the event Australia came within a whisker of winning as Joe Pearce inspired a forward effort which surpassed all expectations. The pace of the game was frenetic and the tackling of both teams was unimaginably relentless.

The game began sensationally. The old maestro, Dally Messenger had kicked off - *a little make-believe that ought to be eliminated in such games,* as one reporter mused. As was normal on such occasions a scrum was formed at the centre and the home team heeled to begin a short-passing movement into British territory. As the ball was worked down the left wing the probability of an Australian score seemed very real as Pearce shaped to pass in-field. The pass never reached the receiver for Ellaby, all elegance and pace and the man Australia feared most, had plucked the ball from the air and was racing over the centre-line before the Aussies could react. McMillan moved to cut off the whirlwind winger but there was never a ghost of a chance as Ellaby flew majestically to the corner for arguably the quickest try in test history. The "hillites" were staggered but breathed a little easier when Sullivan's valiant attempt to convert shaved the outside of the posts.

Weissel had two abortive attempts at goal but then found his shooting boots to land a couple of penalties and Australia led 4-3. As the play intensified one critic wrote, *it was a storm centre in the ruck, a good place for a man to be outside.* Sullivan then landed a marvellous goal from a penalty beyond the "25" on the touch-line but as the ball left his boot the referee caught a Lion off-side and disallowed the goal. Disappointment was followed by elation, however, as the brilliance of the Lions three-quarters was unleashed. Stan Brogden kicked from centre-field to the open right wing causing Cliff Pearce to turn and retrace his steps but before he could blink Ellaby was flashing past him to gather the ball one-handed at break-neck speed. Ellaby ran almost to the corner before being challenged by McMillan who was unable to prevent the winger from sending a scoring pass inside to Arthur Atkinson.

There was no more scoring although Australia tried everything. Weissel had unsuccessful kicks at goal, Ernie Norman created a chance for Dempsey to score under the bar but the ball went to ground when it would have been easier to score and, worst of all, with little time remaining Weissel and Laws overran the ball in the British in-goal.

Sydney, first test 1932.
Top: Australia's captain Herb Steinohrt tackles British second-rower Bill Horton whilst
Fred Laws watches proceedings.
Bottom: Australian forward Sid Pearce prepares to move the ball away from a mid-field ruck.

TEST MATCH 29

AT BRISBANE CRICKET GROUND – 18 June, 1932
AUSTRALIA 15 GREAT BRITAIN 6 (HT 10-0)

F McMillan (Wests)	J Sullivan (Wigan) capt
J Wilson (Ipswich) T	A Ellaby (St. Helens)
EJ Norman (Easts)	A Atkinson (Castleford)
FC Laws (Toowoomba Town)	S Brogden (Huddersfield)
CG Pearce (Wests)	S Smith (Leeds) T
E Weissel (Temora) 2G	E Pollard (Wakefield T) T
H Gee (Ipswich) 2T	†L Adams (Leeds)
H Steinohrt(Toowoomba Valley) capt	N Silcock (Widnes)
DV Dempsey (Ipswich)	LL White (Hunslet)
P Madsen (Toowoomba Brothers)	JF Thompson (Leeds)
†LW Heidke (Ipswich)	M Hodgson (Swinton)
SHW Pearce (Easts) G	W Horton (Wakefield T)
†F O'Connor (Souths)	J Feetham (Salford)

Referee - J Simpson (Queensland)   Crowd - 26,574   Gate - £3,119/6/-

Scoring - 5-0 8-0 10-0 10-3 10-6 15-6

Dubbed "The Battle of Brisbane", the second test match of 1932 was a triumph over adversity for the Australians almost on a par with the performance of Wagstaff's heroic band in the "Rorke's Drift Test" of 1914. For periods in the second half the home side were reduced to eleven men and at one stage were down to ten. Make-shift hooker Dempsey broke his wrist, Weissel suffered a bad ankle injury and Gee, Norman and O'Connor were all temporarily removed from the action. *The Cynic* wrote,

In the second half the forward battle developed on tornadic lines, players being flattened by the cyclonic tackling of heavy, powerful, well-trained men with the full rigor of give-all, take-all tactics ... It became the most desperate and rugged game imaginable. Players were strewn like dead men on the field, or were carried off to touch-lines to recover. They were chiefly Australians.

By the end of the match Australia were packing only three forwards - Steinohrt, Heidke and Madsen. Strangely enough this device served to bottle up the menace of the British three-quarters as nine Australians were free to contain seven Lions backs.

As in the first test there was an almost immediate score but on this occasion it was the home team which had the flying start. Britain kicked off to the right hand side of the field where Dempsey fielded and returned with a cross-field punt aided by the wind. The ball cleared Smith's head and the Australians were quick to profit by initiating a smart passing bout which ended with Laws being tackled just short but from the play-the-ball there was no stopping Gee who skipped over wide out. Weissel left-footed a superb conversion and Australia led 5-0 within the first minute.

Eleven minutes later McMillan, kicking beautifully throughout, found touch inside the Lions' "25" and from the resulting scrum Gee shot round the blind-side to put Wilson over for another try. Britain responded with the most spectacular move of the match which saw superlative handling release Ellaby whose speed and swerve took him over in the corner only for the referee to rule no try because of obstruction on Cliff Pearce. Even the Australians thought the decision harsh. By this stage the play was becoming decidedly heated. Australia were quite happy, however, as they stretched their lead to ten points with a simple Weissel penalty at a scrum under the posts.

As the bodies began to pile up, the game began to swing Britain's way early in the second half. A try to Smith at the corner from quick orthodox passing at a scrum completely demolished the home defence and then Pollard scored a fortuitous try as a mischievously bouncing ball played tricks on the Australian defenders. Ten-six to the home XIII, whose players were being injured in relays, and twenty minutes left. It looked long odds against Australia holding out.

Smith was crowded out at the flag, O'Connor miraculously knocked the ball from Brogden's grasp as he went to touch down and then with only minutes remaining Australia scored an incredible try as Britain lost possession on the home "25". Weissel, forgetful of his lame ankle, grabbed the ball and raced towards Sullivan at half-way, side-stepped the great man and half-ran, half-hobbled straight for the posts. Sullivan gave chase and nailed Weissel a few yards from the line and another Lion toed the ball away only for Hector Gee to sweep up the oval and touch down just to the right of the posts to send the crowd into rapture. Joe Pearce kicked the goal and the crowd bore captain Herb Steinohrt away in triumph at the final whistle.

TEST MATCH 30

AT SYDNEY CRICKET GROUND – 16 July, 1932
AUSTRALIA 13 GREAT BRITAIN 18 (HT 9-3)

F McMillan (Wests)	J Sullivan (Wigan) capt 3G
J Wilson (Ipswich)	A Ellaby (St. Helens)
CG Pearce (Wests)	A Atkinson (Castleford)
FC Laws (Toowoomba Town)	S Brogden (Huddersfield) T
† FWH Neumann (Valleys, Brisbane)	S Smith (Leeds) 3T
E Weissel (Temora) 5G	† AJ Risman (Salford)
H Gee (Ipswich)	B Evans (Swinton)
H Steinohrt(Toowoomba Valley) capt	WA Williams (Salford)
LW Heidke (Ipswich)	LL White (Hunslet)
P Madsen (Toowoomba Brothers)	JF Thompson (Leeds)
SHW Pearce (Easts)	M Hodgson (Swinton)
F O'Connor (Souths) T	AE Fildes (St. Helens Recs)
† W Christie (Coorparoo, Brisbane)	W Horton (Wakefield T)

Referee - L Deane (NSW)   Crowd - 50,053   Gate - £4,252
Scoring - 2-0 4-0 9-0 9-3 11-3 11-6 11-11 11-13 13-13 13-18

After the rage and fury of the first two tests, the decider redeemed the game's image for in all respects it was a wonderfully entertaining affair contested in the best of spirits. For long enough it looked as if the Ashes would go to Australia who at one stage held an advantage of nine points but a combination of tiring forwards and weak tackling amongst the inside backs late in the game made life easy for the quicksilver British three-quarters. Four tries to one was a fair indication of the superiority of the Lions' backs and a poor reward for Australia's pack which for the first 50 minutes had played like men possessed.

The game began with a surprise as Sullivan failed with a comparatively easy penalty and there was a let-off at the other end when McMillan struck the post with a drop-shot. Australia were clearly on top in the early exchanges and were unfortunate when Weissel jinked through and cut out a beautiful opening for Cliff Pearce only for the centre to knock-on with Wilson waiting for the scoring pass. On the quarter hour, however, Weissel landed a superb 40 yard penalty from close to touch and seven minutes later kicked another from 35 yards. Soon 4-0 became 9-0 as Cliff Pearce made a blinding run down the left flank, evaded three tackles and slung inside to Neumann on the Lions' "25". O'Connor was up in support to take the winger's pass and, though seemingly held, managed to stretch himself elastically to touch down just inside the left upright. Weissel converted and Australia seemed to be sitting pretty.

The Lions were far from done, however. Atkinson dropped the ball with a try almost assured after brilliant play by Brogden and then Ellaby scintillated in a run which would have provided a try had any support been forthcoming. Shortly before half-time the pressure finally told. A scrum formed near half-way and the ball went left via Evans, Risman, Brogden and Evans again until it reached Stan Smith at full throttle on the "25". McMillan set his sights on the elfin winger but it was no contest as Smith had plenty of space and more than enough pace. Sullivan again failed with the kick.

Shortly after the change-round Weissel landed another fine goal to put Australia 11-3 up but it was merely the prelude to a terrific barrage from the Lions. Sullivan, strangely off-target, missed a simple penalty and then handed the kicking over to Joe Thompson who fared no better with another shot. Eventually Australia cracked. Ellaby went close before Brogden made monkeys of the home defence as he sliced through to the posts from a 25 yard scrum. Amazingly Sullivan missed the goal again. Australia's defence was on the point of disintegration, however, and a simple try was soon conceded as passing broke down on the home "25" allowing Risman to scoop up the ball and throw a long pass to Smith who streaked unhindered to the corner. Sullivan's luck turned as his conversion from touch smote the post and dropped over the bar.

A few minutes later Gee cleared his line with an ill-directed kick only for Sullivan to field and drop a fine goal. Australia quickly equalised with a Weissel penalty and should have regained the lead but Weissel unaccountably pulled wide another none-too-difficult kick. The winning points fittingly came from that devil on the wing, Stan Smith, following another long pass on the "25". Smith shot down the chalk-line and crossed at the corner, taking the flag with him. He thus became the first player since 1910 to score an Ashes hat-trick. Sullivan, restored to his usual accuracy, made light of the side-line conversion and Britain had won the Ashes for the fifth successive series.

Sydney, third test, 1932.
Stan Smith (9) throws a pass to test debutant Gus Risman as Joe Wilson challenges.

Australia's Test side on the Kangaroo's back.   Will they be on the "pig's back" to-morrow?

A cartoonist's view of the 1932 Australian team.

TEST MATCH 31

AT BELLE VUE, MANCHESTER – 7 October, 1933
GREAT BRITAIN 4 AUSTRALIA 0 (HT 0-0)

J Sullivan (Wigan) capt 2G	F McMillan (Wests) capt
A Ellaby (St. Helens)	† A Ridley (Wests)
AJ Risman (Salford)	† DM Brown (Easts)
S Brogden (Huddersfield)	CG Pearce (Wests)
S Smith (Leeds)	† J Why (Souths)
† WJ Davies (Castleford)	† VJ Hey (Wests)
B Evans (Swinton)	† VA Thicknesse (Easts)
N Silcock (Widnes)	P Madsen (Toowoomba Brothers)
LL White (Hunslet)	DV Dempsey (Ipswich)
† J Miller (Warrington)	† RE Stehr (Easts)
W Horton (Wakefield T)	F O'Connor (Souths)
M Hodgson (Swinton)	SHW Pearce (Easts)
J Feetham (Salford)	WJ Prigg (Central Newcastle)

Referee - F Peel (Bradford)   Crowd - 34,000   Gate - £4,659
Scoring - 2-0 4-0

Australia entered this opening test on the crest of a wave having won all eleven of their tour fixtures, rattling up 275 points (63 tries) against a mere 55 (7 tries). In Vic Hey, an explosively gifted stand-off, and Dave Brown, the most prolific-scoring Kangaroo ever to tour (285 points in his 32 games), Australia had two superb match-winners. The pair would later play English League with Leeds and Warrington respectively but for now they were key figures in a team which excelled in the traditional fast-moving, robust style favoured by so many Australian sides.

Fortunately for the home side the English weather once more threw its weight behind the British cause as rain fell throughout and a greasy ball militated against open play. A press comment summed up the game:

It was a test match purely and simply, and those who had hoped that the men on both sides would reveal the power they are known to possess in combined work to make the play open and attractive had to be satisfied with a fierce struggle in which the tackling was always too keen and too sure for the attackers - a struggle in which the great strength and fine stamina of the forwards, who bore the brunt of what was really a battle, compelled even the admiration of the Rugby League men who were disappointed that the game had not realised its spectacular promise.

As so often before the most influential figure on the field was the charismatic British captain Jim Sullivan. A reporter wrote,

He was England's sheet anchor at the beginning, he nursed his side until it had turned the corner, and then he cared for his forwards as only a great full-back can do. His two penalty goals in the last fifteen minutes merely top-dressed one of the most majestic individual displays ever given in test football. They did, of course, also serve to win the match.

Australia were on top only during the first quarter of an hour when their pack gained possession at a positively alarming rate but the backs surprisingly tried none of their unorthodox moves. During this early period Sullivan and loose-forward Jack Feetham often seemed to be all that stood between Australia and the goal-line. Cliff Pearce with his bumping runs was the most dangerous of the Kangaroos, twice barging Risman out of his path as if he was a child. No real fault could be found in either pack although Thicknesse and Hey clearly had the better of the half-back duel, at least in the first half when there was never a hint of a try for Britain. Their great wingers Ellaby, in his last test, and Smith never had a run.

As Britain gradually gained the ascendancy during the second half a score still seemed unlikely until in the 65th minute the Kangaroos gave away a penalty at a scrum and were duly punished by Sullivan. Shortly afterwards Brown failed to equalise with an easy penalty and the game was sealed when Sullivan landed his second goal after Viv Thicknesse strayed off-side at a scrum. There were scares at both ends, however. First Sullivan made a fielding error, Wally Prigg shot clear and looked all over a scorer but was somehow overhauled by stand-off Davies and then Brogden crossed for a British try only to be recalled for a forward pass. The game ended with mounted police patrolling the touch-lines as an excited crowd spilled over the speedway track and threatened to encroach on the playing area.

TEST MATCH 32

AT HEADINGLEY, LEEDS – 11 November, 1933
GREAT BRITAIN 7 AUSTRALIA 5 (HT 2-5)

J Sullivan (Wigan) capt 2G	† W Smith (Ipswich)
B Hudson (Salford)	A Ridley (Wests)
AJ Risman (Salford)	DM Brown (Easts) T,G
W Dingsdale (Warrington)	CG Pearce (Wests)
† J Woods (Barrow) T	† F Gardner (St. George)
S Brogden (Huddersfield)	VJ Hey (Wests)
B Evans (Swinton)	VA Thicknesse (Easts)
J Miller (Warrington)	P Madsen (Toowoomba Brothers) capt
LL White (Hunslet)	† AF Folwell (Newtown)
N Silcock (Widnes)	† J Gibbs (South Newcastle)
M Hodgson (Swinton)	F O'Connor (Souths)
W Horton (Wakefield T)	† J Doyle (Toowoomba)
J Feetham (Salford)	WJ Prigg (Central Newcastle)

Referee - F Peel (Bradford)   Crowd - 29,618   Gate - £3,873
Scoring - 2-0 2-5 4-5 7-5

For a change the English weather favoured the Australians. Conditions were perfect for rugby. The Kangaroos dominated for most of the 80 minutes. Yet once again they somehow contrived to lose, letting the game slip away with only 90 seconds on the clock. Just as everyone was preparing to applaud them on a well merited triumph the cup of victory was dashed from their lips as Great Britain scored a highly improbable last gasp try through debutant winger "Tank" Woods.

The try was a good one. A scrum went down and Bryn Evans, playing in his last test match and showing his years, at last managed a clean break having been well policed by the quicker Thicknesse and Prigg. Veering towards the mid-field he let the ball out and it travelled faster than it had done all afternoon right down the three-quarter line. There was clearly an air of desperation in the movement but no matter. It reached Woods who was presented with the thinnest of chances but tore to the line to secure the Ashes for his country in his one and only test.

Australia should have been home and dry with the series squared long before Woods' dash for immortality but luck and British cussedness seemed to be against them for three decades following their Ashes win of 1920. This loss at Headingley must have been one of the cruellest mishaps to befall the green and golds throughout that dismal period.

The British press corps castigated the home pack for its lack of finesse and mobility, a notable exception being Feetham, lauded the skills and support play of the Aussie forwards, admired the enterprise and energy of the visiting backs and bemoaned the faulty and wild passing which infected the harrassed home halves and three-quarters. Most of all, however, they wondered why in the last ten minutes the Australians, so confident and superior hitherto, suddenly tried to employ a totally alien close game which cost them the series. Perhaps it was the shock of Dingsdale putting Risman over for a try disallowed for a forward pass which caused them to try to put up the shutters. Whatever the reason, their safety-first tactics cost them the test.

All the best chances went to Australia. Gardner, an alert and clever wing, intercepted but fell to Sullivan. A blind-side move between Thicknesse and Prigg completely baffled Britain but when Gardner had kicked past and outrun Sullivan the ball had taken a malicious bounce and the try had been lost. A third chance went begging when Ridley dropped Brown's bullet-like pass with the line at his mercy. Sullivan had kicked a penalty in the second minute but after 30 minutes the Kangaroos unfolded a magnificent try. Prigg picked up in his own "25", unleashing Ridley who beat two men and lobbed inside to Thicknesse at half-way. The scrum-half performed miracles in taking the ball as it bounced from one hand to the other and finally he took it from his shoulder before handing on to Doyle. Brown finished the masterpiece under the bar and kicked the goal. Otherwise his kicking had been abysmal and probably cost his side the game. Sullivan scored the only other points of the game with a penalty early in the second half. In the final analysis it was yet again the great man's goals which represented the difference between victory and defeat.

TEST MATCH 33

AT STATION ROAD, SWINTON – 16 December, 1933
GREAT BRITAIN 19 AUSTRALIA 16 (HT 12-9)

J Sullivan (Wigan) capt 5G	F McMillan (Wests) capt
B Hudson (Salford) T	J Why (Souths)
A Atkinson (Castleford)	DM Brown (Easts) 5G
AJ Risman (Salford)	FC Laws (Toowoomba)
S Smith (Leeds) T	CG Pearce (Wests)
† E Jenkins (Salford)	VJ Hey (Wests) T
† W Watkins (Salford)	† LE Mead (Wests)
J Miller (Warrington)	P Madsen (Toowoomba Brothers)
† T Armitt (Swinton)	AF Folwell (Newtown)
N Silcock (Widnes)	RE Stehr (Easts)
M Hodgson (Swinton)	J Gibbs (South Newcastle)
W Horton (Wakefield T)	SHW Pearce (Easts)
J Feetham (Salford) T	WJ Prigg (Central Newcastle) T

Referee - F Peel (Bradford)   Crowd - 10,990   Gate - £1,515/14/6
Scoring - 0-5 2-5 7-5 10-5 10-7 10-9 12-9 12-14 17-14 17-16 19-16

In winning the third test of 1933 Great Britain became the first side to complete a "whitewash" in a three match Ashes series notwithstanding that each encounter had been a close run thing. The third test was a thrilling, open affair in direct contrast to the previous five tests played in England which had produced only five tries and 31 points. This Swinton test produced as many tries and more points to indicate how different it was from the previous five grim but gripping confrontations. Not that there was anything short of total commitment from the implacable rivals for the combat was as desperate as usual. Tom Longworth, reporting for *The Daily Express,* wrote,

Three points - ordinarily a mere nothing - was an exaggeration of the difference between the two sides. While England may have deserved to have won, had Australia secured a points majority we could not have begrudged them their success. There was absolutely nothing in it.

Fog was widespread in Lancashire on the day and the match was only declared on an hour before kick-off, the poor crowd being a reflection of the weather conditions.

After Brown had failed with a couple of penalty kicks Australia took the lead when Vic Hey, the star of the match, scored a beautiful try following a mazy run from a scrum twenty yards out. Brown kicked the goal and after thirteen minutes Australia led 5-0. Sullivan soon reduced the deficit with a penalty and it was not long before Britain edged ahead. Risman made a fine break but appeared to have spoilt his good work by failing to pass to Smith. Luckily Billy Watkins was supporting on the inside and Risman lobbed the ball to him. Watkins, no sprinter, sized up his options and kicked out to the right where Hudson gathered a perfect bounce and crossed for a try, converted by Sullivan. With Jenkins and Watkins playing like test veterans on their debuts Britain were able to turn the screw and from a forward foray Feetham snapped up a pass from Hodgson which Silcock had failed to gather and forced his way over. There was no conversion and two penalties from Brown brought the Kangaroos to 10-9 before Sullivan extended Britain's lead to 12-9 at the interval.

Within a minute of half-time Australia grabbed the lead after Mead and Prigg instigated a move carried on by Why down the right wing. Atkinson gambled on an interception but lost and Prigg received an inside pass to score. Brown's conversion was good. Sullivan, persistent as ever, kicked another penalty to level the scores and then Britain gained a crucial try. Australia had survived with difficulty some punishing bursts by Atkinson before a scrum went down. Watkins and Jenkins ensured a swift service out to the left where Smith deftly gathered a wayward pass to dart over in the corner. Australia were then mortified to see Hey apparently clear only to fall to a tackle by Atkinson who *seemed to drop from the clouds.* A fifth goal to Brown brought the score breathtakingly to 17-16 before Sullivan kicked his own fifth to complete the scoring.

For both captains, Frank McMillan and Sullivan, it was the end of great test careers, McMillan having faced the British in nine tests and Sullivan the Kangaroos in fifteen. It was also the last test for Stan Smith (8 Ashes tests), Bill Horton (10), Jack Feetham (8), Cliff Pearce (8) and Frank Laws (6).

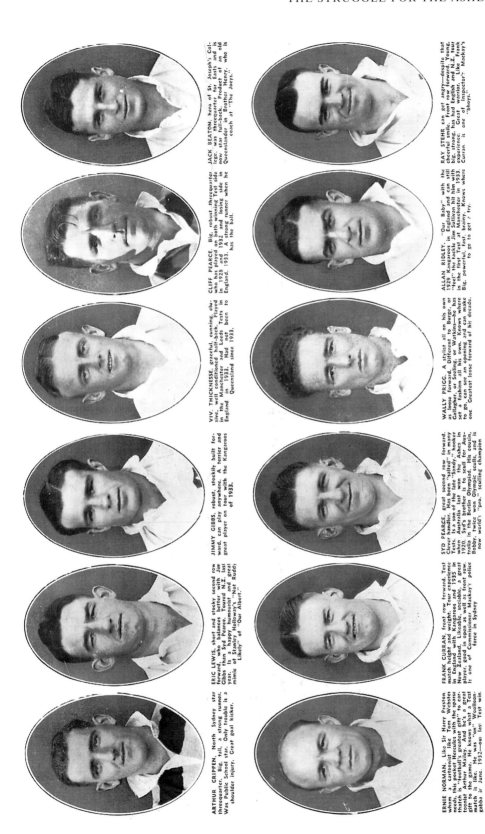

ARTHUR CRIPPEN, North Sydney star threequarter. Big, tall, a strong runner. Was Public School star. Only trouble is a shoulder injury. Great goal kicker.

ERIC LEWIS, short and stocky second row forward, who balances better with Jim Gibbs than Syd Pearce. Toured N.Z. last year. A happy humourist and great mimic of Stanley Holloway's "Not Ruddy Likely," of "Our Albert."

VIV. THICKNESSE, graceful, cunning, elusive, well conditioned half-back. Played in the Manchester and Leeds Tests in England 1933. Had not been to Queensland since 1933.

JACK BEATON, hero of St. Joseph's College, was threequarter for East, and is now star full-back. Product of an old Queenslander in Brother Henry, who is coach at "The Joeys."

JIMMY GIBBS, robust, stockily built forward, can play anywhere. A terrier and great player on tour with the Kangaroos of 1933.

CLIFF PEARCE. Big, robust threequarter who has played on both winning Test side in 1925 and 1932, and losing side in England, 1933. A strong runner when he has the ball.

WALLY PRIGG. A stylist all on his own as loose forward. Different to Burge, or Gallagher, or Sceling, or Watkins—he has set a fashion all his own. Knows where to go, can see an opening and can make one. Greatest loose forward of hit decade.

ALLAN RIDLEY. "Our Baby" with the 1929 Kangaroos in England and can still "roo!" the tackle Jim Sullivan hit him with in the first Test at Manchester in 1933. Big, powerful, fast, brainy. Knows where to go to get a try.

ERNIE NORMAN. Like Sir Harry Preston whom a cartoonist like Tom Webster needs, this pocket Hercules with the sparse thatch is "football's greatest gift" to cartoonist Arthur Mailey. And he's a great gift to the game. He knows what a Test match is like. He was "on" Woolloongabba ir June, 1932—oui last Test win.

FRANK CURRAN, front row forward. Test match height and weight. Tour experience in England with Kangaroos in 1935 when Australia last won the Ashes in 1920. Syd's brother is to scull for Australia in the Berlin Olympiad. His cousin, Bobby, twice won Olympic sculls, and is now one of Commissioner Mackay's police force in Sydney

SYD PEARCE, great second row forward. Clever handler. Has been "salted" in many Tests. Is a son of the late "Sandy," hooker when Australia last won the Ashes in 1920. Syd's brother is to scull for Australia in the Berlin Olympiad. His cousin, Bobby, twice won Olympic sculls, and is now world's "pro." sculling champion

RAY STEHR can get angry—despite that cheerful smile. Front row forward. Young, big, strong, has had English and N.Z. tour experience. Great warrior. Like Frank Curran is one of Inspector Mackay's "bhoys."

A dozen New South Welsh reps who played Ashes tests in the 1930s.

TEST MATCH 34

AT SYDNEY CRICKET GROUND – 29 June, 1936
AUSTRALIA 24 GREAT BRITAIN 8 (HT 4-3)

† JJ Beaton (Easts) 2G	† W Belshaw (Liverpool St)
A Ridley (Wests) T	† JC Morley (Wigan)
DM Brown (Easts) capt 2T,4G	A Atkinson (Castleford) capt
VJ Hey (Toowoomba)	S Brogden (Leeds)
† A Crippin (Norths)	† AS Edwards (Salford)
EJ Norman (Easts)	E Jenkins (Salford)
VA Thicknesse (Easts)	† T McCue (Widnes)
RE Stehr (Easts)	N Silcock (Widnes)
PCC Fairall (St. George)	† H Field (York)
FJ Curran (Souths)	J Miller (Warrington)
SHW Pearce (Easts) T	M Hodgson (Swinton) G
LW Heidke (Ipswich)	† JH Woods (Liverpool St)
WJ Prigg (Central Newcastle)	† H Beverley (Hunslet) 2T

Referee - L Deane (NSW)   Crowd - 63,920   Gate - £6,115
Scoring - 2-0 2-3 4-3 6-3 11-3 14-3 19-3 21-3 24-3 24-8

This was one of those test matches which had everything - brilliant individual performances, sizzling combined movements, ferocious tackling, a couple of dismissals and, for the home fans, the desired result. In the final analysis Australia won with a good deal to spare as their forwards proved too strong, too fast and too skilful for the Lions pack. Having been denied a try in the first half Australia, fielding no fewer than six players from the Eastern Suburbs club, showed uncanny combination in the second period to run up twenty points before Britain replied with a late consolation try. For centre Dave Brown, one of Australia's greatest League sons, it was a particularly memorable day as at the tender age of 23 years 86 days he became his country's youngest test captain and celebrated by scoring more points in an Ashes test than any previous player, eclipsing the record thirteen points haul of Eric Weissel back in 1929.

The first half was a rugged affair with cautions being handed out to Hodgson (twice), Woods and Stehr before the referee finally lost patience after a fracas amongst the forwards just before the interval and sent off rival props Stehr and Silcock who *shook hands as they crossed the touch-line and later disported themselves as though they were the best of pals.* Australia had looked the more dangerous outfit but led by a solitary point at the change-round, Brown having given them the lead with a fine wide-angled penalty before going behind to a cleverly worked try by Beverley from a cute short pass from McCue at a ruck close to the line. Brown restored the home side's lead with a towering penalty from the centre.

Four minutes into the second half another tremendous penalty goal by Brown from 40 yards edged Australia into a 6-3 lead as they began to tighten their grip on the match. Crippin, a nineteen year-old winger, and Prigg were held just short but a try had to come and it was a beauty. Full-back Beaton fielded a kick on his own "25" and began a superb side-stepping run which carried him down the right flank to the Lions' "25" before a desperate ankle-tap caused him to stumble and spill the ball. Brown swept it up and the ball flashed to Pearce, to Heidke and finally to Ridley who strode over near the posts. Brown converted.

Minutes later British passing broke down on the right wing near half-way. Heidke toed the ball on for Hey to gather at top speed. Morley almost got to Hey but the centre parted to Brown who crossed wide out to put Australia out of reach at 14-3. A wonderful try followed as Australia won possession from a scrum 50 yards out. The ball moved through the halves and centres before Atkinson collared Brown who managed to get a marvellous pass out to Ridley. Ridley raced to the "25" and threw inside to Norman who immediately punted infield for Pearce to collect and spurt the last dozen yards for a glorious try. Beaton kicked the goal and then landed a simple penalty when Atkinson wandered off-side at a scrum.

A final Australian score emanated from another scrum near the centre as Thicknesse, Norman and Hey sent Brown racing down the right flank using Ridley as a foil before diving over a few yards from the flag. With the game well won Australia relaxed and just before the close Edwards, Britain's youngest tourist so far, made a lovely swerving run before sending Beverley in for his second try to which Hodgson added the goal. Australia were more than content, however, having halted a British streak of four victorious tests over the green and golds.

THE RUGBY LEAGUE TOURISTS FOR AUSTRALIA

THE 1936 LIONS

Nix's impressions of the 26 Rugby League players who will leave England for Australia on Friday week, April 17, with the exception of those engaged in the Cup final at Wembley the following day.

Reading from the top (left to right) they are:

Three-quarters: Hudson (Salford), F. Harris (Leeds), Atkinson (Castleford), Risman (Salford), Gwyn Davies (Wigan), Smith (Leeds), Edwards (Salford), Morley (Wigan).

Half-backs: Jenkins (Salford), Watkins (Salford), McCue (Widnes), Brogden (Leeds).

Forwards: Jones (Keighley), Field (York), Arkwright (Warrington), Beverley (Hunslet), Exley (Wakefield Trinity), Hodgson (Swinton), Troup (Barrow), Woods (Liverpool Stanley), Silcock (Widnes), Miller (Warrington), Armitt (Swinton), Ellerington (Hull).

Full backs: Brough (Leeds) (captain), Belshaw (Liverpool Stanley).

TEST MATCH 35

AT BRISBANE CRICKET GROUND – 4 July, 1936
AUSTRALIA 7 GREAT BRITAIN 12 (HT 5-5)

JJ Beaton (Easts) G	JW Brough (Leeds) capt
A Crippin (Norths) T	S Brogden (Leeds)
DM Brown (Easts) capt G	W Belshaw (Liverpool St)
VJ Hey (Toowoomba)	AJ Risman (Salford) capt 2G
A Ridley (Wests)	AS Edwards (Salford) 2T
EJ Norman (Easts)	E Jenkins (Salford)
VA Thicknesse (Easts)	W Watkins (Salford)
RE Stehr (Easts)	N Silcock (Widnes)
PCC Fairall (St. George)	T Armitt (Swinton)
FJ Curran (Souths)	JH Woods (Liverpool St)
SHW Pearce (Easts)	†J Arkwright (Warrington)
LW Heidke (Ipswich)	M Hodgson (Swinton) G
WJ Prigg (Central Newcastle)	H Beverley (Hunslet)

Referee - FL Moynihan (Brisbane)   Crowd - 29,486   Gate - £3,908
Scoring - 0-3 0-5 5-5 5-10 7-10 7-12

The first test match had proved that given firm going Australia had a team well capable of wresting back the Ashes. Unfortunately for the home team Brisbane Cricket Ground had suffered heavy rain before the kick-off which rendered the surface soft and tricky. In the circumstances Britain, with a severely restructured team, adapted the better. Aided by Armitt's 51-25 advantage in the tight the Lions were on top for at least three-quarters of the game and adopted a policy of kicking to the wings rather than running the slippery ball. It was a policy which paid off handsomely for both British tries were the results of judicious kicks from stand-off Emlyn Jenkins, who dictated play almost constantly. The game was extremely hard but clean and there was a total absence of the he-man excesses of the first test.

Britain made all the running in the first ten minutes. Hodgson missed a penalty and then Watkins, Beverley and Risman moved dangerously before Heidke saved the situation with a timely interception. Jenkins almost had Edwards over from a teasing kick but Beaton managed to thwart the winger. The kicking tactics soon came off, however, for following a scrum at half-way in the tenth minute Jenkins worked a run-around with Belshaw before booting the ball to the corner for Edwards to chase. The young winger beat Crippin and Beaton to it, toed it over the line and plunged for the try. Hodgson failed to convert and then missed another shot at goal from a penalty. Britain were not to be denied, however, for Brown dropped out on the full and from the resultant scrum under the posts Fairall conceded a penalty which Risman translated into two points. Australia were fortunate not to go further behind when a driving tackle by Belshaw on Hey caused the latter's pass to go astray. Edwards gathered and looked all over a scorer until a magnificent chase and tackle by Crippin saved Australia's line. Against the run of play Australia equalised on the half-hour. The try came from the most unpromising situation as Lions second-rower Hodgson slashed through the middle, shoved Thicknesse out of his path and hurled the ball toward Risman. The ball fell behind Risman and in a flash Crippin was seen racing away on a 60 yards sprint to the corner to outpace Brough and then run along the in-goal to touch down under the bar. Beaton converted and Britain had no advantage to show for all their superiority during the first half.

There were close calls at both ends in the initial stages of the second half. Pearce made a great run for Australia and seemed to be clean away when he was called back and a penalty awarded in Australia's favour. Britain soon regained the upper hand and Brogden was very close to a try before the lead was retaken by the Lions in the 55th minute. From a mid-field scrum Jenkins eschewed his normal kick to the wing and instead broke cleanly past Norman and ran to the Australian "25". At this point he reverted to the kick and Edwards gave chase. Crippin misjudged the bounce and Edwards dashed through to pluck the ball from the air leaving Beaton floundering in his wake. There was a suspicion that Edwards had pushed Crippin but the try was allowed and Risman landed a superb conversion. Australia narrowed the gap to three points when Brown landed a penalty but ten minutes from time Hey was caught off-side under his own posts and Hodgson kicked the goal that sealed the game for Britain. Australia finished the stronger but could not break a defence brilliantly marshalled by Belshaw and Beverley.

TEST MATCH 36

AT SYDNEY CRICKET GROUND – 18 July, 1936
AUSTRALIA 7 GREAT BRITAIN 12 (HT 2-5)

JJ Beaton (Easts)	W Belshaw (Liverpool St)
A Ridley (Wests)	B Hudson (Salford) T
DM Brown (Easts) capt 2G	S Brogden (Leeds) T
EJ Norman (Easts)	AJ Risman (Salford) capt
A Crippin (Norths)	AS Edwards (Salford)
VJ Hey (Toowoomba) T	E Jenkins (Salford)
† FM Gilbert (Toowoomba)	W Watkins (Salford)
RE Stehr (Easts)	N Silcock (Widnes)
P Madsen (Toowoomba Brothers)	T Armitt (Swinton)
FJ Curran (Souths)	J Arkwright (Warrington)
LW Heidke (Ipswich)	JH Woods (Liverpool St)
SHW Pearce (Easts)	M Hodgson (Swinton) 3G
WJ Prigg (Central Newcastle)	H Beverley (Hunslet)

Referee - L Deane (NSW)   Crowd - 53,546   Gate - £4,299
Scoring - 2-0 2-5 2-10 2-12 7-12

A firm ground and a dry day should have been manna from heaven for Australia but the deciding test followed much the same pattern as the previous one. Australia certainly erred in playing an unwilling Madsen as hooker for the British pack again dominated possession and allowed Jenkins to kick the Lions to the Ashes. Britain stuck rigidly to their game plan, made a minimum of errors and denied the Australian backs the opportunity to use their superior pace and skill. With five Salford players in the back division Britain could have been expected to play a more open game but in a classic case of the end justifying the means the feat of carrying off the Ashes was more important than playing pretty rugby.

Australia set off at a fine pace and aided by a sequence of six penalties were unlucky not to take the lead in the opening ten minutes. Heidke dropped the ball twenty yards from the line after lovely passing down the left flank and Edwards did well to stop another dangerous movement on the opposite flank. Hey had hard lines when a bumping run took him into the British "25" only for an ankle-tap to send him tumbling to earth and then Gilbert made a bad decision when punting over Belshaw with support on both sides. Eventually Australia were rewarded when Brown landed a prodigious penalty from five yards inside the Lions' half and wide out on the right wing. Britain began to retaliate and after Hodgson had failed with two penalties Watkins dashed over from a close-in scrum only to lose the ball in crossing. Brogden and Edwards almost made the line as the pressure on the home team mounted and tempers amongst the forwards started to fray. The flash-point came when Stehr was seen to be laid out after a melee and Arkwright was sent off. When Stehr had been revived he too was dismissed becoming the only player to have been marched twice in a series. Worse was to follow for Australia who fell behind just before the break. A scrum went down on the left wing near the home "25", Armitt heeling. Watkins and Jenkins whipped the ball to Risman who punted over Crippin to the right wing, the home winger turning and chasing but being non-plussed by a quirkily high bounce, which caused him to overrun the ball and allowed Hudson to touch down just before the ball rolled dead. Hodgson kicked a magnificent conversion and Australia went in to the second half three points down. Australia pressed strongly for a considerable period but failed to register a score. Brown actually crossed following a pulverising run by Ridley but a forward pass had marred the effort. Beaton and Prigg were both kept out with great difficulty but it was Britain who produced the vital score and once more it was a kick which unlocked the defence. This time Watkins put in a grubber from a scrum 25 yards out. Beverley was first to the ball which was quickly transferred via Risman to Brogden who scorched the few remaining yards to score in the left corner. Hodgson added a mighty goal and as the Australian forward effort subsided, Prigg excepted, Jenkins drove the home XIII back to their "25" for Hodgson to drop a neat goal following a ruck under the posts.

Five minutes from time Australia at last breached the British line with a fine try as Prigg fielded a kick around half-way, veered away from two Lions forwards, shot forward past a couple of surprised backs and fifteen yards from the line threw a long, high pass to Hey who gathered it above his head and sped over near the corner. Brown's conversion was a beauty but there was no real hope for Australia who had succumbed yet again to a tactically superior adversary.

TEST MATCH 37

AT HEADINGLEY, LEEDS – 16 October, 1937
GREAT BRITAIN 5 AUSTRALIA 4 (HT 2-4)

W Belshaw (Liverpool St)	LR Ward (Norths)
† B Cunniffe (Castleford)	† JP Reardon (Norths, Brisbane)
† AJ Croston (Castleford)	JJ Beaton (Easts) 2G
AJ Risman (Salford) capt	RL McKinnon (Easts)
JC Morley (Wigan)	† BH Williams (Bombala)
E Jenkins (Salford) T	EJ Norman (Easts)
T McCue (Widnes)	† PE Williams (Souths)
N Silcock (Widnes)	FJ Curran (Souths)
T Armitt (Swinton)	† HT Pierce (Easts)
JH Woods (Leeds)	RE Stehr (Easts)
J Arkwright (Warrington)	J Gibbs (South Newcastle)
M Hodgson (Swinton) G	EW Lewis (Souths)
H Beverley (Hunslet)	WJ Prigg (Central Newcastle) capt

Referee - AE Harding (Manchester)   Crowd - 31,949   Gate - £3,942
Scoring - 0-2 2-2 2-4 5-4

If there had been any justice Australia would have found themselves one up in the rubber after a gruelling but engrossing 80 minutes at Headingley. Unfortunately for Wally Prigg's weary warriors it is not axiomatic that the better team always wins for there was unanimity that Australia deserved victory. They had played a wonderfully open game in the best Australian tradition. *Little John* of *The Sports Post* (Leeds) wrote,
The Australians played their best football of the tour .... for they gave us a perfect demonstration of the close passing and quick backing-up game. The men were always there in support. The straight short runs were driven in, and it really was remarkable how, even when men were more than half held, they managed to get the ball away to colleagues coming up at speed.
Despite the excellence of Australia's attacking play and the dominance they exerted, the old adage that tackling wins matches held true for a hard pressed British XIII - that and the crucial ability to take the one chance which came their way late in the game.
Australia played the first half with the benefit of a stiff breeze and, in hindsight, should perhaps have made more of their advantage. Early pressure resulted in Beaton kicking a splendid penalty goal from near the right touch-line after six minutes and from then on the Kangaroos seemed to threaten relentlessly without ever quite being able to add the final touch to their incisive approach play. Britain, boasting a pack which one observer described as *big enough to push a house over*, were winning the scrums but their backs were totally unable to put a move together.
Australia, it seemed, must score but somehow just as the line was about to fall British tacklers would spring from nowhere. Bert Williams, playing his first game as winger, was almost over; Beaton shaved the posts with a penalty; Beaton, dashing outside his winger, was held out by three desperate tacklers on the line; Prigg dived agonisingly close to a loose ball over the British line but could not get a hand to the leather .... and still Britain held out. Even more remarkably they levelled the match as McCue and Beverley took them on a rare excursion to the Australian "25" where the Kangaroos conceded a penalty at a play-the-ball for mighty Martin Hodgson, playing in his twelfth and final Ashes test, to boot an easy goal two minutes before the interval. It was scant reward for Australia that they had time to get back to the home "25" to earn a scrum penalty for Beaton to restore their two point lead with the last kick of the half.
The second half continued in the same vein as the first, wave after wave of Australian assaults being hurled back in the face of British grit and guts. As the hour approached Beaton was hurt near his own line but having received attention took up his position at outside-centre as a scrum formed on Australia's "25". Emlyn Jenkins, an auburn-haired genius of a Welsh stand-off, had been bottled up by Ernie Norman all afternoon but now became the game-breaker. Receiving from McCue, whose service thus far had been at best erratic, the little Welshman at last eluded Norman and swerved toward the wing. Australia, anticipating a pass to the flank, calamitously exposed a gap to the alert stand-off and he was through in a flash for the try. A solitary mistake and a game which was won was lost.

TEST MATCH 38

AT STATION ROAD, SWINTON – 13 November, 1937
GREAT BRITAIN 13 AUSTRALIA 3 (HT 3-0)

W Belshaw (Warrington)	LR Ward (Norths)
B Hudson (Salford) T	† L Dawson (Easts, Newcastle) T
S Brogden (Leeds)	JJ Beaton (Easts)
AJ Risman (Salford) capt 2G	EJ Norman (Easts)
AS Edwards (Salford) 2T	BH Williams (Bombala)
E Jenkins (Salford)	JP Reardon (Norths, Brisbane)
W Watkins (Salford)	PE Williams (Souths)
† A Higgins (Widnes)	LW Heidke (Ipswich)
T Armitt (Swinton)	HT Pierce (Easts)
N Silcock (Widnes)	J Gibbs (South Newcastle)
† K Jubb (Leeds)	EW Lewis (Souths)
J Arkwright (Warrington)	† H Narvo (Newtown)
H Beverley (Halifax)	WJ Prigg (Central Newcastle) capt

Referee - AE Harding (Manchester)   Crowd - 31,724   Gate - £3,815
Scoring - 3-0 5-0 5-3 10-3 13-3

Unlike the Headingley test there was no doubting Britain's entitlement to this Ashes clinching victory at Swinton. A much changed XIII brought about the desired result and forced the pace from start to finish. A much more mobile pack than the six at Leeds and the resurrection of the 1936 tourists' back division provided the basis for a triumph which was never really in question.

In the first half it was noticeable that the speed of the home forwards was severely curtailing the Australian short-passing game, hard though the Kangaroos strove to open out. Australia clearly missed the front-row power of the absent Stehr and Curran whilst their rejigged back-line lacked penetration with the absence of McKinnon. Even so, for a considerable time the onlookers must have thought that they were looking at a mirror image of the first test for despite an overwhelming all-round superiority Britain could only manage to score once in the first half. The movement, an all-Salford creation, which produced the try came in the absence of Australian hooker Harry Pierce who had departed the field with a head injury and in that respect might have been considered fortuitous. It began with Hudson storming inside to take a pass from Watkins before transferring to the unflappable Risman. Risman made ground and, as so often in club matches, chose exactly the right time to unleash his wing partner Edwards who raced away for the try.

In the second half the British backs began to emulate their forwards' superiority over their opponents and some of their play was a delight to watch as they spread the ball wide, making optimum use of their pace and of the understanding amongst the five Salford players. Yet despite the pre-eminence of the Salford quintet it was the Leeds centre Stan Brogden who really caught the eye. He was clearly the swiftest man on the field and always used his pace to the best advantage of his team in a display reminiscent of the wonderful performances he had turned in on the tours of 1932 and 1936. In the face of the speed and combination of the home backs the Kangaroo rear-guard had a thankless afternoon, particularly as their half-backs, Percy Williams and Jack Reardon, were clearly unhappy in their association.

Risman, with a penalty, increased the British lead to 5-0 before a brief rally brought a try to winger Les Dawson from a characteristically well supported Australian break-out. The score was immediately wiped out, however, as a fine back-line movement put Edwards over for his second try, converted by Risman, and the lead stretched to 10-3. The scoring, all of which was accomplished by Salford Red Devils, was completed when barn-storming Barney Hudson snapped up a dropped ball from Ernie Norman, dribbled to the line and was first to the touch.

For two notable stalwarts of Anglo-Australian tests the game represented their last at this level. Nat Silcock, that war-horse of a prop, playing in his tenth test against the Kangaroos, no doubt went out a happier man than the versatile Ernie Norman who had tangled with the British on seven occasions, the last four as a loser.

TEST MATCH 39

AT FARTOWN, HUDDERSFIELD – 18 December, 1937
GREAT BRITAIN 3 AUSTRALIA 13 (HT 3-10)

W Belshaw (Warrington)
B Hudson (Salford) T
AJ Risman (Salford) capt
S Brogden (Leeds)
AS Edwards (Salford)
E Jenkins (Salford)
W Watkins (Salford)
† DR Prosser (Leeds)
T Armitt (Swinton)
A Higgins (Widnes)
K Jubb (Leeds)
J Arkwright (Warrington)
H Beverley (Halifax)

LR Ward (Norths)
L Dawson (Easts, Newcastle)
RL McKinnon (Easts)
JJ Beaton (Easts) 2G
† AM Norval (Easts) T
JP Reardon (Norths, Brisbane) T
FM Gilbert (Toowoomba)
FJ Curran (Souths)
HT Pierce (Easts)
LW Heidke (Ipswich)
EW Lewis (Souths)
H Narvo (Newtown) T
WJ Prigg (Central Newcastle) capt

Referee - AE Harding (Manchester)   Crowd - 9,093   Gate - £1,237/2/6
Scoring - 0-5 0-8 3-8 3-10 3-13

That most historic of Rugby League arenas, Fartown staged the final test of the 1937 series. Remarkably it remains the only test to have graced that venerable stadium and for all the players involved, save the indestructible Gus Risman, it was to be their last clash in test rugby. The old enemies would not meet again for another nine years thanks to Hitler's mad machinations.

In the event the day was a much happier one for Australia whose performance silenced the growing band of critics sure that Great Britain would make a clean sweep of the series. Though unexpected, Australia's triumph was well merited and their win was their first in Britain since the first test of 1929, an unhappy sequence of eight tests.

Although the British forwards won an overwhelming supply of possession from the tight their backs, so fluent in the previous test, frittered the ball away alarmingly in the face of some inspired defensive play by the Kangaroo forwards amongst whom Herb Narvo and Wally Prigg proved titans in the loose. The British middle-backs were sickened by the power of Ross McKinnon's tackling and in Beaton and Reardon Australia had the game's smartest schemers. The finest player on the field, however, was Laurie Ward whose full-back play, both in attack and defence, was a revelation.

Most of the early play was enacted in Australian territory as Armitt mopped up the scrums but it was the Kangaroos who soon established a winning lead. After Dawson had been recalled when running clear for an offence which only the referee seemed to have witnessed, Australia hit the front in the fourteenth minute. Beaton, inside his own half, put in a short run beating two defenders and fired the ball out to Andy Norval, an erstwhile loose-forward making his test debut on the wing. Norval was away like a shot and when confronted by Belshaw put in a short kick which bounced perfectly for the novice wing and horrendously for Belshaw. Norval touched down wide out but Beaton was equal to the conversion and Australia were five points to the good. Britain again pressed hard but a scintillating dash by Ward had them back-pedalling before Prigg, Gilbert, McKinnon and Dawson combined in a movement which set the home side at panic stations. The momentum was maintained and a lovely three-quarter move orchestrated by Beaton culminated in Reardon touching down from Norval's inside pass giving Australia an eight points lead after only nineteen minutes.

After several escapes Britain responded around the half-hour when from a scrum inside the Kangaroos' "25" Brogden just managed to hold on to a wild pass before whipping the ball out to Hudson whose speed and power transformed the slimmest of chances into an unconverted try. Before the interval, however, Britain slipped further behind when an unhappy Billy Watkins was penalised for feeding at a scrum and Beaton landed a fine goal from 40 yards.

Ten minutes into the second half Britain lost Belshaw through a shoulder injury but still continued to gain a majority of possession which was promptly forfeited by inept kicking and, apart from one notable effort from the gargantuan Arkwright, all the near misses were at the British goal-line. The final nail in Britain's coffin was a try by Narvo after a scramble near the line a few minutes before time. Britain's misery was complete when Edwards unaccountably lost the ball in the act of touching down.

WHY ENGLAND ha

ENGLAND has held the Rugby League "Ashes" since 1922 because our players have a greatly different approach to the game than is apparent in Australia.

Essential difference is that our teams are not concerned with high-scoring, but in match-winning.

Perhaps you would call it "spoiling."

We prefer to call it "tactics."

Of the 13 series of Test matches played since 1908 Australian teams have won only two to the Englishmen's 11.

And yet Australians have scored 425 points to our 424.

It's a comparison we are happy to concede.

Australian teams may continue to compile a worth-while aggregrate of points, but until they also adopt "tactics" England will win vital matches.

Rugby League is based on scrummaging.

Without powerful forwards, keenly aware of all the possibilities of the game, understanding every advantage that can be taken without breaking the rules, England's game would collapse.

Our teams are moulded, trained, and graded, therefore, to develop forward play.

OUR packs are sent on to the field not just to score points, but to control the game throughout, to form set patterns of play.

Of course, we choose the best men the code can offer to stand behind them, but their play is subsidiary in our style.

Batten, Parkin, Bacon, and Stockwell, who played in the 1921 Test series that began England's winning sequence, were among the finest back-line ever to represent their country.

But don't forget the supermen who formed the pack—Cunliffe, Cartwright, Hilton, Taylor, Skelhorne, and Gallagher.

When we are short of classy backs we send agents to South Wales, noted training ground of Rugby Union's nippy halves and centres, where, without trouble, one can find, "ready made," potential internationals.

And we are always prepared to pay big money for them

Sometimes transfer fees have topped £1000

After all, Rugby League is a game for professionals—the bigger the prizemoney

THESE PLAYER.

GUS RISMAN
(Captain),
(Centre Three-quarter)
5ft. 10in., 13st., 35 yrs.

TED WARD
(Centre three-quarter), 6ft.,
13st. 4lb., 28 yrs.

WILLIE DA'
(Five-eight)
5ft. 8in., 1
29 yrs.

JOE JONES
(Full-back),
5ft. 10in., 12st.
11lb., 27 yrs.

ERIC BATTEN
(Wing three-quarter), 5ft.
9½in., 12st. 2lb.,
29 yrs.

J. LEWTHWAITE
(Wing three-quarter), 5ft.
11in., 13st., 25 yrs.

A. BASSET
(Wing thr
quarter),
10½in., 12st. 1
30 yrs.

TOMMY McCUE
(Vice-Captain)
(Half-back),
5ft. 6in., 11st.
8lb., 32yrs.

A. JOHNSON
(Wing three-quarter), 5ft.
10½in., 13st.,
27 yrs.

ERN WARD
(Centre three-quarter), 5ft.
11in., 13st., 26 yrs.

B. KNOWEL'
(Centre th
quarter),
8in., 11st. (
24 yrs.

the higher the incentive to near-perfect play.

English clubs have also imported classy backs from Australia.

These Australian players, among them Dinny Campbell, Ray Markham, Dave Brown, Bill Shankland, Jeff Moores, could not play for England, but their presence in club teams helped develop our players.

In the team now touring there are 12 Welshmen, who, although eligible to play for Britain against Australia, are not permitted to represent England in matches against Wales or France.

In Brita only for t

Australi and usual have beer cipally on

And Au "open gan close-up s stand the

But our to win m pleasers."

For thi to the ga

d THE ASHES by Eddie Waring

DEFEND THEM

VOR FOSTER (Forward), ., 13st. 10lb., 29 yrs.

IKE OWENS (Forward), 6ft., 14st. 2lb., 26 yrs.

HARRY MURPHY (Full-back), 6ft., 13st. 12lb., 24 yrs.

MARTIN RYAN (Full-back), 5ft. 10in., 12st. 11lb., 22 yrs.

OE EGAN (Hooker), 8in., 13st., 26 yrs.

GEO. CURRAN (Hooker), 5ft. 10in., 13st. 3lb., 28 yrs.

F. WHITCOMBE (Forward), 5ft. 10in., 17st. 8lb., 31 yrs.

KEN GEE (Forward), 5ft. 9in., 15st. 3lb., 29 yrs.

ED HUGHES (Forward), ., 14st. 13lb., 30 yrs.

DOUG. PHILLIPS (Forward), 6ft. 2in., 14st. 7lb., 26 yrs.

BOB NICHOLSON (Forward), 5ft. 10in., 13st. 7lb., 24 yrs.

LES WHITE (Forward), 5ft. 11in., 13st. 7lb., 24 yrs.

ble to play
oirth.

conditioned
t than ours,
based prin-
ormations.

used to the
the rugged,
you under-
ctacular.
ected solely
be "crowd

ir approach
icated.

Our best forwards have, for a generation, come from Yorkshire and Lancashire.

Although Yorkshiremen are uncharitably dubbed "strong in the back and weak in the head," they have planned many of the stratagems that have given us such a grip on "The Ashes."

And despite their supposed incoherence, these same Yorkshiremen are great tutors.

We take our football seriously, and even schoolboy and junior teams are trained by former internationals in the essence of match tactics and control.

taught never to promote play that may cost vital points.

One of England's best-trained packs was that which came to Australia in 1936 —giants in every sense of Rugby League.

Tom Armitt, the hooker, knew every trick and counter of his position; Woods and Silcock were super-props, with power and cunning; Arkwright and Hodgson were highly mobile in the second row; and the lock, Harry Beverly, was a quick-running tackler who "buried 'em" from any angle.

They used to say that when Armitt and his supports packed down, the half-back, without exchange of a word or glance, knew what to expect.

IN moulding the Cup Tie or Test pack an English coach never depends solely on his own opinions and ideas. It is not rare for half a dozen "guest coaches"—all former internationals—to co-operate in the preparation of the forward line.

Despite wartime conditions every chance of regular coaching was given our players, to the neglect of conditioning. It was left mainly to the men themselves to reach peak physical fitness.

Another important feature in England's success and the strength of our forwards is our setting of alternate positions in scrums.

We specially grade men for open scrummage and "blind" side play, because we consider it of great importance

Australians frequently take up scrum positions in the same formation without change, regardless of the side on which the ball will be coming in.

Finally, statistics prove the superiority of England's players.

Australians readily agree that Englishmen have won most Tests because they have made fewer mistakes.

We, in turn, admit that we have been a shade luckier than Australians.

Outstanding example of our luck was in the 1929-30 series.

That year Australian half-back Joe Busch's disallowed try, in the scoreless third Test at Swinton, should have won "The Ashes" for Australia.

The try was legitimate. but the touch judge, in his excitement, ruled against it. His mistake was our luck.

But when you look at that long series of wins you can't put it all down to luck.

EDDIE WARING

TEST MATCH 40

AT SYDNEY CRICKET GROUND – 17 June, 1946
AUSTRALIA 8 GREAT BRITAIN 8 (HT 2-6)

† D Parkinson (Balmain)	AJ Risman (Salford) capt G
† E Newham (Cowra)	† E Batten (Bradford N)
† J Jorgenson (Balmain) capt G	† E Ward (Bradford N)
† R Bailey (Canterbury) T	† J Kitching (Bradford N)
† LW Cooper (Easts) T	† AE Johnson (Warrington)
† PC Devery (Balmain)	† W Horne (Barrow) T
† J Grice (Souths, Brisbane)	T McCue (Widnes)
† F Farrell (Newtown)	† K Gee (Wigan)
† G Watt (Easts)	† J Egan (Wigan)
† R Westaway (Valleys, Brisbane)	† FW Whitcombe (Bradford N) T
† AC Clues (Wests)	† L White (York)
† R Kay (Souths, Brisbane)	† DV Phillips (Oldham)
† NG Mulligan (Newtown)	† IA Owens (Leeds)

Referee - T McMahon (NSW)   Crowd - 64,527   Gate - £10,130
Scoring - 0-3 2-3 2-6 5-6 5-8 8-8

Of the 26 players who took the field for this first test only the British veterans Gus Risman and Tommy McCue had previously played at this level. Nonetheless the game exhibited all the traits so well established in test football - hard and typically tense, yet clean, except for one isolated incident. This occurred in the 28th minute when British centre Jack Kitching tackled Australia's captain, Joe Jorgenson, and in the aftermath punched him. Kitching was sent off and Britain, ahead by a point, faced a numerically superior foe for over 50 minutes. In such circumstances Australia should have obtained a better result but Joe Egan and his five-man pack outscrummaged the Australians to the tune of 28-17 and with Ike Owens, McCue and Ernest Ward excelling in attack and defence the game could have gone either way. Both goal-kickers, Jorgenson and Risman, normally models of accuracy, had enough chances to win several games but missed six and seven shots respectively.

The game began sensationally as Britain harassed Australia on the goal-line until Bailey threw out a wild pass which Jorgenson had to touch down in the in-goal. At the resulting five-yard scrimmage Grice fumbled with dire consequences for Horne nipped in to gather and score before the defence could react. Risman missed the conversion from a comfortable position and five minutes later Jorgenson landed a good 35 yard penalty, his only bull's-eye of the afternoon. Between the ninth and twentieth minutes Risman failed with three penalties and Jorgenson with one before Australia had a very narrow escape. Egan caught the ball from an Australian goal-line drop-out and amazed everyone by dummying through and diving over at the corner only for the referee to rule that the ball had not been grounded.

When Kitching's dismissal occurred shortly afterwards it seemed to spur rather than inhibit the Lions who went further ahead on the half-hour following a clever piece of play by Ward who short punted over the defence, regathered after a juggling act and fed Johnson. Johnson was baulked near the corner but got in a pass to the mountainous Whitcombe who barged over near the flag.

The first few minutes of the second half saw Jorgenson and Risman fail with more penalty kicks but eleven minutes into the half Australia hit back with a delightful try. Inside his own half hooker George Watt cannily switched play at a ruck and the ball was worked out to Bailey who broke away down the right wing before being challenged by Risman near the "25". A cheeky dummy left Risman behind as Bailey raced to the line. There was no conversion but four minutes later the force-field which seemed to be operating round the goal posts at both ends temporarily short-circuited to allow Risman to kick a simple penalty after "Bumper" Farrell had gone off-side. The scores were tied after 70 minutes when Lionel Cooper scored a superlative try after receiving from a scrum 70 yards out. Good passing had released the winger and a beautiful change of pace carried him past Risman. Jorgenson missed the conversion but even more crucially he failed three minutes later to land a straight 25 yard penalty which could have given Australia the match.

The last few minutes saw Britain almost snatch the game as Owens was thrown into touch at the corner and a last gasp penalty from Risman had the crowd on tenterhooks. Farrell was deemed off-side at the centre but Risman's kick drifted wide and Australia breathed again.

TEST MATCH 41

AT THE EXHIBITION GROUND, BRISBANE – 6 July, 1946
AUSTRALIA 5 GREAT BRITAIN 14 (HT 0-5)

D Parkinson (Balmain)	E Ward (Bradford N) G
E Newham (Cowra)	† A Bassett (Halifax) 3T
R Bailey (Canterbury) capt	AJ Risman (Salford) capt
J Jorgenson (Balmain) G	† EH Ward (Wigan)
LW Cooper (Easts) T	AE Johnson (Warrington) T
PC Devery (Balmain)	W Horne (Barrow)
J Grice (Souths, Brisbane)	T McCue (Widnes)
F Farrell (Newtown)	K Gee (Wigan)
G Watt (Easts)	J Egan (Wigan)
R Westaway (Valleys, Brisbane)	FW Whitcombe (Bradford N)
AC Clues (Wests)	L White (York)
R Kay (Souths, Brisbane)	DV Phillips (Oldham)
† J Hutchinson (Newcastle)	IA Owens (Leeds)

Referee - SW Chambers (Queensland)   Crowd - 40,500   Gate - £5,190
Scoring - 0-3 0-5 2-5 2-8 5-8 5-11 5-14

Despite the fact that coal shortages had caused drastic cuts in public transport the second test created such interest in Brisbane that the attendance broke all sporting records for the city. Crowds began to gather at 4 a.m. The gates were thrown open at 7 a.m. and closed at 11.40 a.m. with the ground bursting at the seams. Even so, more than 10,000 fans gained free entry by nefarious means after the gates had been closed and so great was the press that the referee had to clear the lines of encroaching bodies before the first scrum could go down.

The match was no classic, being more notable for its robust defence and relentless covering than for any particular brilliance in combination or openness of play. Some of the exchanges would have been staged more appropriately in a boxing ring and when British hooker Joe Egan was sent off just before the end he was no more than a sacrificial lamb for what had gone before. Britain won with some ease, the forwards clearly outplaying their opposites. Les White led the pack in brilliant fashion but it was in the scrum base triangle of Owens, McCue and Horne that the Lions had the trump card. McCue, in particular, was at his best and virtually ran the game. Though McCue was undoubtedly the dictator, the executioner was the powerful Welsh winger Arthur Bassett whose lethal finishing brought him a remarkable hat-trick on his test debut.

The first half provided little in the way of constructive football yet Australia defended magnificently to restrict the Lions to two scores. McCue was the architect of the first after fifteen minutes. Securing from a scrum just inside Australian territory the wily scrum-half short-kicked smartly for Bassett to burst through, take the ball in his stride and cross at the corner. Ernest Ward failed with the conversion but six minutes before the interval landed a stunning touch-line penalty goal.

Australia began the second half aggressively as Farrell and Westaway took play to the British line forcing Gee to concede a penalty from which Jorgenson landed a goal. Britain's response was swift and again engineered by McCue who gained the Lions a dangerous position by finding touch five yards from the home line and from the ensuing scrum it was child's play for the British halves to work the blind-side enabling Bassett to stroll over for his second try.

Australia rallied and on the hour they conjured a splendid try to reduce the British lead to 8-5. The movement was initiated by Bailey 40 yards out and carried on by Jorgenson who served Lionel Cooper in a seemingly hopeless position. Faced with at least four defenders and little space in which to manoeuvre, Cooper made light of the odds to score a characteristically belligerent try at the corner. Australian hopes evaporated five minutes from time, however, when Johnson scored a remarkable try for the Lions. Chasing a kick the winger outstripped Newham but had to juggle with the ball above his head for fully fifteen yards before finally managing to cradle it and race over at the flag. Three minutes later the final nail was driven into Australia's coffin as Ted Ward raced down-field from Phillips' pass, veered to the right wing and sent Bassett cruising over wide out for his third touchdown.

Britain's victory meant that the Ashes had been retained and marked a quarter of a century's domination of the series for Australia had never recovered them since their loss in 1921-22.

TEST MATCH 42

AT SYDNEY CRICKET GROUND – 20 July, 1946
AUSTRALIA 7 GREAT BRITAIN 20 (HT 7-2)

D Parkinson (Balmain)	E Ward (Bradford N)
† N White (Kurri)	A Bassett (Halifax) 2T
J Jorgenson (Balmain) capt 2G	AJ Risman (Salford) capt 3G
† TN Eather (Boggabri)	EH Ward (Wigan) G
LW Cooper (Easts)	E Batten (Bradford N)
PC Devery (Balmain)	W Horne (Barrow)
† C Kennedy (Souths) T	T McCue (Widnes)
F Farrell (Newtown)	K Gee (Wigan)
G Watt (Easts)	J Egan (Wigan)
† J Armstrong (Souths)	† G Curran (Salford) T
AC Clues (Wests)	L White (York)
R Kay (Souths, Brisbane)	DV Phillips (Oldham)
NG Mulligan (Newtown)	IA Owens (Leeds) T

Referee - T McMahon (NSW) Crowd - 35,294 Gate - £4,572
Scoring - 2-0 2-2 7-2 7-4 7-7 7-10 7-15 7-20

Britain's victory enabled Gus Risman's "Indomitables" to become the only Lions team to complete a three-match series Down-under undefeated. The victory was, however, by no means as clear-cut as the score implied. Australia led into the second half, had a man sent off and had to contend with a 46-15 deficit in the scrummaging. Moreover, they had to play for 73 minutes with full-back Dave Parkinson in agony having suffered a broken leg when being heavily dumped in a tackle. In such circumstances Australia performed miracles in defence, Britain's last five points coming at the final bell.

The first half saw Britain squander countless opportunities as Australia clung like grim death to their adversaries and made the most of the chances which came their way. Cooper twice made dangerous interceptions, first falling to weight of numbers and then just being toppled by Risman's ankle-tap before Jorgenson gave the green and golds the lead with a well-struck penalty from the "25" after seventeen minutes. British pressure failed to bring any reward as Noel White beat Bassett to a tantalising McCue kick to the home in-goal and both Owens and Bassett mishandled when well placed to score. With Risman making a hash of a simple penalty it seemed as if the Lions were jinxed for the day until Risman made amends by coolly dropping a goal from outside the "25" to level the scores.

Australia soon recovered the lead when Jorgenson potted a 30 yards penalty as Britain continued to fritter away possession and worse was to follow for the Lions as Ernest Ward entered a passing movement from a scrum in Australia's "25". Ward tried a short kick but the ball went straight to Clem Kennedy who raced into open space, reached half-way and kicked. Amazingly it was Australian hooker George Watt who was first to the ball and, as he was tackled, managed to fire a difficult pass to Kennedy. The scrum-half got his finger-tips to the ball, juggled momentarily and finally gained control to score a sensational try.

The six minutes following the break saw the Lions in an altogether different frame of mind as they posted eight points to take a lead they never lost. Risman began by landing a simple penalty and then sweet handling from a scrum saw McCue, Owens, Horne and Ernest Ward release Bassett for the winger to evade White's challenge and touch down near the flag. Britain piled on the pressure and faulty Australian handling allowed McCue to work an opening for Curran to give the Lions a 10-7 lead. Australia lost the game irretrievably in the 63rd minute when Arthur Clues was sent off for striking at Horne in a tackle. After that the game became something of a scramble with the Lions proving more adept in the art. Batten created a try with a wonderfully sinuous run from his "25" almost to the Australian line where he was eventually run to ground but not before he had given Owens a scoring pass. Risman goaled from under the sticks and as time ran out Britain scored again as Gee fired a long pass from the ruck to send Bassett cavorting 40 yards to touch down wide out. Ted Ward booted the conversion after the final bell had sounded and Britain had recorded a victory which was overpoweringly flattering to their efforts and scant justice to those of the Australians.

The game marked the end of Gus Risman's wonderful test career which had begun back in 1932 on the same ground. No other player has ever enjoyed such longevity in Anglo-Australian conflict.

TEST MATCH 43

AT HEADINGLEY, LEEDS – 9 October, 1948
GREAT BRITAIN 23 AUSTRALIA 21 (HT 11-6)

JA Ledgard (Leigh)	CB Churchill (Souths)
†J Lawrenson (Wigan)	P McMahon (Toowoomba) 2T
†AJ Pimblett (Warrington) 2T	†DA McRitchie (St. George)
E Ward (Bradford N) capt G	†NJ Hawke (Canberra)
†S McCormick (Belle Vue R) 2T	JN Graves (Souths) T,3G
W Horne (Barrow)	WP O'Connell (Easts) capt
†GJ Helme (Warrington)	GK Froome (Newtown) T
K Gee (Wigan)	†A Gibbs (South Newcastle)
J Egan (Wigan)	KB Schubert (Wollongong)
G Curran (Salford)	D Hall (Valleys, Brisbane) T
R Nicholson (Huddersfield)	JF Holland (St. George)
TJF Foster (Bradford N) 2T	RJ Rayner (Souths)
†DD Valentine (Huddersfield) T	NG Mulligan (Newtown)

Referee - AS Dobson (Pontefract)   Crowd - 36,529   Gate - £8,020/8/6
Scoring - 0-3 0-6 5-6 8-6 11-6 14-6 17-6 17-11 20-11 20-16 23-16 23-21

Headingley was the stage for an orgy of open rugby, an extravaganza of entertainment, a game which broke the mould as far as test football was concerned. A record twelve tries spoke volumes for the attacking powers of the teams even allowing for the fact that the defences may not have exhibited the traditional ferocity of test teams. The match, too breathtaking to allow any skullduggery, was played in the best of spirits with only nine penalties (seven to the Kangaroos) being awarded, mostly for offences at the scrums, which crucially went to Britain 40-18. So enthralling was the action that Alfred Drewry of *The Yorkshire Post & Leeds Mercury* was moved to write, *Fifty years hence the recital of its story will be a sore trial to bored grandchildren.*

Australia rocked Britain in the early exchanges with some tellingly direct forward play and within quarter of an hour had run in two tries. The first, in the fifth minute, went to prop Duncan Hall who crashed irresistibly past three defenders who were too slow to see the danger. Froome missed a sitter of a conversion. Ten minutes later a planned move saw O'Connell spurt through a gap before feeding McMahon who slipped over at the corner and Australia led 6-0.

At this point Britain suddenly threw off the Australian yoke and began to play inspired football. Ward appeared to score from a kick-through by McCormick but Britain were recalled to receive a penalty for a previous obstruction on the winger. After twenty minutes, however, perfect rugby produced a try as Pimblett drove to the right allowing Nicholson to scissor with Lawrenson. The winger handed off a posse of tacklers before providing Foster with the scoring pass. Ward landed the goal, his only successful kick of the match. Seven minutes later Ledgard made a run down the wing and tried to pass inside but the ball ricocheted back to him off a defender and the full-back carried on to the "25" before parting to Horne and there was Foster, the great man of this match, to bag a second try. Five minutes before the break quick thinking by Foster enabled McCormick to break clear, side-step Churchill and dive past Froome for a superb try.

Britain kept up their momentum. Five minutes after the break the ball was whipped along the line for McCormick to swallow dive in at the flag. Australia had a brief look at the home line but McMahon knocked on three yards out and in the 56th minute Britain took their lead to 17-6 as crisp passing created an overlap for Valentine, temporarily on the wing, to score wide out. On the hour Australia struck back as Froome crept over at the corner and Graves hit a mighty conversion but within two minutes Britain had scored again with Pimblett tearing through for a fine try.

The game ebbed and flowed gloriously and in the 65th minute British passing disintegrated well inside Kangaroo territory. Hawke was quickly away and by the time he gave the ball to Graves at half-way there was no one to stop the winger who converted his own try and suddenly Australia were only four points adrift and threatening to win. Ten minutes from time, however, Pimblett dashed through for a try to give Britain breathing space at 23-16. Even then the Kangaroos refused to yield and magnificent passing brought a 75th minute try to McMahon, converted by Graves. British hearts leapt into their mouths in the dying seconds as a dramatic run by Clive Churchill almost snatched the game but "the Little Master" fell to a last ditch tackle from behind inches short of everlasting glory.

Headingley, 1948.
The first Ashes team to bear the title "Great Britain" lines up. Left to right, they are Egan, Valentine, Foster, Nicholson, Curran, Gee, Helme, Horne, McCormick, Pimblett, Lawrenson, Ledgard, Ward (capt).

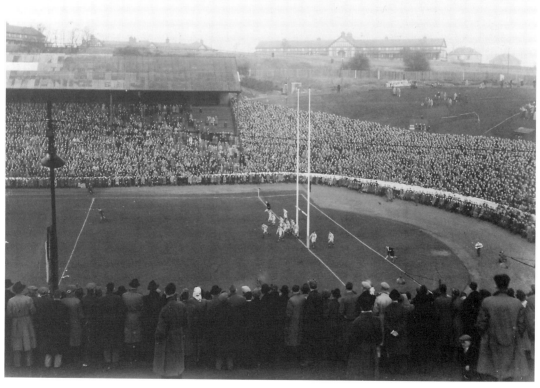

Odsal Stadium, 1949.
A record crowd for an Ashes Test in Britain at the time watch as an Australian conversion misses the mark.

TEST MATCH 44

AT STATION ROAD, SWINTON – 11 November, 1948
GREAT BRITAIN 16 AUSTRALIA 7 (HT 10-2)

M Ryan (Wigan)	CB Churchill (Souths)
J Lawrenson (Wigan) 2T	P McMahon (Toowoomba)
AJ Pimblett (Warrington) 2T	† J Horrigan (Valleys, Brisbane) T
E Ward (Bradford N) capt 2G	† CM Maxwell (Wests) capt
S McCormick (Belle Vue R)	JN Graves (Souths) 2G
† RL Williams (Leeds)	WP O'Connell (Easts)
GJ Helme (Warrington)	† WH Thompson (Toowoomba)
K Gee (Wigan)	A Gibbs (South Newcastle)
J Egan (Wigan)	KB Schubert (Wollongong)
G Curran (Salford)	NR Hand (Norths)
R Nicholson (Huddersfield)	NG Mulligan (Newtown)
TJF Foster (Bradford N)	RJ Rayner (Souths)
DD Valentine (Huddersfield)	IW Tyquin (Souths, Brisbane)

Referee - GS Phillips (Widnes)   Crowd - 36,354   Gate - £6,702
Scoring - 2-0 5-0 10-0 10-2 13-2 13-7 16-7

After the exuberance of the play at Headingley the second test saw a reversion to a style of play more in keeping with the traditions of test rugby as both teams defended more stubbornly. Once again the match was scrupulously cleanly contested and for a change Australia managed to obtain an almost equal share of possession from the scrums, Egan shading Schubert 27-23 in this respect. Unfortunately they were unable to profit from this relative glut of ball and Britain, playing measured football, were able to dictate affairs throughout. The home lead was never seriously threatened and Australia, strangely subdued, became too obsessed with passing for its own sake and were altogether too slow and stereotyped, particularly amongst the middle backs.

Conditions on the day were ideal although the ground was a little soft from rain earlier in the week. Australia had the first opportunity to put points on the board but Graves was inches short with a touch-line penalty. Ward made no mistake with a simple penalty for Britain, however, when Churchill fouled Helme as he broke from a scrum. Mulligan, Australia's only real success of the match, almost made it to the line with a lovely run but Ryan nailed him on the touch-line. Britain stepped up the pace and Lawrenson and Ryan were both kept out with great difficulty by the sorely pressed Kangaroos before Britain finally breached the line after nineteen minutes. The Australian rear-guard buckled as Williams stole through and handed on to Ward for the British captain to time his pass perfectly for Pimblett to score not far from the posts. Ward surprisingly fluffed the conversion.

On the half-hour Britain doubled their advantage with a vintage touchdown. Helme and Williams worked a run-around which released Ward who quickly served Pimblett - an absolute revelation in this series - for the centre to streak to the line using Lawrenson as a foil and without a finger being laid on him. Ward's goal took Britain ten points clear and they might have gone even further ahead had not Churchill pulled off a cracking tackle on McCormick after a typical piece of wizardry by Ward. On the stroke of half-time Australia pulled back two points when Graves landed a fine goal.

Australia held the upper hand for the first fifteen minutes of the second half but wasted chance after chance, most blatantly when Graves dropped a pass a yard from the goal-line. Britain weathered the storm but wasted a good opportunity when Foster failed to part to Williams in a scoring position and then Lawrenson was grounded in the shadow of the Australian posts after a cute scissors move with Pimblett. The killer blow was not long in coming, however, as Williams ghosted through on the left before play switched to the right for quick passing to outflank the Kangaroos. Lawrenson applied the final touch and put Britain out of reach at 13-2. Australia finally obtained a try six minutes from time when Horrigan snapped up a stray pass and ran strongly for a consolation try goaled by Graves. Even then Britain had time to sweep to the other end for Lawrenson to score his second try just before the final whistle.

Britain, who played well to a man, were best served by Valentine, a tackling-machine, Ryan and Pimblett, whilst two debutants on opposite sides had distinctly varying experiences. Dickie Williams, a future Lions captain, looked born to test rugby whilst Col Maxwell, the tour skipper, would never play test rugby again.

TEST MATCH 45

AT ODSAL STADIUM, BRADFORD – 29 January, 1949
GREAT BRITAIN 23 AUSTRALIA 9 (HT 5-6)

M Ryan (Wigan)	CB Churchill (Souths)
J Lawrenson (Wigan)	P McMahon (Toowoomba)
AJ Pimblett (Warrington)	† RJ Lulham (Balmain) T
E Ward (Bradford N) capt T,4G	DA McRitchie (St. George)
S McCormick (Belle Vue R) T	NJ Hawke (Canberra)
RL Williams (Leeds) T	WP O'Connell (Easts)
GJ Helme (Warrington)	GK Froome (Newtown)
K Gee (Wigan)	A Gibbs (South Newcastle)
J Egan (Wigan)	KB Schubert (Wollongong)
G Curran (Salford) 2T	D Hall (Valleys, Brisbane) T
† JJ Featherstone (Warrington)	NG Mulligan (Newtown)
† W Hudson (Wigan)	IW Tyquin (Souths, Brisbane) capt
DD Valentine (Huddersfield)	FL De Belin (Balmain) T

Referee - GS Phillips (Widnes)   Crowd - 42,000   Gate - £6,875
Scoring - 5-0 5-3 5-6 8-6 13-6 18-6 23-6 23-9

The third test had originally been scheduled for 18 December but had been fogged off and Australia had crossed the Channel to complete a ten-match tour of France winning both tests played. Despite the fact that the destination of the Ashes had already been decided and foul weather still threatened, a record crowd for an Australian test in England turned up hoping for a repeat of the Headingley epic. In the event the match never reached those heights but was nonetheless an enjoyable affair with the final score totally belying the efforts of the Kangaroos. For almost an hour Australia held the whip hand but crumbled to an eight minute blitz mid-way through the second half when Britain turned the match on its head with a rush of three tries.

The Kangaroos gave Britain a torrid time in the early stages. Churchill failed with a drop at goal, Froome was narrowly wide with a penalty and smooth passing ended with McMahon being scythed down a yard short. It was against the run of play therefore when a snap try gave Britain the lead. Scrum-half Helme cheekily broke the defence and sent Ward over unmolested. Ward added a grand touch-line improvement and Britain were undeservedly five points to the good. Australia were undaunted and Fred De Belin, excelling in the Kangaroo pack, drove deep into home territory before sending Lulham ploughing through Lawrenson's grasp for a smart try. Froome's goal attempt sailed wide but Australia continued to hammer the British defence. De Belin almost had Lulham in for a second try but Ward brought the centre down with a perfect tackle. O'Connell was at the heart of most of Australia's most dangerous assaults and it came as no surprise when one of his labyrinthine runs ended in Hall crashing over to give the Kangaroos a deserved lead. Just before the break O'Connell varied his tactics beautifully with a searching kick to the corner from which Lulham almost scored.

Australia continued to have the better of things in the second half until Britain entered their purple patch in the 55th minute when Ryan linked delightfully with his three-quarters to send McCormick flying past the last defender for a super try. Having regained the lead Britain seemed rejuvenated. Valentine smashed through and almost had McCormick over again and in quick succession Helme, Williams and Lawrenson were held on the line before a choice Egan pass enabled Curran to struggle over festooned with defenders. Ward converted and Britain led 13-6. There was no respite for Australia as a mesmeric passing bout stretched a harassed defence to breaking point before the direction of the attack was switched when Pimblett drove sharply inside to send Williams scuttling 40 yards and fending off Lulham before dotting down under the bar. Ward converted and repeated the dose soon afterwards when Curran dived over for his second try. To their credit Australia refused to throw in the towel and De Belin was rewarded with a last minute try.

An interesting statistic from the series revealed that for the first time Australia fielded three different captains in the tests. They have subsequently done likewise in the series of 1962, 1967, 1970 and 1973 whilst Britain have used three skippers in the series of 1929-30, 1936 and 1982.

TEST MATCH 46

AT SYDNEY CRICKET GROUND – 12 June, 1950
AUSTRALIA 4 GREAT BRITAIN 6 (HT 4-6)

CB Churchill (Souths) capt	M Ryan (Wigan)
ND Pidding (St. George) 2G	GW Ratcliffe (Wigan)
D McRitchie (St. George)	E Ward (Bradford N) capt
† K Middleton (Norths)	EJ Ashcroft (Wigan)
† J Troy (Newtown)	† J Hilton (Wigan) 2T
† FS Stanmore (Wests)	RL Williams (Leeds)
† KV Holman (Wests)	T Bradshaw (Wigan)
JF Holland (St. George)	K Gee (Wigan)
KB Schubert (Manly)	J Egan (Wigan)
D Hall (Valleys, Brisbane)	E Gwyther (Belle Vue R)
FL De Belin (Balmain)	† R Ryan (Warrington)
† A Thompson (Souths, Brisbane)	† F Higgins (Widnes)
LG Cowie (Souths)	† H Street (Dewsbury)

Referee - G Bishop (NSW)   Crowd - 47,275   Gate - £6,792

Scoring - 0-3 2-3 4-3 4-6

Great Britain emerged worthy winners from a match which took place under some of the worst conditions imaginable. Heavy rains had reduced the SCG to a quagmire and two curtain-raisers had merely served to churn the morass into an even more uninviting, cloying, oozing paddy-field. Within minutes of the start most of the players were simply unrecognisable bearing more resemblance to a potter's figures than to flesh and blood. There was a constant procession of players waiting to have buckets of clean water thrown into their faces to clear their mud-clogged eyes. If Rudyard Kipling had ever needed models to portray his "muddied oafs" he would have found his fill on this Monday afternoon in Sydney.

Wigan provided a record seven players to the British XIII but it was the least experienced of the septet, debutant winger Jack Hilton, who had the biggest influence on a remarkable match, fought out with an intense ferocity but which belied the appalling conditions to produce some fine football at times. Australia had opened strongly and pressure had enabled Pidding to attempt two long-range penalties within the first ten minutes. Neither succeeded but the second struck the bar and bounced out. Then in the thirteenth minute, quite against the run of play, Britain took the lead. A scrum went down 40 yards from the home line, Britain heeled and Bradshaw broke to the blind-side and served Ashcroft. Martin Ryan entered the line, a move which clearly foxed the Aussies, and an all-Wigan move ended with Hilton scorching down the flank through Churchill's tackle to score a peach of a try at the corner.

Pidding had a chance to reduce the arrears but he muffed a comparatively easy penalty - if any goal-kick could be described thus in such conditions. After 22 minutes, however, the same player landed a very fine 35 yard goal and repeated the dose on the half-hour to edge Australia into a 4-3 lead, as play became increasingly venomous. Two minutes before half-time the score which effectively settled the issue came like a bolt from the blue. Australia were battering at the British defence and looking likely scorers when Hall threw out a pass which Ashcroft intercepted ten yards from his line and close to the right touch-line. Hilton, improbably supporting on the wrong wing, accompanied Ashcroft as he dashed towards half-way with Frank Stanmore in hot pursuit. The Australian stand-off grassed Ashcroft just inside the Australian half despite being somewhat impeded by Hilton but not before the centre had parted to his out-of-position winger. Holman dived at Hilton's fast disappearing heels but to no avail and the winger shattered a last challenge from Churchill to score a glorious try at the corner.

The second half saw no more scoring. Britain, thanks to Egan's 39-27 pull in the scrums, kept the ball tight although they clearly had the better three-quarters and risked little. Even so, Australia might have won. Six minutes into the half Stanmore kicked through, the ball plopped dead and "Dutchy" Holland hacked on and dived as the ball crossed the British line. The ball spurted free and Hilton grounded but most witnesses swear that a fair try was scored. George Bishop, the first ex-test player to referee a test match, ruled no try and the ground erupted in disbelief. Pidding then struck the post with a penalty and a dribbling rush by Middleton and McRitchie was thwarted by the mud when it seemed easier to score than not to and eight minutes from time Pidding's long-range penalty dropped tantalisingly short. On such trifles are test matches won and lost.

Above: Sydney, first test, 1950. The pitch is a morass as Lions prop Ken Gee straddles the ball. To the right Ernest Ward drags an Australian away from the ball. *Below:* Brisbane, second test, 1950. Australian second-rower Fred De Belin runs at a Lions trio of Gordon Ratcliffe, Ernest Ward and Fred Higgins.

TEST MATCH 47

AT BRISBANE CRICKET GROUND – 1 July, 1950
AUSTRALIA 15 GREAT BRITAIN 3 (HT 5-3)

CB Churchill (Souths) capt G	JA Ledgard (Leigh)
† DJ Flannery (Ipswich)	GW Ratcliffe (Wigan)
† N Andrews (Mackay)	E Ward (Bradford N) capt
K Middleton (Norths)	EJ Ashcroft (Wigan)
JN Graves (Souths) T,G	† T Danby (Salford) T
FS Stanmore (Wests)	RL Williams (Leeds)
KV Holman (Wests) T	T Bradshaw (Wigan)
A Thompson (Souths, Brisbane)	K Gee (Wigan)
KB Schubert (Manly)	J Egan (Wigan)
JF Holland (St. George) G	E Gwyther (Belle Vue R)
† H Crocker (Souths, Brisbane)	† H Murphy (Wakefield T)
FL De Belin (Balmain)	F Higgins (Widnes)
LG Cowie (Souths) T	H Street (Dewsbury)

Referee - F Ballard (Queensland)   Crowd - 35,000   Gate - £7,376
Scoring - 0-3 2-3 5-3 7-3 12-3 15-3

A controversial and gripping match saw Australia beat Great Britain for the first time since 1937 to square the series. Australia had lost six successive tests to the Poms but enthusiasm to see the match was so high that the game was made an all-ticket affair - the first such occasion in Australia.

Conditions at the "Gabba" could not have contrasted more from those at Sydney for the previous test. A beautiful day and a dry ground seemed likely to be more to Australia's advantage than to the Lions who lacked arch-schemer Willie Horne. Within four minutes, however, Australia were rocked by a gem of a try by Tom Danby, an ex-England RU cap making his test debut. There seemed very little to worry about when an exchange of long kicks between Ledgard and Churchill developed. Eventually Churchill manoeuvred the British full-back out of position but Tommy Bradshaw fielded the ball ten yards inside his own half and broke down the right wing with Danby steaming inside him in support. Thirty-five yards out the scrum-half passed to Danby who appeared well covered but bustled Flannery out of his path, swept past a couple of coverers and accelerated past a despairing Churchill for a try which stunned the crowd.

Three minutes later Johnny Graves landed a huge penalty from a wide position seven yards inside the British half and only one point separated the sides. For a time Australia pressed as Schubert bossed the scrums and Holman kicked judiciously but there was no reward for Graves who missed two shots at goal nor for a fine Holman break from which Middleton dropped a scoring pass. The Lions hit back strongly and a tremendous movement developed when Ward and Ashcroft broke from their "25" to send Danby past De Belin's flying challenge on a 50 yards burst. At the home "25" Danby threw inside to Bradshaw who sent Williams scooting to the posts only for the referee to rule a forward pass. Three minutes before the break Australia rubbed salt into Britain's wound by snatching the lead. Andrews cross-kicked to the left wing. The kick seemed innocuous but instead of bouncing into touch the ball perversely stopped dead. Two defenders left it to each other and allowed Graves to pick up at his leisure, fend off Williams and score a soft try.

Two points adrift despite having the better of the play, Britain continued to hold the upper hand after the interval but to no effect. Nine minutes into the half Holland kicked an angled penalty goal - his first goal for eight years - and Australia led 7-3. After 62 minutes, however, Ashcroft brilliantly intercepted on the home "25" and claimed a try although grassed on the line by Churchill. The referee ruled a double movement. Bradshaw disagreed, said so and was sent off. Worse followed a couple of minutes later when Murphy and Street sent Williams over only for the referee to rule a forward pass. Ken Gee did a Bradshaw and reaped a similar reward. Four points down, having had three tries disallowed and two men dismissed, Britain soldiered on with a three-man pack but had to bow to the inevitable. In the 70th minute Churchill mesmerised three defenders in a run from half-way. Stanmore, Middleton and Graves made more ground and Cowie finished the business with a try at the corner, superbly converted by Churchill.

Four minutes from time Holman secured from a scrum, sent Flannery on a decoy run infield but kept the leather and bolted down the blind-side, sent Ledgard sprawling and scored at the flag to seal a momentous triumph for Australia.

TEST MATCH 48

AT SYDNEY CRICKET GROUND – 22 July, 1950
AUSTRALIA 5 GREAT BRITAIN 2 (HT 2-2)

CB Churchill (Souths) capt G	JA Ledgard (Leigh)
R Roberts (St. George) T	T Danby (Salford)
K Middleton (Norths)	E Ward (Bradford N) capt G
D McRitchie (St. George)	EJ Ashcroft (Wigan)
J Troy (Newtown)	J Hilton (Wigan)
FS Stanmore (Wests)	† J Cunliffe (Wigan)
KV Holman (Wests)	T Bradshaw (Wigan)
JF Holland (St. George)	K Gee (Wigan)
KB Schubert (Manly)	J Egan (Wigan)
D Hall (Valleys, Brisbane)	E Gwyther (Belle Vue R)
H Crocker (Souths, Brisbane)	DV Phillips (Belle Vue R)
† BM Purcell (Souths)	F Higgins (Widnes)
LG Cowie (Souths)	H Street (Dewsbury)

Referee - T McMahon (NSW)   Crowd - 47,178   Gate - £8,072
Scoring - 2-0 2-2 5-2

Conditions for this deciding test were marginally less dreadful than for the first test but only because the SCG had been covered by 40 tons of sand in an attempt to make the pitch more like a sporting arena than a gigantic sago pudding. Such was the public interest in the game that the gates were opened at 7 a.m. and the stands filled by 9 a.m. The crowd was rewarded with a contest as stirring and close as any in test history and at the conclusion Australia had at last won back the Ashes after an interval of 30 years.

None of the Australian three-quarters ever appeared in another test match nor did forwards Jack Holland, the best on the field, and Bernie Purcell. All went out of test football as happy men, however, as the green and golds ended the longest hoodoo test rugby had seen. For that stalwart British pair, Ken Gee and Joe Egan, as well as Doug Phillips it was also the end of the road as far as Ashes tests were concerned. They went out beaten but unbowed.

Ground conditions dictated that there would be precious few chances to play flowing football and two demonic defences ensured that no one would run too far too often. The first half was practically all Australia yet the teams turned round all-square having each kicked a penalty. Churchill had given Australia the lead when Britain had strayed off-side in the 28th minute at which point the Lions had hardly set foot in their opponents' half. Australia should have had a bigger advantage but Purcell had fluffed three shots at goal and only a courageous tackle by Ledgard had stopped Troy from scoring at the corner. Four minutes before half-time Britain managed a rare incursion into Australian territory through a fine burst by Ashcroft which ended in a penalty after McRitchie recklessly barged into Bradshaw causing the half-back to retire temporarily. Ward kicked the goal and Australia had no advantage to show for all their effort.

Purcell failed with two penalty kicks within the first couple of minutes after the restart and for a time it looked as if Australia would rue their mistakes as Britain, inspired by Bradshaw and Ward, began to get their second wind. Ward failed narrowly with a shot at goal and then was brought down just short of the line as the battle intensified. Australia weathered the storm and in the 65th minute scored one of the most crucial tries in test history. Oddly enough on such a vile day the try was the result of a perfect, orthodox three-quarter movement, remarkably simple in conception and faultlessly executed. From a play-the-ball 30 yards from the British line the ball was moved via Holman, Stanmore, McRitchie and Middleton along the line and a classic overlap situation developed. Hilton was faced with the age-old dilemma - two men to tackle and only one pair of arms. He elected to take the centre. Middleton, only nineteen, kept his head and sent the ball out to the lanky Ron Roberts, whose handling hitherto had been erratic. The mud-splattered ball was safely gathered in and Roberts raced with giant's strides to the corner flag and immortality. The crowd went collectively berserk and the Ashes went to Australia.

Everyone knew that in such a game there was unlikely to be a chance of another score. Ernest Ward urged his weary warriors to a last-ditch effort but nothing could force Churchill's heroes to yield their hard-won spoils.

ASHES TO AUSTRALIA

"LUMPS FORMED IN MY THROAT"

(By HARRY SUNDERLAND)

Harry Sunderland, most travelled of all Rugby Leaguites, Manager of many Kangaroo teams on world tours, broadcaster for the B.B.C. and A.B.C. on this tour, and a journalist who has been writing for the "Sunday Despatch" (England), Sydney "Sunday Sun" and Brisbane "Telegraph," is here with the Rugby League "Lions." Here is his story of a talk he gave to the B.B.C. on Australia's Test Victory.

IN the dusk of a recent Saturday on the Sydney Cricket Ground when broadcasting the third and deciding Test, I went all emotional! Lumps came into my throat. As an Australian I naturally wanted the Kangaroos to win. I had been one of the selectors when we last won the Ashes in 1920—and I had been four times to England and seen our teams beaten by the narrowest of margins. After all these years, triumph had come at last.

With the running commentary in company with ace sportscaster Bernie Kerr finished, I had to broadcast a Test Review to England for the B.B.C. What could I say—with six minutes twenty seconds allotted to me? Well, here is what I told England through the B.B.C.

"It has taken Australia over 28 years to win back the Rugby League Ashes Cup and I think no man was more thrilled at the end of to-day's game than Vic Hey, the man who coached the Australians in all three Tests, and who learned what he knows about British methods in the mud in the 10 years he spent in the services of Yorkshire Clubs, like Leeds, Dewsbury and Hunslet.

"There was more mud than I have ever seen on any Rugby ground anywhere, and that includes Salford in 1922 when Hilton and Gallagher scored England's winning tries. Now Australia, after being level with a penalty goal by Ward to Churchill's

at half-time, won by 5 to 2 after Ron Roberts had scored a magnificent second half try.

"First let me tell of these abnormal weather conditions that left the Sydney Cricket Ground like a bog, despite the covering of 40 tons of sand given to it this week.

"There has been rain every day in Sydney since the team returned from Queensland via Gunnedah, and although it cleared for a period on Friday, the downpour came again to-day.

"And this final deluge undid all the work the ground staff had performed this week. This time we could not broadcast our running commentaries from the exposed position on the touchline. So heavy was the rain that we had to seek the sheltering cover of the M. A. Noble pavilion. But the players had to wallow in the mud, with play frequently held up for Ambulance men to come onto the field with buckets of water so that players could wash the mud out of their eyes. Don't allow anyone to ever be cynical with me again about Manchester rain. I'll not argue with them.

"All this rain left the team manager, Tom Spedding, dubious about whether to play Tom Bradshaw or Albert Pepperill at half-back. The vote went to Bradshaw and the little man from Wigan nearly made a draw of the match in the second half when he ran round the blind side with

Danby on his right touchline and nearly shoved the dummy right down the neck of the Australian defence. It was a perfect dummy. Even Danby snatched at the imaginary ball. But Bradshaw hadn't the pace in the mud to get clear.

"Referee Tom McMahon handled the game with extreme calm and I don't think that there is another Australian man with the whistle who could have given the visitors so many penalties early in the game and not been chided by a crowd that went positively crazy when, in the 26th minute of the second half, McRitchie and Middleton proved superior to the British centres and sent right winger Ron Roberts sailing for his try in the corner.

"Every person in this crowd of 47,000 appeared to have torn up newspapers and programmes to hurl it into the air like confetti. Even then the Britishers fought back and had nearly a quarter of an hour to recovery their leeway.

"It is interesting to note that the Australian 13 included four forwards, Holland, Schubert, Hall—all in the front row—and Cowie, who had experience of English football in the last tour. But only two of the backs (McRitchie at centre and Churchill at full-back) had been through an English tour.

"Five backs (Roberts and Troy on the wings, the two half-backs, Holman and Stanmore) and Middleton, were hardly known at the start of the season. They are all very young and have ten years of football in front of them.

"I like this accent on youth. I must quote Shakespeare's—'Age is cold, youth is bold, youth I do adore thee, age I do abhor thee.'

"Two young forwards, Purcell and Crocker, were magnificent.

'Obviously there were too many men in the British team in this Test match struggle in the mud who were in their autumn.

"Look at this 13 who wore the red, white and blue: Gee, Egan, Gwyther, Phillips, Higgins, Street in the pack,

Bradshaw, Danby, Cunliffe, Ward, Ashcroft, Hilton and Ledgard in the backs. There were some smart young men there who could last the full 80 minutes but not enough of them.

"The sequence of the scoring is interesting. Purcell failed at three good attempts and then Churchill took a kick himself in the 26th minute and raised the flags.

"McRitchie tackled Ledgard into touch after he had kicked clear in the 37th minute and referee McMahon gave a full penalty — a free kick where the ball landed. Ward kicked the goal. That left them two all at half-time.

"The tourists had both the drizzling rain and the wind at their backs in the second half, but failed to use the low kicks past the defence that might have worried the Australians. They punted high and the Australians had time to get back to the ball.

"One glorious spell when Bradshaw fed a dummy pass towards his right winger and then threw an infield pass to Phillips nearly cut a hole in the defence. That was in the 8th minute after the interval, and a try at that stage might have won the game for England.

"But they were driven back and when the Australians kept passing the ball from the base of the rucks it was inevitable that the switch from the left to the right flank would find the hole that enabled the new man for Australia, Ron Roberts, playing in his first test, to go for the corner like Billy Batten used to. "The crowd rode him for the whole 40 yards he ran, and when he dived over about four yards inside the flag the confetti that was hurled in the air presented a sight like a snowstorm as it fell back amongst the spectators who had thrown it.

"The Ashes Cup will be left in Sydney, but the tour is not over yet. New Zealand has to be tackled, and as we expect the Kiwis in England in 1951 I look forward to the final games in Auckland with great eagerness."

TEST MATCH 49

AT HEADINGLEY, LEEDS – 4 October, 1952
GREAT BRITAIN 19 AUSTRALIA 6 (HT 12-2)

JD Evans (Hunslet)	CB Churchill (Souths) capt
† AH Daniels (Halifax) T	ND Pidding (St. George) 3G
† R Ryder (Warrington) T	NG Hazzard (Bundaberg)
E Ward (Bradford N)	† HJ Wells (Wollongong)
† F Castle (Barrow) T	† BP Carlson (Norths, Newcastle)
W Horne (Barrow) capt 5G	† GR Hawick (Souths)
† AE Toohey (Barrow)	KV Holman (Wests)
GA Prescott (St. Helens)	D Hall (Toowoomba)
† A Ackerley (Halifax)	KB Schubert (Manly)
JJ Featherstone (Warrington)	B Davies (Brothers, Brisbane)
R Ryan (Warrington)	FA Ashton (Easts)
† CH Pawsey (Leigh)	A Paul (Lakes, Newcastle)
K Traill (Bradford N)	H Crocker (Souths, Brisbane)

Referee - GS Phillips (Widnes) Crowd - 34,505 Gate - £8,628
Scoring - 0-2 2-2 7-2 12-2 12-4 17-4 17-6 19-6

Clive Churchill's 1952-53 Kangaroos left Australia billed as *the weakest team ever to represent Australia abroad* yet contrived to win 23 and draw one of their 27 matches in Britain scoring a record 816 points in the process. Unfortunately two of their three defeats were suffered in the tests and the Ashes, which they were defending in England for the first time for over 30 years, were disappointingly forfeited after the first two tests. By the time the first test dawned the Kangaroos were clear favourites for the Ashes and an unusually experimental British XIII had been comprehensively poo-poohed by the home press.

In the event Australia turned in a miserable performance, completely out of character from their virile displays in the club games, and Great Britain hardly had to break sweat as the Kangaroos dithered and frittered away their meagre possession by aimless and unproductive kicking.

After two minutes Australia established a footing inside the home "25" where Pawsey was caught off-side allowing Pidding to land an easy penalty goal. It was to be the only time Australia held the lead. There were fruitless kicks at goal for Ward (twice) and for Pidding during the first quarter when the most conspicuous feature of the play was the faulty handling of both sides. The best chance of a try fell to Britain when Ryder chased a kick and harried the defence so much that he regained possession only to see his pass to Pawsey, who otherwise had a splendid debut, go to ground. In the eighteenth minute Horne levelled the scores with a penalty goal and it became increasingly obvious that the Australian pack was distinctly off colour and presenting Britain with few problems.

Evans and Daniels went close for Britain before a ten point burst in the last eight minutes of the half effectively ended the Aussie challenge. First Hawick, having a bad game opposite Willie Horne, lost the ball which was gobbled up by Ryder. Horne and Ward carried the movement on before Castle was put in possession. The winger stepped smartly inside, beat two coverers in the process and then eluded another before arcing into the posts for a lovely try. Horne, relieving Ward of the kicking, added the goal. A few minutes later a scrum was formed around the Australian "25", Ackerley heeled and Toohey picked up. Australia were so preoccupied with watching the wily Willie Horne that they failed to notice Ryder careering between the two half-backs and he was under the posts before the defence could move. Horne smiled and kicked the conversion.

Just before the interval Churchill limped off injured but returned to take up a roving commission but was clearly not his usual self. Australian hopes rose momentarily when Pidding kicked a goal after 45 minutes but a superb solo try by Arthur Daniels killed off any lingering Australian ambitions and provided the high spot of the game. Churchill kicked to touch following a scrum but Daniels stopped the ball with his foot near the touch-line, picked up and weaved in and out of the defence before crossing at the corner for a try which brought the house down. Horne's conversion was magnificent and Britain were home and dry at 17-4. Penalties to Pidding and Horne were the only further scores although Australia were still striving for a try which was never going to materialise. Britain had displayed much the better combination and in Traill and Horne had individuals who dictated the play.

Headingley, 1952. Legends Clive Churchill and Willie Horne lead out their sides. Behind Churchill are Duncan Hall and Noel Hazzard. Horne is followed by Alan Prescott, Ted Toohey, Ron Ryder and Jim Featherstone.

TEST MATCH 50

AT STATION ROAD, SWINTON – 8 November, 1952
GREAT BRITAIN 21 AUSTRALIA 5 (HT 8-0)

JD Evans (Hunslet)	CB Churchill (Souths) capt
AH Daniels (Halifax)	DJ Flannery (Ipswich)
D Greenall (St. Helens) 2T	NG Hazzard (Bundaberg)
E Ward (Bradford N) T,2G	CS Geelan (Newtown) T
F Castle (Barrow) 2T	BP Carlson (Norths, Newcastle) G
W Horne (Barrow) capt G	FS Stanmore (Wests)
AE Toohey (Barrow)	CM Donohoe (Easts)
GA Prescott (St. Helens)	D Hall (Toowoomba)
T McKinney (Salford)	KB Schubert (Manly)
JJ Featherstone (Warrington)	CM Gill (Norths, Newcastle)
CH Pawsey (Leigh)	B Davies (Brothers, Brisbane)
DD Valentine (Huddersfield)	TW Tyrell (Balmain)
K Traill (Bradford N)	† AL Collinson (Wests)

Referee - JW Jackson (Barrow)   Crowd - 32,421   Gate - £6,776
Scoring - 3-0 6-0 8-0 8-2 10-2 13-2 16-2 16-5 21-5

A beautiful, crisp autumnal day should have presaged a classic encounter in this 50th Anglo-Australian test match. Perversely the game turned out to be one of the more forgettable jousts the series has produced. Australia, with the springboard of eight successive victories since the first test, simply failed to compete and having conceded the lead after quarter of an hour never seriously threatened the home line until Geelan scored their solitary try close to full time.

Despite the fine weather which blessed the match the pitch was in an appalling state thanks to heavy rain in the preceding days and this may have inhibited the Kangaroos to some extent. In all fairness, however, Australia seemed to rely on sheer brute strength and appeared to have no tactical plan. Moreover, they were handicapped by Schubert, playing the last of his nineteen tests, failing to match McKinney in securing scrum possession, Britain winning the heels 32-17.

The major feature of the match, however, was the virtuoso performance of Ernest Ward, the 32 year-old Great Britain centre. Ward was magnificent, rapier-like in attack, sure in defence, master of every situation, a veritable god on the day. At the final whistle, the Ashes having been regained, the British players spontaneously chaired Ward in triumph from the field along with Willie Horne, the skipper.

The game began badly for the Kangaroos when Churchill miscued a simple penalty in the first minute, the first of four relatively easy shots he would miss in the opening 40 minutes. One reporter noted, *it was almost possible to feel the depressing effect it had on the team.* Britain responded with a flurry of assaults but were unable to breach the line although Toohey came desperately near before being hurled into touch five yards short. Eventually the pressure told and after fifteen minutes Evans, Prescott and Valentine worked the ball deep into the opposition half. Featherstone moved the ball onto Ward who flipped the ball deliciously to the onrushing Greenall. Greenall and his winger, Daniels, exchanged passes and Greenall plunged over at the corner taking Churchill and the flag with him for a disputed try.

A brief Australian rally ensued and Flannery was kept out only by a fine tackle by Evans but Britain struck again after 26 minutes. Ward was the mainspring, for after feinting to drive up the middle, he spotted a weakness on the Australian right flank and was through in a twinkling. He served Castle and the winger nonplussed Churchill with a debilitating side-step to put the home team six points ahead. Ward stretched the lead to eight points before the interval with a long-range penalty goal.

Eight minutes into the second half Australia pulled back to 8-2 when Carlson kicked a penalty but this was quickly cancelled out when Horne dropped a masterpiece of a goal and Australia were counted out when Ward made a monkey out of Tyrell to score a delightful try. The crowd rose as one to this effort and was soon applauding again as the maestro combined with Horne to get Castle over. Geelan's try followed to reduce the deficit to 16-5 but Ward fittingly had the last word when with the final act of the game he converted Greenall's second try.

TEST MATCH 51

AT ODSAL STADIUM, BRADFORD – 13 December, 1952
GREAT BRITAIN 7 AUSTRALIA 27 (HT 7-9)

JD Evans (Hunslet) 2G	CB Churchill (Souths) capt
† DR Bevan (Wigan)	ND Pidding (St. George) T,6G
D Greenall (St. Helens)	NG Hazzard (Bundaberg)
E Ward (Bradford N)	CS Geelan (Newtown)
F Castle (Barrow)	† TA Ryan (St. George) 2T
W Horne (Barrow) capt T	FS Stanmore (Wests)
AE Toohey (Barrow)	KV Holman (Wests) T
GA Prescott (St. Helens)	ER Bull (Manly)
T McKinney (Salford)	† KH Kearney (St. George)
JJ Featherstone (Warrington)	D Hall (Toowoomba)
CH Pawsey (Leigh)	B Davies (Brothers, Brisbane) T
DD Valentine (Huddersfield)	FA Ashton (Easts)
K Traill (Bradford N)	AL Collinson (Wests)

Referee - AS Dobson (Pontefract)   Crowd - 30,509   Gate - £5,478

Scoring - 0-2 0-4 0-9 2-9 7-9 7-14 7-19 7-24 7-27

Writing in *The Rugby League Review,* Vincent Firth had this to say of the third test of 1952:
What might and certainly ought to have been a grand game of Rugby quickly degenerated into an ugly and unseemly brawl which very nearly ended in a blood-bath.

The post-match reports were full of expressions such as *disgraceful, disgusting, shameful* and *nauseating.* Many of the match reports appeared more like dispatches from war correspondents than accounts of a sporting encounter. Certainly this Odsal horror was the most ill-tempered and violent clash between Australia and Britain since the infamous "Battle of Brisbane" twenty years earlier. The game was punctuated by mass punch-ups, individual assaults and all manner of clandestine skullduggery and the real wonder for those present was that only one man, Australian prop Duncan Hall, was dismissed. Hall was sent off after 52 minutes following an incident in which Ernest Ward was injured over his own line. Hall thus became the first Aussie to be marched in a test in England although he was by no means the worst offender. By the time Noel Pidding had kicked Australia into a 4-0 lead in the first quarter tempers were already fraying as the tackling reached a frightening intensity and stern action early on may have averted the open warfare which broke out in the second half. Britain had lost winger Castle with a shoulder injury causing Valentine to play on the wing for an hour thus depleting the British pack for most of the "game".

Australia, in between the fistcuffs, played some fine football and must have wished they had produced some of it in the first two tests. Holman and Stanmore formed a sublime half-back partnership. Had the game been played under more harmonious circumstances they would have been lauded to the heavens but amid the mayhem their brilliance was sadly of secondary interest. It was following a sumptuous piece of running by Stanmore that the position was set up for Geelan to send in Pidding after 24 minutes. Pidding converted for a 9-0 lead. Evans, the best British back, pulled back two points with a penalty before converting a try by Horne a minute before half-time as the home team rallied well.

Five minutes after the break Hazzard cut through after a fine passing bout and was half-stopped by Evans but found Davies backing up inside to touch down at the posts for Pidding to convert. Down 14-7, Britain stormed back only to see Pawsey somehow lose the ball a yard from the line when under no pressure. At that juncture the brawling started in earnest and Holman's dash for a try from a ruck and two more fine tries from debutant winger Tom Ryan were greeted by an eerie silence where normally they would have been cheered to the echo.

Amidst the welter of press condemnation and public outrage it was easy to overlook the performance of Noel Pidding, the "Bradman of Australian Rugby League", in beating the record number of points for a player in Anglo-Australian tests. His tally of fifteen was one more than the feat of Dave Brown in 1936, whilst his six goals were also a new record. The excesses also overshadowed the fact that the game marked the end of Ernest Ward's career as a test player. One of Britain's finest and fairest players, Ward could hardly have envisaged bowing out in such an unsavoury encounter.

TEST MATCH 52

AT SYDNEY CRICKET GROUND – 12 June, 1954
AUSTRALIA 37 GREAT BRITAIN 12 (HT 10-5)

CB Churchill (Souths) capt	J Cunliffe (Wigan)
ND Pidding (Maitland) T,8G	† BL Jones (Leeds) 3G
K McCaffery (Toowoomba) 2T	EJ Ashcroft (Wigan) capt
† A Watson (Wests, Brisbane)	† PB Jackson (Barrow) T
BP Carlson (Wollongong) T	F Castle (Barrow)
RB Banks (Toowoomba)	† HR Price (Warrington)
KV Holman (Wests)	GJ Helme (Warrington)
ER Bull (Manly)	GA Prescott (St. Helens)
KH Kearney (St. George)	T McKinney (Salford)
D Hall (Valleys, Brisbane) T	† J Wilkinson (Halifax)
† ND Provan (St. George) T	DD Valentine (Huddersfield)
† KJ O'Shea (Colts, Ayr) T	† ND Silcock (Wigan) T
H Crocker (Parramatta)	K Traill (Bradford N)

Referee - D Lawler (NSW)   Crowd - 65,884   Gate - £16,842/6/-
Scoring - 3-0 3-5 8-5 10-5 10-10 12-10 12-12 17-12 22-12 27-12 32-12 37-12

Twenty-five minutes from time the scores in this spendidly contested test had been locked at 12-12 and the Lions, winners of only two of their previous six tour matches, had confounded the Jeremiahs who had written them off as a lost cause. During those last 25 minutes, however, Australia ripped in for 25 points to register the highest score yet in Ashes conflict. Noel Pidding set new records by kicking eight goals and scoring nineteen points, eclipsing his own marks set in 1952. Pidding also shattered the Australian record aggregate for points against Britain previously held by the celebrated Dave Brown (35 points) in lifting his tally to 44.

Australia won the game in the forwards amongst whom none shone brighter than the debutant second-row pair of Norm Provan and Kel O'Shea. By the final quarter the whole of the British back three were crocked and just before time winger Frank Castle was stretchered off with a gashed knee after tackling Keith Holman. Although these injuries undoubtedly gave the score a distortedly lopsided look, Australia had always seemed likely victors.

The home team hit the front after only eight minutes. Hall broke the Lions' defence near half-way before being grounded on the "25". From the play-the-ball Kearney shot a long pass to Holman and there was Hall again backing up like a half-back to send Provan the last five yards to the line. Pidding astounded everyone by missing the simplest of conversions. Another tremendous effort by Provan was stopped on the line and Australia mounted incessant pressure until the 25th minute when Britain retaliated with a glorious try. Traill ran wide from a ruck on his own "25" and worked a reverse pass to Valentine who quickly made ground up the middle, drew Churchill and despatched Nat Silcock on a 40 yard run to the posts. Jones converted and Britain led 5-3 but only for three minutes as Holman dashed blind-side of a ruck and passed inside to Bull. The big prop broke a tackle and served O'Shea who forced his way over near the sticks for Pidding to goal. Six minutes before the interval Pidding stretched his side's lead to 10-5 with a fine angled penalty.

Within four minutes of the resumption Britain were level. A scrum heel saw Helme and Price whip the ball to Jackson who took advantage of McCaffery's faulty positioning and easily beat Churchill to score at the posts. Jones added the goal but within two minutes Australia were ahead again thanks to a prodigious 50 yard penalty goal into the wind by Pidding. A minute later the scores were level as Jones landed a goal from the touch-line almost on half-way.

The flood-gates opened after 55 minutes when Hall proved unstoppable in a mighty surge to the corner flag. A super goal from Pidding seemed to deflate the Lions and within minutes the Aussies held a ten points advantage as beautiful passing between the halves and three-quarters enabled Pidding to touch down. Two rapid tries by McCaffery put the game beyond recall for the Lions and a final try was scored just before the end when Crocker and Churchill unleashed Carlson who gathered his own kick to cross at the flag. Pidding landed his eighth goal and Australia had one hand on the Ashes Cup.

AUSTRALIAN RUGBY LEAGUE TEAM — Second Test v. England — Brisbane, 3rd July, 1954

Front Row: N. D. PIDDING, C. B. CHURCHILL (Capt.), VIC. HEY (Coach), K. V. HOLMAN, R. W. SULLIVAN
2nd Row: K. KEARNEY, H. CROCKER, R. BULL, N. PROVAN, K. O'SHEA, D. HALL
Back Row: C. CONNELL, N. HAZZARD, B. DAVIES, B. CARLSON, A. J. WATSON

The 1954 Lions in high spirits as
they leave London for Australia

TEST MATCH 53

AT BRISBANE CRICKET GROUND – 3 July, 1954
AUSTRALIA 21 GREAT BRITAIN 38 (HT 10-19)

CB Churchill (Souths) capt	BL Jones (Leeds) 10G
ND Pidding (Maitland) 3G	† WJ Boston (Wigan) 2T
NG Hazzard (Roma)	PB Jackson (Barrow) T
A Watson (Wests, Brisbane)	EJ Ashcroft (Wigan)
BP Carlson (Wollongong) 2T	† TP O'Grady (Oldham)
† R Sullivan (Norths)	RL Williams (Hunslet) capt T
KV Holman (Wests) T	GJ Helme (Warrington) T
ER Bull (Manly)	GA Prescott (St. Helens)
KH Kearney (St. George)	T McKinney (Salford)
D Hall (Wests, Brisbane) T	† J Bowden (Huddersfield)
ND Provan (St. George) T	CH Pawsey (Leigh) T
KJ O'Shea (Colts, Ayr)	ND Silcock (Wigan)
H Crocker (Parramatta)	DD Valentine (Huddersfield)

Referee - D Lawler (NSW)   Crowd - 46,355   Gate - £13,190

Scoring - 0-2 5-2 5-7 5-12 10-12 10-14 10-19 13-19 13-24 13-26 13-31 13-33 13-38 16-38 21-38

In a staggering reversal of form and fortune from the first test all the records established at Sydney were obliterated only three weeks later as the Lions ran riot on a treacherous surface. Great Britain hit a new high with their 38 points whilst the aggregate of 59 points had never been exceeded. On a personal level Lewis Jones eclipsed Noel Pidding's short-lived record by kicking ten goals and scoring twenty points. By a remarkable coincidence Jones set his record on the same ground as he had set a record of seventeen points as a Union Lion four years previously. The crowd and takings had also never been beaten in Queensland.

Whilst it was soon clear that Britain appeared the livelier side Australia managed to stay in the game for 50 minutes after which their cause became increasingly hopeless. Britain had gone into an early lead when Jones popped over an easy penalty but Australia had replied with a lovely try after twelve minutes when O'Shea had broken up a British thrust on the home "25". Dashing down the wing he served Carlson who rushed inside O'Grady and short-kicked ahead. Boston covered but slipped and Carlson scored a fine try near enough the posts to give Pidding an easy goal. It was to be the only time Britain trailed.

Eight minutes elapsed before the Lions took control as O'Grady made a long run down the flank before sending inside to Pawsey who romped over at the corner for Jones to kick a magnificent conversion. In the 27th minute Billy Boston, beginning his illustrious test career, scored a classic try running from half-way after Valentine and Jackson had shredded the defence. Jones added the goal. Australia took only three minutes to reply as Sullivan began a movement in which Pidding did well to elude two opponents before sending Provan in. Pidding's goal reduced Britain's lead to two points but by half-time they had stretched it to nine. First Jones landed a simple penalty and then Ashcroft made the running for skipper Dickie Williams to cross. Jones made light of the conversion to land his fifth goal.

Australian hopes rose briefly soon after the break when Ashcroft failed to collect a kick-through by Watson and Hall was quick to profit with a try which took Australia to within six points. The Lions scored the next nineteen points, however, and as a contest the game was over. A superbly worked try from a scrum on the home "25" following a hypnotic dummy-scissors between Williams and Ashcroft saw Jackson send Boston over. Jones landed a touch-line conversion and soon afterwards, whilst running across the face of the Australian defence, suddenly hooked over a wonderful 30 yard drop goal.

Ashcroft then took Churchill's tackle to present Jackson with a try. Jones converted to equal Pidding's record of eight goals and then coolly broke the record with a drop-goal from 35 yards. His tenth goal followed a try by Helme who ran over unopposed from a scrum. Twenty-five points clear, Britain eased off and during the last six minutes allowed Australia to run in tries through Holman and Carlson, the latter improved by Pidding.

From being something of a laughing stock following the humiliation of the first test Great Britain had suddenly become favourites for the Ashes.

TEST MATCH 54

AT SYDNEY CRICKET GROUND – 17 July, 1954
AUSTRALIA 20 GREAT BRITAIN 16 (HT 10-8)

CB Churchill (Souths) capt
BP Carlson (Wollongong)
HJ Wells (Wollongong) T
A Watson (Wests, Brisbane) T
ND Pidding (Maitland) T,4G
RB Banks (Toowoomba)
KV Holman (Wests)
B Davies (Brothers, Brisbane)
KH Kearney (St. George)
D Hall (Wests, Brisbane)
ND Provan (St. George)
KJ O'Shea (Colts, Ayr)
† P Diversi (Norths) T

BL Jones (Leeds) 2G
WJ Boston (Wigan)
PB Jackson (Barrow)
EJ Ashcroft (Wigan) T
TP O'Grady (Oldham)
RL Williams (Hunslet) capt 2T
GJ Helme (Warrington)
GA Prescott (St. Helens)
T McKinney (Salford)
J Bowden (Huddersfield)
CH Pawsey (Leigh)
ND Silcock (Wigan)
DD Valentine (Huddersfield) T

Referee - D Lawler (NSW)   Crowd - 67,577   Gate - £17,217

Scoring - 0-3 0-8 5-8 10-8 15-8 15-11 20-11 20-16

Australia regained the Ashes surrendered two years earlier in a thrill-laden, fluctuating encounter played in the most sporting of spirits. Both sides scored four tries and although Australia deserved the spoils victory could easily have gone to the Lions.

For the first half-hour Great Britain were absolute masters, established an eight points lead and were unlucky not to have gained a more substantial advantage. Yet by half-time Australia had nosed in front and never again fell behind.

On a heavy, slippery pitch Britain pressed from the kick-off. Twice Boston could have scored but knocked on after superb work by Helme before O'Grady pulled off a miraculous tackle on Harry Wells a yard from the British line. Britain swept to the other end and a marvellous run by Boston was terminated by an equally marvellous tackle by Churchill. After thirteen minutes the British barrage yielded the first try. Churchill kicked to clear his line but instead of finding touch the ball was gathered by O'Grady 40 yards out. The young winger immediately dashed up the touch-line, disposed of Carlson's challenge and, finding his way blocked by Churchill and Holman, tossed the leather back inside to Ashcroft who sped the last twenty yards to touch down wide out. Five minutes later Churchill and Jones were engaged in a kicking duel when Wells intervened. His kick was badly directed and Williams gathered near half-way, grubber-kicked past a posse of Australian forwards and gave chase. Churchill hesitated in going for the ball and Williams took full advantage to secure and race over from the "25". Jones goaled splendidly and at 8-0 the Lions seemed unstoppable.

Boston slipped fifteen yards out with the line beckoning and after 22 minutes Ashcroft made a glorious run before kicking ahead on Australia's "25". O'Grady looked all over a scorer as he pursued the ball but O'Shea crashed him to the ground before he could finish the business. A penalty was awarded but not the obstruction try that many thought the incident warranted.

Following this narrow escape Australia began to wake up and in the six minutes before half-time turned the game on its head. There appeared to be no danger as a scrum formed on Australia's "25" and the halves worked the ball away. Churchill joined the line and served Wells who embarked on a damaging run to half-way before parting to Watson who proceeded to burst through Jones' tackle before cutting inside Boston to race 50 yards for a sensational try. Pidding converted as he did a couple of minutes later when Diversi struggled over from a ruck close to the line.

The crucial score was recorded five minutes into the second half when Wells, the dominating figure of the game, burst through a tackle by Jones and clattered into Prescott. Arguments raged as to whether the big centre was held before he slithered over the line but the try was allowed and duly converted. Still Britain were not done and after 65 minutes Williams and Silcock contrived to send Valentine scything through to reduce the deficit to four points. Five minutes later Holman shot down the short side 40 yards out and fed Wells who drew Jones and Boston before sending Pidding racing over and round behind the posts for a try converted by the scorer. Seven minutes before time Helme made a try of true artistry, breaking from a mid-field scrum, dummying outrageously several times before Williams took over to score under the bar. Jones converted but amidst pulsating excitement Australia held out to win the Ashes for only the fourth time.

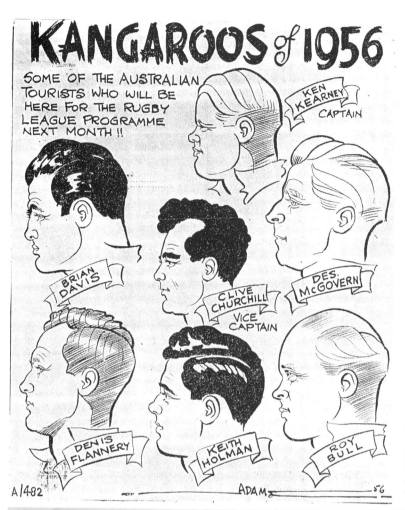

Top: Seven Kangaroos of 1956 as seen by cartoonist Ken Adams. Adams has spelled Davies incorrectly!
Bottom: Wigan, first test, 1956. Kangaroo winger 'Bandy' Adams prepares to tackle the great Billy Boston.

TEST MATCH 55

AT CENTRAL PARK, WIGAN – 17 November, 1956
GREAT BRITAIN 21 AUSTRALIA 10 (HT 9-5)

† F Mortimer (Wakefield T) 3G	CB Churchill (Souths)
WJ Boston (Wigan) 2T	IJ Moir (Souths) T
PB Jackson (Barrow)	RH Poole (Newtown) T
A Davies (Oldham) T	A Watson (Wests, Brisbane)
M Sullivan (Huddersfield) T	DP Adams (Maitland)
HR Price (Warrington)	RB Banks (Cunnamulla)
JM Stevenson (Leeds)	KV Holman (Wests) 2G
GA Prescott (St. Helens) capt	B Davies (Brothers, Brisbane)
PT Harris (Hull)	KH Kearney (St. George) capt
† B Shaw (Hunslet)	ER Bull (Manly)
JJ Grundy (Barrow) T	TJ Tyquin (Souths, Brisbane)
D Robinson (Leeds)	† WL Marsh (Cootamundra)
† EW Dawson (York)	KJ O'Shea (Wests)

Referee - NT Railton (Wigan)   Crowd - 22,473   Gate - £4,837

Scoring - 0-3 3-3 3-5 6-5 9-5 14-5 16-5 21-5 21-10

On a miserable wet November afternoon the Australians failed to brighten a cheerless Central Park. Kearney's Kangaroos scored first and last but in between they hardly competed as Britain handled a greasy ball with almost uncanny dexterity. Despite winning the scrums 18-9 and having an 11-8 advantage in penalties Australia played a very uncharacteristically inept game, failing to cover, wasting possession and making wallflowers out of their talented backs. It was a soul destroying finale for Clive Churchill, Australia's champion full-back, who was playing his thirteenth test against the old enemy. The only real success for the tourists was scrum-half Keith Holman who fought manfully to stem the British tide. Great Britain should have been out of sight by half-time but for some appalling goal-kicking by Frank Mortimer who failed with five attempts.

Australia began superbly. At the first scrum in the seventh minute Holman and Banks combined smoothly before centres Poole and Watson drew the defence to put Moir over in the corner for an unimproved try. It was the only pass Moir received whilst Adams on the other wing had to wait until the 73rd minute for his first pass! In the twelfth minute Britain levelled. Robinson and Grundy led a forward break which fragmented the Australian defence. Boston and Stevenson carried on the move and Alan Davies trotted the last ten yards to the posts unmolested only to see Mortimer make a horrendous mess of the easy conversion. Nine minutes later Australia went in front for the last time when Holman landed a simple penalty.

Britain now began to dictate affairs, scoring tries in the 29th and 35th minutes. First Stevenson, a live-wire scrum-half, slung out a long pass to Sullivan who, finding himself baulked on the wing, short-kicked ahead and was clearly obstructed in trying to touch down but as Jack Grundy got the decisive touch a try was scored anyway. More British pressure saw Alan Davies burst through to serve his co-centre Phil Jackson who quickly got the ball to Boston. Tyquin almost stopped the winger but was slipped. Boston stumbled but still had time to scramble over for the try. Just before half-time Australia mounted a rare raid ending in Holman being grassed five yards out but the break arrived with the Kangaroos somewhat lucky to be only four points down.

It was Boston who provided the high spot of the afternoon in the 49th minute and effectively ended the Aussie challenge. At a play-the-ball just inside the visitors' "25" Boston took a ball from Prescott, veered in-field and threaded his way through the Australian cover to score under the posts. Mortimer at last kicked the goal. Of course, Australia should have stopped Boston but it would not be the last time the Wigan Wonder would torture Australia with impossible tries. Nine minutes later Mortimer kicked a fine penalty before Britain added a final try through Sullivan capitalising on fine work by Harris. Mortimer's conversion made the score 21-5 before Australia had the last, meaningless, word with a try at the corner from Poole and a glorious conversion from Holman.

TEST MATCH 56

AT ODSAL STADIUM, BRADFORD – 1 December, 1956
GREAT BRITAIN 9 AUSTRALIA 22 (HT 7-7)

F Mortimer (Wakefield T) 3G	GL Clifford (Newtown) 5G
WJ Boston (Wigan)	DJ Flannery (Ipswich)
PB Jackson (Barrow)	A Watson (Wests, Brisbane)
A Davies (Oldham)	RH Poole (Newtown)
M Sullivan (Huddersfield)	DJ McGovern (Toowoomba)
HR Price (Warrington)	RB Banks (Cunnamulla) T
JM Stevenson (Leeds) T	KV Holman (Wests) T
GA Prescott (St. Helens) capt	ER Bull (Manly) T
PT Harris (Hull)	KH Kearney (St. George) capt
B Shaw (Hunslet)	B Davies (Brothers, Brisbane) T
D Robinson (Leeds)	† DA Furner (Toowoomba)
JJ Grundy (Barrow)	KJ O'Shea (Wests)
† D Turner (Oldham)	IRP Doyle (Toowoomba)

Referee - M Coates (Pudsey)   Crowd - 23,634   Gate - £4,172
Scoring - 0-2 2-2 2-7 4-7 7-7 9-7 9-9 9-14 9-19 9-22

Australia, written off as no-hopers and showing five alterations from the first test, confounded the critics by at first holding the British and ultimately crushing them. Conditions underfoot were no less treacherous than at Wigan, for Odsal's infamous mud was ankle-deep despite the day being dry and fair but the Kangaroos adapted much better to the heavy ground this time.

Even though the Australians won handsomely enough in the end, Britain had the better of the first half but were profligate with the opportunities which came their way. All the time that Britain were throwing away golden chances Australia grew in confidence and took greedily the chances which fell to them.

In the first minute Stevenson was penalised for feeding his own forwards and Gordon Clifford, near faultless at full-back, kicked Australia into a 2-0 lead which was wiped out ten minutes later when Mortimer struck a penalty home after Bull went off-side. There followed a period of intense but fruitless British pressure. Grundy went over following a scrum but was adjudged to have knocked on and only excellent covering kept out Robinson and Sullivan whilst Stevenson and Davies were held inches short. McGovern relieved the pressure with a splendid run in which he eluded four men but back stormed the British again and again only to be foiled by desperate defence.

In the 27th minute Britain seemed to have things well under control as they moved the ball out of their own "25" only for disaster to overtake them when Harris passed straight to Holman who needed no second invitation to scoot to the line, neatly side-stepping Mortimer en route. Clifford converted. Britain came back strongly and Sullivan lost the ball in crossing the Australian line before Mortimer landed his second goal after 35 minutes. A minute before half-time a scrum formed twelve yards from Australia's line, Holman secured and passed to the blind-side but the ball was not taken allowing Stevenson, opportunist as always, to toe on and score unchallenged.

When after 47 minutes Mortimer put Britain ahead for the first time with his third penalty, it seemed that the Ashes were slipping from Australia's grip, especially when McGovern knocked on three yards out with no one to beat. Turner and Harris were ordered from the field but only to change into clean jerseys, having become unrecognisable. Unfortunately for Harris in the 58th minute his nice white arm was distinctly seen loose in a scrum and Clifford levelled the scores at 9-9.

Four minutes later the vital score occurred. Holman threw the ball to Bobby Banks' feet which the off-half miraculously scooped out of the mud, short-kicked, gathered and finally side-stepped three bewildered defenders within the space of fifteen yards before touching down under the posts for an absolute gem of a try. Clifford's conversion was a formality as was his next only three minutes later following Brian Davies' bullocking try which put the game out of Britain's reach. A similar try to Roy Bull in the last minute was suitable reward for a tremendous display of grafting by the prop-forward. Australia's pack, so feeble in the first test, rose magnificently to their challenge in this gruelling encounter in the mud and were ably abetted by a cracking pair of half-backs, whilst the three-quarters stifled the home backs to distraction.

TEST MATCH 57

AT STATION ROAD, SWINTON – 15 December, 1956
GREAT BRITAIN 19 AUSTRALIA 0 (HT 8-0)

GA Moses (St. Helens)	GL Clifford (Newtown)
WJ Boston (Wigan) T	DJ Flannery (Ipswich)
PB Jackson (Barrow)	RH Poole (Newtown)
A Davies (Oldham) 2G	A Watson (Wests, Brisbane)
M Sullivan (Huddersfield) T	DJ McGovern (Toowoomba)
HR Price (Warrington)	RB Banks (Cunnamulla)
JM Stevenson (Leeds)	KV Holman (Wests)
GA Prescott (St. Helens) capt	ER Bull (Manly)
PT Harris (Hull)	KH Kearney (St. George) capt
†SD Little (Oldham) T	†BJ Orrock (St. George)
G Gunney (Hunslet) T	TJ Tyquin (Souths, Brisbane)
JJ Grundy (Barrow)	KJ O'Shea (Wests)
D Turner (Oldham) T	IRP Doyle (Toowoomba)

Referee - R Gelder (Wakefield)   Crowd - 17,542   Gate - £4,224
Scoring - 5-0 8-0 13-0 16-0 19-0

With the series locked at one victory each the scene was set for a classic Ashes decider but what transpired was a total let-down. There was none of the fury or passion traditionally associated with an Anglo-Australian clash, no really scintillating passages of play and no towering displays by individuals. Worst of all, there was virtually no contest. The Australians, who should have been cockahoop after their success at Odsal, were unaccountably feeble even allowing for the absence of key forwards Davies and Provan. Faced with such indifferent opposition Britain never needed to extend themselves. Even so the nineteen points margin represented the largest yet recorded by Britain on home soil and equalled their largest ever triumph over Australia of 22-3 back in the first test at Sydney in 1924.

Unfortunately the afternoon was again miserable and mud was once more the order of the day - conditions hardly to be unexpected in mid-December and an indictment of the tour arrangements.

Australia began well enough but flattered to deceive. Des McGovern was almost in at the corner but a shattering tackle by Moses saved a certain score and in the process dislocated the winger's shoulder. McGovern gamely played 77 minutes with the injury. Off-setting this, Phil Jackson spent most of the match on Britain's wing after suffering concussion, Sullivan taking his place at centre. Clifford missed two penalties for the Kangaroos and Gunney one for Britain before the opening try came to the home team in the 24th minute, Tommy Harris providing the pass for prop debutant Syd Little to run through a diffident bunch of defenders. Davies converted. After this first score Australia seemed to resign themselves to defeat even though Britain were far from rampant and only added one further try during the first half when Moses, excelling at full-back, ran beautifully to set up Turner whose strength took him over.

Five minutes after half-time any hopes the Kangaroos may have nurtured of a rally were shattered when Geoff Gunney flung himself over for a try under the bar. Davies' conversion gave Britain a lead of 13-0 and the Ashes were as good as recovered. With such a commanding lead Britain began to move the ball more freely. Grundy went 30 yards as a move three-quarters the length of the field ended in Prescott just being grassed in time by Flannery and then Prescott was a leading figure in a marvellous passing movement to allow Sullivan to make the fourth touch-down. Boston hammered the final nail in Australia's coffin, roaring over after snapping up a loose ball 30 yards out.

Writing in *The Sunday Pictorial,* Eddie Waring summed up the game succinctly:
There was nothing awe-inspiring about Britain's win. It was too easy. But where were the crowd's cheers? It was a win without a wallop.

Six months later Australia were crowned World Cup winners counting among their crushed victims a Great Britain side containing ten of the Ashes-winning XIII, the score-line of 31-6 making a nonsense of their efforts in the series of 1956.

The 1958 Lions:
Back: Huddart, Terry, Carlton, P. Jackson, Karalius, Fraser, Davies, K. Jackson, Sullivan, Challinor.
Middle: Ackerley, Moses, Murphy, Mitchell, McTigue.
Front: Martyn, Pitchford, Prescott, Bolton, Ashton, Manson.

AUSTRALIA'S FIRST TEST WIN AT SYDNEY WAS A TRIUMPH OF
PLANNING AND BLUFF.

A SMASHING TEST VICTORY . . . WITH 11½ PLAYERS

A cartoonist's view of the first and second tests of 1958.

TEST MATCH 58

AT SYDNEY CRICKET GROUND – 14 June, 1958
AUSTRALIA 25 GREAT BRITAIN 8 (HT 18-0)

GL Clifford (Newtown) 5G	† EG Fraser (Warrington)
R Kite (Wagga) T	† I Southward (Workington T) T,G
HJ Wells (Wests)	PB Jackson (Barrow)
BP Carlson (Norths) T	A Davies (Oldham)
IJ Moir (Souths)	M Sullivan (Wigan)
† AJ Brown (Newtown)	DR Bolton (Wigan) T
KV Holman (Wests)	† AJ Murphy (St. Helens)
B Davies (Brothers, Brisbane) capt	GA Prescott (St. Helens) capt
KH Kearney (St. George)	PT Harris (Hull)
WL Marsh (Balmain)	† A Terry (St. Helens)
† RP Mossop (Manly) T	† M Martyn (Leigh)
ND Provan (St. George) T	† JB Edgar (Workington T)
KJ O'Shea (Wests) T	JW Whiteley (Hull)

Referee - D Lawler (NSW)   Crowd - 68,777   Gate - £29,548

Scoring - 5-0 10-0 13-0 18-0 20-0 20-3 20-8 25-8

Hot favourites before the match, Great Britain were heavily dumped by an unfancied Australian team superbly marshalled by captain-prop Brian Davies, the only Queenslander in the side. Davies, the game's outstanding performer, led a pack which completely outplayed the British six. The front row of Davies, Kearney and Marsh ruled the ruck area and the back three of Provan, Mossop and O'Shea repeatedly punctured the British defence. Each scored a try to severely embarrass the British back-row. The Australian backs were no less superior to their counterparts. Holman gave a lesson in scrum-half play to Alex Murphy, a nineteen-year-old debutant, who, however, would have much to say for humself, literally and metaphorically, in subsequent clashes.

Although the match was by no means vicious, referee Darcy Lawler was at pains to stop the lid from blowing off, issuing cautions to Holman twice, Kite, Clifford, Sullivan and Murphy. Quite the worst offence was Clifford's laying out of spring-heeled stand-off David Bolton as he raced through with "try" etched all over his face. Bolton was stretchered off but returned to score Britain's best try with a 40 yard run to the posts after smart play by Harris.

Britain were never really in the game. Barely five minutes had elapsed before full-back Fraser, declared fit only two hours prior to kick-off, blundered badly in failing to secure a play-the-ball on his own line. O'Shea simply dived onto the loose ball as if Christmas had arrived six months early. Clifford kicked the easiest of conversions. Australia piled on the pressure and in the eleventh minute Rex Mossop, an ex-Wallaby, was banging the ball down for the second try. Clifford's conversion made it 10-0. Worse was to follow for after quarter of an hour Carlson careered over at the corner without a hand being laid on him. By half-time Australia had stretched their lead to eighteen points, Provan having engineered a try for Ross Kite who crossed at the flag. Clifford's conversion was a beauty.

Not long into the second session Australia were twenty points clear when Clifford slotted over a penalty from 25 yards following a foul on Kearney. The Lions belatedly began to play some football but their first score was disputed. Jackson broke through and kicked toward the Australian line where Southward plunged for the touch-down. The try was allowed much to the displeasure of the onlookers who claimed the winger did not ground the ball. Bolton's try followed in the 65th minute and with a conversion from Southward Britain had pulled back to 20-8.

Provan was knocked out in a heavy tackle but the Australian forwards reasserted their authority and it was Provan who had the last laugh after crashing over from a ruck close to the Lions' line. Clifford's conversion completed the scoring. The score-line was, if anything, flattering to Great Britain whose approach had been altogether too casual.

Brisbane, second test, 1958. Dave Bolton (on ground) fractures his collar-bone as he and Ike Southward tackle Greg Hawick.

Brisbane, second test, 1958. British hooker Tommy Harris is grounded by Norm Provan and Billy Marsh. Rex Mossop is ready to lend a hand.

Australian winger Brian Carlson cannot prevent Jim Challinor from touching down for Britain's first try.

Alan Prescott, his right arm broken, grabs Gordon Clifford with his good arm. Johnny Whiteley and Tommy Harris support their captain.

TEST MATCH 59

AT THE EXHIBITION GROUND, BRISBANE – 5 July, 1958
AUSTRALIA 18 GREAT BRITAIN 25 (HT 2-10)

GL Clifford (Newtown) 3G
R Kite (Wagga)
GR Hawick (Wagga)
BP Carlson (Norths) T
†P Dimond (Wests) T
AJ Brown (Newtown)
KV Holman (Wests) T
B Davies (Brothers, Brisbane) capt
KH Kearney (St. George)
WL Marsh (Balmain) T
RP Mossop (Manly)
ND Provan (St. George)
KJ O'Shea (Wests)

EG Fraser (Warrington) 5G
I Southward (Workington T) 2T
E Ashton (Wigan)
†JP Challinor (Warrington) T
M Sullivan (Wigan) T
DR Bolton (Wigan)
AJ Murphy (St. Helens) T
GA Prescott (St. Helens) capt
PT Harris (Hull)
†B McTigue (Wigan)
†R Huddart (Whitehaven)
JW Whiteley (Hull)
†VPP Karalius (St. Helens)

Referee - D Lawler (NSW)   Crowd - 32,965   Gate - £17,101

Scoring - 0-3 2-3 2-5 2-7 2-10 2-15 7-15 7-20 10-20 13-20 13-25 18-25

"Rorke's Drift Revisited" - Forty-four years on from the epic triumph of Wagstaff's wounded warriors in the third test of 1914 another bruised and battered band of Brits battled to undying glory. Alan Prescott broke his right forearm in the third minute but like some latter-day Nelson stayed on the field to lead his men to an unforgettable victory. Stand-off Dave Bolton left the field for good in the seventeenth minute, his collarbone shattered in trying to get Sullivan away. Eric Fraser (elbow), Jim Challinor (shoulder) and Vince Karalius (back) all ended up in hospital after the match. Yet Great Britain won and won well. They never surrendered the lead and denied the Australians a try until the 55th minute and even that was disputed. It was certainly the stuff of which legends are made and only those who were present can really appreciate the heroics of the stricken Lions who so bravely wrote their names into the annals of test rugby.

Despite their handicaps the Lions never stopped playing football. As early as the fourth minute they struck the lead. Murphy, playing the game of his young life, shot away devastatingly, found support in McTigue and Ashton and there was Challinor flying over at the corner. Clifford reduced the arrears with a penalty five minutes later but 3-2 became 7-2 as Fraser booted a couple of goals for the Lions, who were now reduced to 4½ effective forwards with Karalius having moved to stand-off.

It seemed only a matter of time before Australia took control but despite tremendous pressure the British refused to buckle. The Lions just kept playing football and in the 34th minute Murphy struck again. From a scrum he was away like a worried whippet. McTigue, already detached from the sawn-off scrum, was up in support to send Sullivan plunging in at the corner and Britain went in at the break with an unexpected eight point advantage.

Four minutes into the second half Britain's lead had been stretched to 15-2 and the Australians were decidedly worried. Again it was Murphy who did the damage. Bursting away from a tackle he left Brown and Holman for dead and handed on to Whiteley who passed inside to Southward for the winger to outpace Dimond over the last twenty yards. Fraser added the goal. In the 55th minute Australia at last scored a try, Marsh flinging himself over from a ruck. Clifford's conversion brought the score to 7-15 but the Lions hit back hard within five minutes. Whiteley drove devastatingly up-field before serving McTigue who was grounded but played the ball so swiftly that the Aussies could not reorganise before Southward booted on, chased, gathered and sauntered under the posts for Fraser to convert.

Australia replied with two tries, the first to Carlson after a lovely run and dummy and the second to Dimond who just squeezed in at the corner. At this stage it seemed that Britain must surely capitulate but Murphy struck the killer blow. A scrum went down and in the twinkling of an eye Murphy had fed Karalius who ran strongly before being buried by a horde of tacklers but somehow managed to pop a pass to the ubiquitous scrum-half who zoomed in from 30 yards to plant the ball under the bar. Fraser's conversion was good and not even Holman's kick and rush try four minutes from time could save Australia from abject humiliation. The thin white line had held.

TEST MATCH 60

AT SYDNEY CRICKET GROUND – 19 July, 1958
AUSTRALIA 17 GREAT BRITAIN 40 (HT 12-14)

GL Clifford (Newtown) 4G	EG Fraser (Warrington) 8G
IJ Moir (Souths)	I Southward (Workington T) T
HJ Wells (Wests)	E Ashton (Wigan)
BP Carlson (Norths)	A Davies (Oldham) T
P Dimond (Wests)	M Sullivan (Wigan) 3T
GR Hawick (Wagga) T	PB Jackson (Barrow) capt
KV Holman (Wests) T	AJ Murphy (St. Helens) T
B Davies (Brisbane, Brothers) capt	A Terry (St. Helens) T
KH Kearney (St. George)	PT Harris (Hull)
WL Marsh (Balmain)	B McTigue (Wigan)
RP Mossop (Manly)	R Huddart (Whitehaven)
ND Provan (St. George) T	JW Whiteley (Hull) T
KJ O'Shea (Wests)	VPP Karalius (St. Helens)

Referee - J Casey (Queensland)   Crowd - 68,720   Gate £29,458
Scoring - 0-5 2-5 2-7 2-12 7-12 7-14 12-14 12-17 12-22 12-25 12-30 17-30 17-35 17-40

Working on the assumption that lightning rarely strikes twice in the same place, the Australian selectors rather touchingly kept faith with the side humbled at Brisbane, retaining the entire pack and replacing only two of the backs. Their belief that the Lions, minus Prescott, Bolton and Challinor, could not possibly play so well again was cruelly disproved as Britain piled up a record score in Anglo-Australian tests, ran the home side ragged and won the Ashes on Australian soil for the first time since 1946.

For Keith Holman it was a sad finale to a tremendous test career which had begun on the same ground eight years previously. He was appearing in his fourteenth test against the British - an Australian record - and it was also the last test for other notable Kangaroos in Clifford, Davies, Hawick, Kearney and O'Shea.

The Lions continued in the same vein they had struck in Brisbane with Southward scoring brilliantly after only seven minutes. By the 22nd minute they were 12-2 up after Abe Terry, a monumental prop, had lightly tripped through the defence for try number two. Eric Fraser, kicking unerringly, had landed three goals to a solitary penalty by Clifford. Australia rallied strongly and in the period before half-time hauled themselves to within two points of Britain. Provan crossed for a converted try but a fourth goal to Fraser kept Australia at arm's length. Hope was restored just before the break when Holman scored a lovely individualist try, chipping over Fraser to touch down beneath the bar. Clifford's conversion brought the score to 12-14.

After the interval Australia continued to threaten but the crucial score came in the 53rd minute and inevitably the game-breaker was Murphy who somehow contrived to beat Wells twice on the home "25" before accelerating past a rooted Clifford. It was the first of three tries within nine minutes, Sullivan scoring in the 58th and 62nd minutes. The second almost sparked a riot as the referee was pelted with fruit, bottles and rubbish. It had begun with Moir kicking through to the British line whereupon he was blatantly obstructed. Full-back Fraser, however, made a hash of gathering the ball and Moir had a chance to profit but hesitated. To the disgust of the mob the referee waved play-on and Britain swept to the other end to score an amazing try. The stuffing had been knocked out of the home side and within five minutes a converted try to Alan Davies had taken Britain to an unassailable 30-12 advantage.

Little matter that Hawick cleverly touched down after 72 minutes for Britain still had time to score through Whiteley and Sullivan. Sullivan's try paralysed the Australians as he sped the length of the field to complete only the fifth hat-trick by a Briton in tests against Australia. The last one had been scored by Arthur Bassett in 1946 and since Sullivan's effort the feat has not been repeated. On the other wing Ike Southward's try had enabled him to become only the fourth Briton to score tries in each test of a series. He thus emulated George Tyson and Johnny Thomas (both 1908-09) and Jonty Parkin (1924).

A series which had begun in ignominy for the Lions had ended in the rout of the Australians. Britain had uncovered a new glittering generation of test stars in Murphy, Ashton, McTigue, Huddart, Bolton and Karalius as Australia's old stars had faded.

Swinton, first test, 1959.
'Rocky' Turner wins an aerial battle against Dud Beattie. Turner and Beattie clashed more violently three years later in the third test at Sydney and were both sent off.

TEST MATCH 61

AT STATION ROAD, SWINTON – 17 October, 1959
GREAT BRITAIN 14 AUSTRALIA 22 (HT 4-12)

EG Fraser (Warrington) 4G	WK Barnes (Balmain) capt 5G
WJ Boston (Wigan) T	E Lumsden (St. George)
E Ashton (Wigan) capt	RW Gasnier (St. George) 3T
A Davies (Oldham)	HJ Wells (Wests) T
M Sullivan (Wigan)	† JE Riley (St. George)
DR Bolton (Wigan)	BJ Clay (St. George)
AJ Murphy (St. Helens)	BA Muir (Wests, Brisbane)
A Terry (St. Helens)	WA Wilson (St. George)
PT Harris (Hull)	† IJ Walsh (Eugowra)
B McTigue (Wigan)	DR Beattie (Ipswich)
R Huddart (St. Helens)	† GK Parcell (Ipswich)
M Martyn (Leigh)	RP Mossop (Manly)
D Turner (Wakefield T) T	† BC Hambly (Wagga)

Referee - R Gelder (Wakefield)   Crowd - 35,224   Gate - £7,412
Scoring - 0-2 0-5 0-7 2-7 4-7 4-10 4-12 4-15 4-20 9-20 9-22 14-22

After the humiliations suffered in the series of 1958 Australia restructured her test XIII so successfully that the first test of 1959 saw a Great Britain side, essentially the same as the great team of '58, dazed, demoralised and defeated. The main agents of Australia's first ever test victory at Swinton (five defeats and a draw hitherto) were Brian Clay, a balding barrel of a loose-forward turned stand-off, rock solid as a defender and the principal director of the attack, and a sensational young centre in Reg Gasnier. Gasnier, scorer of five tries in three games against New Zealand during the summer, electrified the Swinton crowd and millions of television viewers as he ripped the British defence to shreds with a virtuoso display of pace and penetration. His hat-trick of tries was the first by an Australian against Britain since the very first Anglo-Australian test back in 1908, when Jimmy Devereux performed the feat. Gasnier's combination with the more robust Harry Wells was certainly the equal of any centre pairing in test history.

From the outset the Kangaroo forwards established their superiority and were much more disciplined than their lacklustre opposites. During the first quarter the home side threatened only once, when Boston intercepted, and Australia took a seven point lead. After ten minutes Barnes kicked a simple penalty when Harris went off-side and two minutes later Wells was the prime mover in a majestic score. The burly centre made it all look so simple as he cut out two men with a precision pass to Gasnier who screamed down the touch-line from half-way leaving Fraser gasping in vain pursuit. In the eighteenth minute another penalty to Barnes edged Australia further ahead before Fraser was able to narrow the gap with two well-struck goals. It was as near to the lead as Britain would come. Wells almost had Barnes over before he himself took a sweet reverse pass from Mossop to score an unconverted try after 33 minutes. Barnes added a fine long-range penalty shortly afterwards and Britain's cause was not helped when Murphy twisted his knee just on half-time. Two minutes into the second half the Kangaroos produced the killer try. Muir provided the service for Gasnier 40 yards out. Ashton and Boston were dumbfounded as sheer pace and marvellous acceleration took the young centre past them to touch down wide out. Britain rallied, Fraser hitting the post with a penalty, McTigue creating two fine openings and Sullivan being hurled into touch a foot from the line. Australia weathered the storm, however, and, from a drop-out by Bolton, Gasnier burst through a large gap for his hat-trick. Barnes converted and Australia led 20-4. The last ten minutes saw Britain render the score-line more palatable. Bolton grubber-kicked through for Boston to dribble on to score under the bar with Fraser converting before Barnes stilled the crowd's enthusiasm with another penalty. In the final seconds McTigue provided Turner with the opportunity to force his way over for a consolation try converted by Fraser but Britain's best efforts had all come much too late. Heads had to roll.

Swinton, first test, 1959.
Top: Hat-trick hero, Reg Gasnier plants the ball down supported by Johnny Riley.
Billy Boston arrives too late.
Bottom: Great Britain centre Alan Davies cops it from Brian Clay and Barry Muir.

TEST MATCH 62

AT HEADINGLEY, LEEDS – 21 November, 1959
GREAT BRITAIN 11 AUSTRALIA 10 (HT 6-2)

† F Dyson (Huddersfield)	WK Barnes (Balmain) capt G
I Southward (Oldham)	BP Carlson (Norths) 2T,G
E Ashton (Wigan)	HJ Wells (Wests)
N Fox (Wakefield T) T,G	RW Gasnier (St. George)
M Sullivan (Wigan)	E Lumsden (St. George)
DR Bolton (Wigan)	BJ Clay (St. George)
JM Stevenson (York) capt	BA Muir (Wests, Brisbane)
A Terry (St. Helens)	WA Wilson (St. George)
PT Harris (Hull)	IJ Walsh (Eugowra)
D Robinson (Leeds) T	GK Parcell (Ipswich)
B McTigue (Wigan)	RP Mossop (Manly)
DG Vines (Wakefield T)	† EW Rasmussen (Toowoomba)
JW Whiteley (Hull) T	BC Hambly (Wagga)

Referee - R Gelder (Wakefield)   Crowd - 30,184   Gate - £6,480
Scoring - 3-0 3-2 6-2 6-7 6-10 11-10

At Swinton the Kangaroos had shown that given a firm ground and a little freedom they were more than a match for Great Britain. Conditions and history were not on their side at Headingley, however. Phil King, of *The Sunday People*, noted impishly that *good old English mud cloaked a slight lack of mobility in the home "six"*. Britain had indeed selected a gargantuan pack but with the skills of McTigue and Whiteley to call upon there was much more than brute force in their armoury. Traditionally Headingley was a grave-yard for Australian test hopes, the Kangaroos already having lost six times there in six outings. Still why should Barnes' men fear tradition? Had they not just laid their 30 year-old Swinton bogey?

It would be difficult to imagine a tighter, tenser test match than this one, fought out by two splendid teams with never more than four points separating them. By no means a spectacular affair but hard, unremitting and played in a good spirit, here was a contest which held the crowd in thrall from beginning to end. That the laurels ultimately went to Britain was largely due to the excellence of their pack in securing scrum possession to the tune of 17-6, thereby denying Clay and Gasnier their opportunity to wreak havoc. Bolton, at stand-off, played one of the games of his life and with Stevenson, an inspiring captain, the British half-backs called the shots.

Britain had the best of starts, scoring a try after 55 seconds - possibly the quickest try scored in a test on home ground. From the kick-off Southward sent the leather dead. Barnes dropped out from the "25" straight to Southward who kicked and chased but was obstructed and a penalty was awarded ten yards out and close to touch. Stevenson, disdaining the goal chance, caught the Kangaroos cold by sending Robinson plunging through on the blind side where he managed to force the ball down despite the three Aussies who were intent upon holding him upright. After eleven minutes Barnes kicked a fine 45 yard penalty, having already failed with two, and in the process pulled a ham-string. Only one other score accrued in the first half and it fell to Britain in the 32nd minute. Robinson was almost over as a heroic Australian defence harried and covered for all it was worth but the ball was worked wide via McTigue, Whiteley and Bolton before a perfect reverse pass from Ashton sent Fox through Wells' tackle for the first three points of 61 he would plunder from Australia in four Ashes series.

Four points ahead at the break, Britain were four points behind within eight minutes of the restart as Australia hit a purple patch. In the 46th minute Australia forced play into the home "25" and from a scrum Clay served Wells, the outstanding Australian on the day. Wells completely bamboozled the defence by swivelling and passing to Carlson rushing in-field from the wing. Carlson simply flew past an astonished British defence to score a glorious try under the posts which he converted himself.

Two minutes later Gasnier at last escaped his gaolers to make a bewildering run up the middle, beat five opponents, drew the full-back and fired out a scoring pass to Carlson. Carlson missed the conversion and soon afterwards hit the post with a relatively simple penalty - failures which cost the match in the final analysis. The decisive score came sixteen minutes from time from one of the oldest tricks in the book. A five yard scrum went down under the posts, Harris struck, Stevenson secured and flipped an inside pass to Whiteley who ploughed over for the winning try. Fox converted and the series was squared. A stunningly simple try had simply stunned Australia.

TEST MATCH 63

AT CENTRAL PARK, WIGAN – 12 December, 1959
GREAT BRITAIN 18 AUSTRALIA 12 (HT 6-2)

† GV Round (Wakefield T)	WK Barnes (Balmain) capt 3G
I Southward (Oldham) T	BP Carlson (Norths) T
E Ashton (Wigan)	HJ Wells (Wests)
N Fox (Wakefield T) T,6G	RW Gasnier (St. George)
M Sullivan (Wigan)	E Lumsden (St. George)
DR Bolton (Wigan)	BJ Clay (St. George)
JM Stevenson (York) capt	BA Muir (Wests, Brisbane)
A Terry (St. Helens)	DR Beattie (Ipswich)
PT Harris (Hull)	IJ Walsh (Eugowra)
J Wilkinson (Wakefield T)	WA Wilson (St. George)
B McTigue (Wigan)	RP Mossop (Manly)
D Robinson (Leeds)	BC Hambly (Wagga)
JW Whiteley (Hull)	JW Raper (St. George) T

Referee - E Clay (Rothwell)   Crowd - 26,089   Gate - £5,498
Scoring - 2-0 4-0 4-2 6-2 8-2 13-2 13-7 15-7 15-12 18-12

In a drab, uninspiring Ashes decider Australia scored as many tries as Great Britain, played most of what little good football there was but threw away the series through poor tactical play. As so often in the past, a team with superior back power neglected its advantages to allow its forwards to demonstrate their virility against a heavier pack. Australia proved their virility all right and won their opponents' respect but lost the match. Britain were content to allow the Kangaroo forwards an extended trial of strength, for concentrating on the battle they lost the war. Both sets of three-quarters were largely ornamental for the first hour when thrills were few and far between but that was a situation which suited the home team admirably.

In the first half there was never a glimmer of a try as "Sergeant-Major" Clay ruled with an iron fist and the whistle constantly at his lips. In the first fourteen minutes he doled out ten penalties, albeit evenly, and during the first half lectured warring props Wilson and Wilkinson on no fewer than three occasions. Wells and Walsh were also treated to words of warning in a stop-start first 40 minutes.

Fox opened the scoring in the fifth minute with a prodigious 50 yard penalty after a stiff-arm by Hambly and the only other scores of the half were further penalties, all for scrum offences, kicked by Fox (8 and 27 minutes) and Barnes (18 minutes).

The second half opened with Wilkinson being led from the field with a split nose and cheek as a stud ripped his face. Five minutes later he was back by which time Fox had landed another penalty goal, scored a try and kicked a conversion to stretch the British lead to 13-2. There had not seemed much possibility of a try when Fox lofted a high kick some 30 yards from Australia's line in the 48th minute. Bolton, Robinson and a good proportion of the Australian team failed to gather but Fox made no mistake as he followed up and calmly ran behind the posts for a try which he converted.

The game began to open up as Australia realised at last that there was no percentage in locking horns with the British pack. Gasnier demonstrated just how bad the Australian tactics had been when during the last quarter the ball began to reach the three-quarters. A devastating burst by Gasnier breached the British defence and although Round was there to take the flying centre down he could not prevent the great man from sending Johnny Raper over unchallenged. Barnes' goal brought the Kangaroos back into contention at 13-7 but yet another penalty from Fox eased the pressure a little for Britain. Britain, or Neil Fox, now led 15-7 with ten minutes remaining but were certainly not out of the woods. Again it was Gasnier who dragged Australia back. From his own "25" he tore to the opposite end of the field, mesmerised Round and sent Carlson on a clear run to the line. It was a superb effort and with Barnes' conversion Australia were only three points adrift and looking the livelier team. There was to be no fairy-tale ending for Australia, however, for in the dying moments a handling error enabled Whiteley to gift a try to Southward.

Britain had retained the Ashes. Australia may have been the better footballers but Britain had been superior tacticians. It was time for the British to rejoice. The Rugby League world could hardly have anticipated that the 1959 series would be the last occasion the Ashes were to be won by the Brits on home ground for at least 35 years.

Headingley, second test, 1959. Don Robinson crashes over for a try after only 55 seconds.

Sydney, first test, 1962. "Rocky" Turner tries to escape the attentions of Aussies Johnny Raper,
Barry Muir and Reg Gasnier. Norm Herbert tracks Turner.

TEST MATCH 64

AT SYDNEY CRICKET GROUND – 9 July, 1962
AUSTRALIA 12 GREAT BRITAIN 31 (HT 7-9)

D Parish (Wests) 3G	GV Round (Wakefield T)
† MA Cleary (Souths)	WJ Boston (Wigan) T
RW Gasnier (St. George) capt T	E Ashton (Wigan) capt 2T
† RJ Hagan (Townsville)	N Fox (Wakefield T) 5G
KJ Irvine (Norths) T	M Sullivan (St. Helens) 2T
AJ Summons (Wests)	DR Bolton (Wigan)
BA Muir (Wests, Brisbane)	AJ Murphy (St. Helens)
GK Parcell (Ipswich)	N Herbert (Workington T)
IJ Walsh (St. George)	W Sayer (Wigan)
DR Beattie (Ipswich)	B McTigue (Wigan)
EW Rasmussen (St. George)	R Huddart (St. Helens) T
RJ Lynch (Parramatta)	JB Edgar (Workington T)
JW Raper (ST. George)	D Turner (Wakefield T) T

Referee - D Lawler (NSW)   Crowd - 69,990   Gate - £29,576

Scoring - 5-0 7-0 7-3 7-6 7-9 7-14 12-14 12-19 12-21 12-26 12-31

A test which looked a good thing for Australia, who shot into a seven points lead within five minutes, turned into a triumphal procession for the Lions. By the game's conclusion Australia had been savagely demoralised and humiliated. Yet it took Britain until the 37th minute to get their noses in front largely because of Australian hooker Walsh's domination of the scrums. Walsh took the first half scrums 10-2 and overall had a 17-10 advantage over Sayer. With a penalty count of 20-8 in the home team's favour, the performance of the Lions assumed epic proportions. The source of Britain's strength was the superb play of the forwards in the loose. Had Britain had an equal share of possession a record score would surely have been registered. Prop Brian McTigue was simply magnificent, scheming and creating play for damaging runners like Huddart, Edgar and Turner, whilst the Lions backs, on meagre rations, were full of guile and lethal finishing.

The game opened sensationally as Australia rocked Britain in the third minute with an excellent try. Summons dashed toward the right flank and when challenged by Bolton put in a telling cross-kick. Irvine, rushing up at break-neck pace, took a benign bounce, handed off Boston and touched down. Parish converted and two minutes later added a penalty. Undaunted, the Lions hit back after eighteen minutes following a remarkable passage of play. Britain drove the ball deep into Australian territory only for Australia to bring the ball back almost to the British line, where Huddart ripped the ball from Rasmussen and sailed clear of the defence. Cleary eventually caught him but from the play-the-ball McTigue fed Turner a blind-side pass and the loose-forward adroitly used Sullivan as a foil before straightening up to score himself. Eleven minutes later Turner swatted several tacklers and parted to Fox, who disposed of Parish and held off Cleary and Hagan before sending Sullivan diving in at the flag. Three minutes before the break Sullivan equalled Brian Carlson's record by scoring his eighth try in Ashes matches after wonderful handling by McTigue, Herbert, Bolton, Ashton and Fox, who was unable to convert any of the three first-half tries.

Early in the second half a little piece of McTigue magic sent Huddart tearing to the posts from the home "25". Fox converted but after 54 minutes Gasnier, the youngest captain of Australia (23 years, 28 days), gave hope to his side as he sprinted from half-way, left Fox and Sullivan in his wake, shrugged off Round and scored a glorious try at the corner. Parish's fine conversion brought the score to 14-12 but Australia were not to threaten again. After 58 minutes McTigue stormed 30 yards, bumping off tacklers before presenting Ashton with a try under the bar. Fox's conversion and a penalty soon afterwards gave the Lions a nine points cushion. Raper prevented Fox from extending the lead with a marvellous tackle on the big centre on the line but Britain would not be denied as McTigue and Ashton worked another smart manoeuvre for the British skipper to score his second try and Boston scored the final try by which time Australia were thoroughly dispirited.

Britain's display was unquestionably one of the most devastating in the history of test match rugby for by any standards Australia fielded a powerful team but encountered a Lions XIII which simply could not be contained on the day. If anything, the lop-sided score-line was flattering to the vanquished.

TEST MATCH 65

AT LANG PARK, BRISBANE – 30 June, 1962
AUSTRALIA 10 GREAT BRITAIN 17 (HT 3-10)

WK Barnes (Balmain) capt 2G	GV Round (Wakefield T)
E Lumsden (St. George)	WJ Boston (Wigan) 2T
†A Gil (Cairns)	E Ashton (Wigan) capt G
RW Gasnier (St. George)	N Fox (Wakefield T) 3G
KJ Irvine (Norths) T	M Sullivan (St. Helens)
RB Banks (Toowoomba)	†H Poynton (Wakefield T)
AJ Summons (Wests) T	AJ Murphy (St. Helens) T
DR Beattie (Ipswich)	N Herbert (Workington T)
IJ Walsh (St. George)	W Sayer (Wigan)
†W Carson (Wests)	B McTigue (Wigan)
†M Veivers (Souths, Brisbane)	R Huddart (St. Helens)
†W Owen (Newcastle)	JB Edgar (Workington T)
†G Smith (Lithgow)	†L Gilfedder (Warrington)

Referee - J Casey (Queensland)   Crowd - 34,760   Gate - £20,204/17/-

Scoring - 0-2 0-7 3-7 3-10 5-10 5-15 5-17 10-17

Reeling from the pummelling received at Sydney, the Australian selectors panicked and reconstituted the pack by bringing in four new caps. It made no difference to the Lions who won more convincingly than the score suggested despite losing mercurial Alex Murphy with an ankle injury after 55 minutes. It was the first time since 1928 that Britain had won the Ashes in Australia after only two tests. Although Australia improved somewhat on their first test showing, they were still unable to restrain the British forwards in open play and this time were beaten 18-13 in the scrums.

Britain took the lead after seven minutes and never surrendered it, Fox opening the scoring with a penalty. For a time Australia attacked furiously, directing a series of kicks at Boston's wing in the mistaken belief that they could unnerve the Wigan wonder-wing but after eighteen minutes it was the Australians who were unnerved as Britain rolled them back from their "25". As usual McTigue instigated the assault driving 25 yards before back-flipping the ball to Huddart on half-way. "Hurricane" swept past Owen and careered for the line but was grounded just short by Lumsden. A quick play-the-ball saw Poynton throw out a long bobbling pass which Boston collected to stroll over unmolested for a try which Fox converted.

Australia struck back in the 25th minute. Walsh was quick to seize a loose ball, enabling Summons to make ground before lobbing a finger-tip pass to Gasnier, who penetrated the Lions' "25" before giving Irvine a clear run to the corner. The kick was too much for Barnes but Australia were back in the game at 3-7. With McTigue bossing the forward exchanges and Murphy constantly breaking through it was only a matter of time before Britain regained the initiative, however. Sure enough, Australia's defences succumbed after 34 minutes. Gilfedder made the initial thrust before Ashton released Boston on the wing and there was no stopping the mighty Welshman who fended off first Irvine and then Veivers before riding Summons' low tackle to cross at the corner for a dazzling touchdown - his ninth in tests against Australia, enabling him to wrest the record from Carlson and his own team-mate Sullivan.

Australia pressed hard at the start of the second half with full-back Barnes setting a fine captain's example. First he ran elusively before serving Lumsden but the winger could not return what would have been a scoring pass. Then Barnes landed a 44th minute penalty goal and shortly afterwards saved his line with a beautiful tackle on Boston. After 47 minutes Britain struck the decisive blow as from a scrum near the home line Murphy mesmerised Smith and Banks to shoot over without a finger being laid on him. Fox goaled and Britain seemed set to go on a spree similar to that in the first test. They received a setback, however, when Murphy was carried off with 25 minutes to play but Ashton, now at stand-off, shrewdly stretched the British lead with a well-timed drop goal. Despite their numerical supremacy Australia could not dominate and they were fortunate when Poynton, now at scrum-half, ran evasively to send Sullivan over only for the referee to rule that the winger had not grounded the leather. By the time Summons had claimed a resourceful solo try, converted by Barnes, Britain were home and dry, the Ashes theirs for the fourth consecutive series.

TEST MATCH 66

AT SYDNEY CRICKET GROUND – 14 July, 1962
AUSTRALIA 18 GREAT BRITAIN 17 (HT 11-12)

† F Drake (Souths, Brisbane) T	GV Round (Wakefield T)
E Lumsden (St. George)	WJ Boston (Wigan)
A Gil (Cairns)	E Ashton (Wigan) capt T
P Dimond (Wests)	N Fox (Wakefield T) T,4G
KJ Irvine (Norths) 2T,3G	M Sullivan (St. Helens)
† RJ Lisle (Souths)	H Poynton (Wakefield T)
AJ Summons (Wests) capt T	AJ Murphy (St. Helens) T
DR Beattie (Ipswich)	N Herbert (Workington T)
IJ Walsh (St. George)	W Sayer (Wigan)
W Carson (Wests)	B McTigue (Wigan)
M Veivers (Souths, Brisbane)	JB Edgar (Workington T)
EW Rasmussen (St. George)	R Huddart (St. Helens)
JW Raper (St. George)	D Turner (Wakefield T)

Referee - D Lawler (NSW)   Crowd - 42,104   Gate - £18,403/11/-
Scoring - 3-0 8-0 8-5 8-10 8-12 11-12 11-17 13-17 18-17

Although the Ashes had already been won and lost this third test at Sydney went down in the game's annals as one of the most thrilling of all tests, packed with incident, laced with memorable tries and the result hanging on a last-gasp goal-kick by a makeshift marksman. Australia had to fight hard for victory, which many felt was not a just result but they regained lost pride and saved themselves the embarrassment of becoming the first team to lose all three tests. They took the chances which came their way and reaped the reward.

Australia got a flying start and raced to an 8-0 lead after quarter of an hour. Eight minutes into the game the Australian captain Summons scored a dazzling try which took him fully 60 yards, beating Poynton near half-way, rounding the full-back and selling a peach of a dummy to Boston as he went hard for the corner. Seven minutes later Summons collected a kick by Round inside his own half, found the gap and linked with Lumsden who made progress down the wing until challenged by Round whereupon he cross-kicked for Drake to take the ball on the full and touch down. Irvine converted. Drake's try was the first ever scored by a full-back in an Ashes test.

The Lions came back in fine style as Edgar broke the defence. Poynton received a pass 35 yards out, dashed across the field and fed Murphy who drew the tacklers and exquisitely flicked the ball inside to Fox who charged over for a try to which he added the goal. Eleven minutes later Murphy turned the Australian defence inside-out to send Ashton over. Fox's conversion gave the Lions a 10-8 lead with 36 minutes on the clock and this was soon extended when Fox kicked a penalty after Walsh strayed off-side. Australia responded with a try on the stroke of half-time, Dimond, a rugged customer, plunging downfield before kicking to the line where Irvine got to the ball before Round. Australia were well satisfied to go in only a point down at the break.

Six minutes after the restart Murphy and Sullivan tackled Dimond in a manner which induced the referee to dismiss the fiery Sullivan, Huddart being taken out of the pack and employed on the wing. Australia had to make their extra man pay but seemed at a loss as to how to profit. After 56 minutes Beattie, already injured, provoked Turner into a scrap and the pair got their marching orders. Down to eleven men Britain astonishingly went further ahead with a stupendous try by Murphy. The scrum-half showed everyone a clean pair of heels as he raced 50 yards from a scrum at electrifying pace. Fox's goal made it 17-11 with fifteen minutes remaining. Summons was laid out after being crash-tackled by Boston but gamely returned after a few minutes attention to see Irvine kick an easy goal after 71 minutes to place Australia within striking distance of an improbable victory. The minutes crept by until only two remained at which point Lisle broke from his own "25", found Summons in support and the scrum-half was away. Boston poised himself for another crash-tackle but Summons, once bitten, was not about to be bitten again and ducked under Boston's arms before firing the ball to Carson who quickly parted to Irvine. The winger could not be caught and scored at the flag. Everything depended on his touch-line conversion. Irvine's preparations seemed to take an eternity but destiny was on his side and the ball flew straight and true.

Australia's first test team, 1952.
Standing: Paul, Hazzard, Ashton, Davies, Crocker.
Seated: Wells, Hall, Churchill (capt), Hawick.
Front: Pidding, Schubert, Carlson, Holman

Great Britain's first test team, 1963.
Back: Armour (physio), Measures, Tembey, Bowman, Field, Tyson, Sayer, Burgess.
Front: Bolton, Gowers, Karalius, Ashton (capt), Murphy, Fox, Fallowfield (Coach-manager)

TEST MATCH 67

AT WEMBLEY STADIUM, LONDON – 16 October, 1963
GREAT BRITAIN 2 AUSTRALIA 28 (HT 2-10)

K Gowers (Swinton)	K Thornett (Parramatta) T
W Burgess (Barrow)	KJ Irvine (Norths) T
E Ashton (Wigan) capt	GF Langlands (St. George) T,5G
N Fox (Wakefield T) G	RW Gasnier (St. George) 3T
† N Field (Batley)	P Dimond (Wests)
DR Bolton (Wigan)	E Harrison (Gilgandra)
AJ Murphy (St. Helens)	BA Muir (Wests, Brisbane)
† J Tembey (St. Helens)	PM Gallagher (Brothers, Brisbane)
W Sayer (Wigan)	IJ Walsh (St. George) capt
† B Tyson (Hull KR)	NR Kelly (Wests)
KD Bowman (Huddersfield)	RN Thornett (Parramatta)
† J Measures (Widnes)	BC Hambly (Parramatta)
VPP Karalius (Widnes)	JW Raper (St. George)

Referee - DTH Davies (Manchester)   Crowd - 13,946   Gate - £6,251
Scoring - 0-2 2-2 2-5 2-10 2-15 2-20 2-25 2-28

Wembley on a wet and wintery Wednesday night in October is a far cry from one of those magical May afternoons which shine on Challenge Cup Finals at the great stadium. Australia, however, were keen to sample the experience of playing a test at the Empire Stadium and were rewarded with a winning margin greater than they had ever recorded in tests against the British. It was also the first test match to be played under floodlights and the sparseness of the crowd lent a certain eeriness to the proceedings.

There were mitigating factors in Britain's heavy defeat. They had played a man short from the eighteenth minute when stand-off Dave Bolton had retired with a sprung shoulder after being driven into the ground by Earl Harrison's tackle and their other half-back, Alex Murphy, had played all but fourteen minutes with a broken nose. Upto the point of Bolton's withdrawal Britain had held their own and only conceded a penalty to Graeme Langlands but the handicap of playing a five-man pack for such a long period was too much and Australia made the most of their advantage to exploit virtually every error that the home side committed.

Britain had made most of the early running but had not been able to master the slippery turf or control a ball which had the properties of a wet bar of soap. Even so they must have been heartened when shortly after Bolton's departure Neil Fox bounced a 50 yard penalty onto and over the cross-bar to level the scores. It was to be their final act of defiance as the Kangaroo forwards ran riot to provide a set of jet-like three-quarters with the running chances they could only have fantasised about.

It was not until the 34th minute, however, that the British line was breached as Ken Thornett thundered onto Barry Muir's pass from the edge of a ruck and crossed without opposition. Two minutes before the break Reg Gasnier swooped on a British fumble and away went Langlands for a try at the corner to which he added a beautiful goal.

For the first ten minutes of the second period Britain resisted commendably but hopelessly before Australia carved out a magnificent try. Superb supporting play featuring Raper and Dick Thornett opened up the British mid-field defence and there was no catching Gasnier as he majestically raced straight down the middle to the posts. Langlands converted and Australia led 15-2. It was not long before Irvine was streaking away from yet another British fumble to score Australia's fourth try, duly converted by Langlands. Two further tries in the 69th and 76th minutes, one a stunning 70-yarder, gave the merciless Gasnier a hat-trick making him the first man to perform the feat twice in Ashes tests. Langlands converted the first and when the final whistle sounded who could blame the Australians for believing that Wembley really was wonderful? For the first time in over half a century a pair of brothers - the Thornetts - had appeared in a test together, the last pair having been Billy and Viv Farnsworth of the 1911 Kangaroos.

TEST MATCH 68

AT STATION ROAD, SWINTON – 9 November, 1963
GREAT BRITAIN 12 AUSTRALIA 50 (HT 8-31)

K Gowers (Swinton)	K Thornett (Parramatta)
M Sullivan (York)	KJ Irvine (Norths) 3T
E Ashton (Wigan) capt	GF Langlands (St. George) 2T,7G
N Fox (Wakefield T) 3G	RW Gasnier (St. George) 2T
J Stopford (Swinton) T	P Dimond (Wests) 2T
F Myler (Widnes)	E Harrison (Gilgandra) T
AJ Murphy (St. Helens)	BA Muir (Wests, Brisbane)
W Robinson (Leigh)	P Quinn (Gerringong)
† L McIntyre (Oldham)	IJ Walsh (St. George) capt
† CH Watson (St. Helens)	NR Kelly (Wests) T
R Morgan (Swinton)	RN Thornett (Parramatta) T
J Measures (Widnes) T	K Day (Wests, Brisbane)
VPP Karalius (Widnes)	JW Raper (St. George)

Referee - DTH Davies (Manchester)   Crowd - 30,843   Gate - £7,362
Scoring - 3-0 3-5 3-10 3-13 3-18 3-23 3-26 3-31 8-31 8-34 8-39 8-42 8-47 10-47 12-47 12-50

If Great Britain had felt sorry for themselves after their tribulations at Wembley they must have been positively suicidal following the traumas of this second test at Swinton. Australia ran in a record twelve tries in becoming the first team to reach a half century of points in the history of the series as for the first time since 1911-12 Great Britain surrendered the Ashes on home soil. Graeme Langlands bagged twenty points to equal the record set by Lewis Jones in 1954; springheeled Ken Irvine's hat-trick enabled him to equal Brian Carlson's Australian record of eight tries against Britain; Reg Gasnier brought his try tally for the series to five to set another Australian record and, in so doing, passed Carlson's record.

Britain had their excuses, of course. Three of the original forward selections - Huddart, Turner and Edgar - were unavailable and for three-quarters of the match they were without the services of Myler whilst Ashton missed the whole of the second half and a good portion of the first. Both suffered rib injuries. Seven of the British players never played test match football again. For such maestros as Ashton, Sullivan and Karalius it was a sad farewell.

Excuses notwithstanding, the Kangaroos played a wonderfully effective and entertaining game and even at full strength it is doubtful whether they could have been contained. Whilst the three-quarter line fired the bullets with nine tries between them it was loose-forward Johnny Raper who provided the ammunition as he constantly shredded the British defence, having a hand in no fewer than nine of the scores.

Oddly enough it was Britain who struck first in the tenth minute with a fine try. Australia won a scrum deep in the British half but Harrison's pass to Gasnier ricocheted to Fox who strode 60 yards before being overhauled by Irvine. Stopford was up in support, however, to take the centre's pass for a shock try. Then came the deluge as Australia ripped in for seven tries and 31 points within 25 minutes.

Gasnier set the ball rolling in the fourteenth minute as he simply left the defence for dead with a searing burst of acceleration from 25 yards out. Three minutes later Dick Thornett and Raper enabled Irvine to race through a bemused defence and Australia led 10-3. In the nineteenth minute Raper put Langlands over by the flag and six minutes passed before the same combination worked another beautiful try with Langlands this time cleverly using Irvine as a decoy. After 32 minutes Gasnier capitalised on faulty British handling to streak over from the "25" untouched and two minutes later smooth passing released Irvine on half-way for the winger to show a clean pair of heels to all and sundry. Two minutes before the break Kelly went over following a bewildering run by Langlands who also potted his fifth conversion. There was still time for Britain to respond with a scrambled try by Measures from an up-and-under penalty from Gowers. Fox converted and Britain went in for the lemons in a state of shell-shock.

The second half was scarcely less horrendous than the first for Britain. The Australian centres broke from their own line for Irvine to saunter 75 yards for his hat-trick; Dick Thornett forced his way over; Dimond ran over from half-way unopposed; Harrison deservedly scored after a long run; Fox kicked Britain into double figures with two penalty goals but Dimond brought up the 50 after smart work by Muir and Day .... The Ashes to Australia, sackcloth to Great Britain.

Swinton, second test, 1963. Kangaroo hooker Noel Kelly struggles to break John Stopford's tackle.
Len McIntyre moves to help Stopford. Cliff Watson flounders on the ground.
Ken Irvine is in support for Australia.

Headingley, third test, 1963. Ken Irvine scores Australia's solitary try.
Dick Huddart and John Stopford arrive too late whilst Ken Gowers' tackle fails.

TEST MATCH 69

AT HEADINGLEY, LEEDS – 30 November, 1963
GREAT BRITAIN 16 AUSTRALIA 5 (HT 10-5)

K Gowers (Swinton)	K Thornett (Parramatta)
†G Smith (York) T	KJ Irvine (Norths) T
†KC Holden (Warrington)	GF Langlands (St. George) G
†A Buckley (Swinton)	RW Gasnier (St. George)
J Stopford (Swinton) T	P Dimond (Wests)
DR Bolton (Wigan)	E Harrison (Gilgandra)
T Smales (Huddersfield) capt	BA Muir (Wests, Brisbane)
†F Collier (Wigan)	P Quinn (Gerringong)
†J Ward (Castleford) T	IJ Walsh (St. George) capt
CH Watson (St. Helens)	NR Kelly (Wests)
R Huddart (St. Helens)	RN Thornett (Parramatta)
†K Roberts (Halifax)	BC Hambly (Parramatta)
†D Fox (Featherstone R) T,2G	JW Raper (St. George)

Referee - E Clay (Leeds)   Crowd - 20,497   Gate - £6,126
Scoring - 2-0 5-0 5-3 8-3 8-5 10-5 13-5 16-5

Periodically Australia-Britain test matches have thrown up unedifying exhibitions hardly fit to be dignified by the word sport. Brisbane 1932 ... Odsal 1952 ... Headingley 1963. The players' virility, the crowd's tolerance, the referee's patience? This encounter at a gloomy Headingley in November was a test of all these but as a test of Rugby League skills it was a non-starter.

Australia finished the game with only ten men, two of their number having been sent off and one carried off. Britain finished with twelve also having had a man banished. Eric Clay handed out cautions running into double figures. He stood no nonsense and yet the mayhem went on unabated. Dante's Inferno could scarcely have been hotter.

For Britain at least there was the salvaging of pride, so grievously dented by the routs of the previous two tests. Seven new caps were blooded, almost literally, and all came through with flying colours. For Australia there was only disappointment. They had failed to complete the expected whitewashing and had abandoned the enthralling style that had reaped eighteen touchdowns at Wembley and Swinton. How the mighty were fallen. It was Britain who mounted the early pressure, Thornett being forced to save as Smales chased a kick through by Stopford before Don Fox landed a good goal after only 90 seconds following a scrum infringement. Already things were happening which should not happen on a football field and within the first quarter-hour Langlands, Kelly, Dimond, Hambly and Holden received cautions. The atmosphere was heavily charged and it came as no real surprise when a scrum erupted in a flurry of fists and feet in the eighteenth minute. Australian forward Brian Hambly was deemed the main culprit and dismissed. Play continued to be punctuated by episodes of brutality but after 21 minutes a finely worked try fell to Britain. Fox got Bolton moving and although the lively stand-off was collared Fox was there again to link with Buckley in a surge down the left flank which resulted in a try for the fast supporting hooker, Johnny Ward. Australia came back strongly, Gasnier, Harrison and Raper all going near before Ken Thornett made one of his characteristic incursions into the three-quarters, broke Buckley's tackle and threw a pass to Irvine who rounded Stopford in style to equal the record tally of nine tries in Ashes tests held by Gasnier and Boston. Five minutes later it was Stopford's turn to beat Irvine as from a scrum he gathered a deft kick by Bolton to score wide out. Thus with 35 minutes gone Britain led 8-3. The last five minutes of the half saw Langlands and Fox exchange penalty goals for Britain to turn round 10-5 ahead.

The half-time break did nothing to cool the atmosphere. Gasnier, Holden and Dimond felt the lash of referee Clay's strictures but the skullduggery never relented and after 51 minutes Britain's Cliff Watson found himself banned from the field. Two minutes later Britain scored the decisive try as Bolton again kicked high from a scrum. Full-back Thornett appeared to misjudge the flight of the ball and winger Geoff Smith dashed in for the try. In the 55th minute Australian scrum-half Barry Muir was sent off after an altercation with Tommy Smales and there followed an all too brief period of real football. It ended when Irvine was injured in a ferocious tackle a few minutes before time and as he was carried off Fox and Stopford combined sweetly for the loose-forward to finish the scoring.

Sydney, third test, 1966. Australian centre Peter Dimond takes on Cliff Watson and Geoff Wriglesworth.

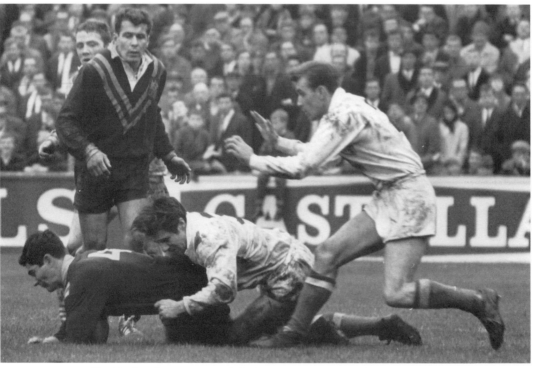

Headingley, first test, 1967. Britain's Ian Brooke grounds Johnny King.
Chris Young races to assist whilst Tommy Bishop and Billy Smith look on.

TEST MATCH 70

AT SYDNEY CRICKET GROUND – 25 June, 1966
AUSTRALIA 13 GREAT BRITAIN 17 (HT 8-7)

WK Barnes (Balmain) 5G	† A Keegan (Hull) 3G
KJ Irvine (Norths)	W Burgess (Barrow) T
† JN McDonald (Toowoomba)	† I Brooke (Bradford N)
GF Langlands (St. George)	A Buckley (Swinton)
† JC King (St. George)	J Stopford (Swinton)
† G Banks (South Newcastle) T	A Hardisty (Castleford) T
WJ Smith (St. George)	† T Bishop (St. Helens) G
R Crowe (West Wyalong)	JB Edgar (Workington T) capt
IJ Walsh (St. George) capt	PJ Flanagan (Hull KR)
L Weier (Norths)	CH Watson (St. Helens) T
† A Crema (Tully)	J Mantle (St. Helens)
† W Bradstreet (Manly)	W Bryant (Castleford)
JW Raper (St. George)	D Robinson (Swinton)
SUB JW Gleeson (Brothers, Brisbane) DNP	SUB WR Aspinall (Warrington) DNP
SUB M Veivers (Manly) DNP	SUB TH Fogerty (Halifax) DNP

Referee - J Bradley (NSW)   Crowd - 57,962   Gate - $51,361
Scoring - 2-0 2-5 4-5 6-5 6-7 8-7 8-9 8-14 8-17 13-17

According to the critics Great Britain were complete no-hopers before this test having already lost four of their nine tour fixtures and having to take the field without tour skipper, Harry Poole, who was afflicted with tonsilitis. In the event the Lions were convincing victors in an exciting encounter during which the lead changed hands five times. For much of the game, however, Australia threatened to sneak home on the basis of Keith Barnes' accurate goal-kicking. Britain displayed admirable patience allowing Australia to wear themselves out before applying the *coup de grâce* in the final quarter. The game was played under international laws which required teams to retire three yards at the play-the-ball as opposed to the local version of five yards which undoubtedly helped to frustrate the home team.

Within five minutes Barnes had booted his first goal but it was Britain who scored the first try when Cliff Watson swept like a juggernaut through the Australian pack in a twenty yard burst to score wide out. Last-minute replacement full-back Arthur Keegan converted with a soaring kick and Britain led 5-2 after eleven minutes. Lions second-rower John Mantle was rendered senseless by a stiff-arm from Langlands but much to the crowd's amusement the referee cautioned the innocent Aussie winger Ken Irvine. By the 25th minute Australia had edged ahead, Brooke and Flanagan having transgressed to permit Barnes to land two prodigious penalties. Four minutes before half-time the lead passed to Britain as Keegan landed a straight 35 yard penalty but the see-saw tipped again when Bishop conceded a penalty in the 39th minute and Barnes potted his fourth goal.

Neither side could gain an advantage in the third quarter when McDonald was seen to be a limping passenger on the Australian wing. Just after the hour Bryant drove fifteen yards to the Australian posts to set up a play-the-ball from which Bishop dropped a simple but crucial goal. The Australian forwards were clearly a spent force by this stage and in the 68th minute Hardisty grabbed a stunning solo try, dashing away from acting-half on a swerving run before kicking past Barnes on the "25" and getting to the ball before the Australian defence could recover. The try cost Hardisty a hip injury and he finished the match on the wing. Keegan's goal gave Britain daylight at 14-8 and seven minutes from time the match was sealed when Bishop, a real bundle of devilment, and Brooke made the running for Burgess, now at centre, to shoot past King and dive triumphantly for a try at the corner. Keegan failed with the kick but at 17-8 Britain were laughing.

Australia had hardly threatened to create a try but with four minutes remaining the British line at last capitulated. The try owed as much to luck as skill, however, as Barnes, in desperation, lofted an up-and-under from a penalty and in the general confusion Banks gathered and crossed for a try. Barnes kicked his fifth goal but it was a case of too little too late. Australia had little to offer apart from Barnes' golden boot and a sterling display of tackling by Johnny Raper whilst Britain had exceeded all expectations. The forwards, well led by stand-in skipper Brian Edgar, had been much the more virile set and Australia could not handle the speed of Hardisty and the trickery of Bishop at half-back.

TEST MATCH 71

AT LANG PARK, BRISBANE – 16 July, 1966
AUSTRALIA 6 GREAT BRITAIN 4 (HT 2-0)

WK Barnes (Balmain) 3G	A Keegan (Hull) 2G
KJ Irvine (Norths)	W Burgess (Barrow)
GF Langlands (St. George)	I Brooke (Bradford N)
†JW Greaves (Canterbury)	F Myler (Widnes)
JC King (St. George)	G Wriglesworth (Leeds)
JW Gleeson (Brothers, Brisbane)	A Hardisty (Castleford)
WJ Smith (St. George)	T Bishop (St. Helens)
NR Kelly (Wests)	JB Edgar (Workington T) capt
IJ Walsh (St. George) capt	PJ Flanagan (Hull KR)
†J Wittenberg (Theodore)	CH Watson (St. Helens)
M Veivers (Manly)	J Mantle (St. Helens)
RN Thornett (Parramatta)	W Ramsey (Hunslet)
RJ Lynch (Parramatta)	D Robinson (Swinton)
SUB G Wellington (Burdekin) DNP	SUB WR Aspinall (Warrington) DNP
SUB J Morgan (Souths) DNP	SUB W Bryant (Castleford) DNP

Referee - C Pearce (NSW)   Crowd - 45,057   Gate - $51,321
Scoring - 2-0 2-2 2-4 4-4 6-4

Great Britain were desperately unlucky to lose a fierce, unsavoury battle after playing a man short for 36 minutes following the dismissal of second-rower Bill Ramsey for alleged kicking. In a game largely devoid of skilful, open rugby Britain had created the few try-scoring chances that arose and were unquestionably the better side. However, instead of securing the Ashes they were robbed of victory by the master marksmanship of Keith Barnes whose final goal was kicked four minutes from the end. The fact that Australia won the scrums 12-5, had a penalty advantage of 15-9 and faced a depleted adversary for almost half the match and yet failed to score a solitary try was as much a reflection on the paucity of their attacking ideas and tactical awareness as on the dreadnought nature of the Lions' defence.

The roughness of the play transmitted itself to the terraces where fighting broke out and at times players and spectators became embroiled in *mêlées* as the disturbances spilled over onto the pitch. All in all the match was a most unsatisfactory affair with even the victors emerging with little honour.

The first half was bereft of spectacle as the two teams played on top of each other preferring to engage in pugilism rather than football. Australian prop John Wittenberg, a debutant, soon found out what test football is sometimes about when he was laid out in the eighth minute. In the aftermath Barnes landed his first penalty goal and that concluded the first half scoring.

Immediately the second half began British centre Ian Brooke was pole-axed by a stiff-arm and in the ensuing mayhem Ramsey received his marching orders. Ramsey had been laid out in the first half and was certainly not the only player who deserved the ultimate sanction. The dismissal seemed to strengthen the British resolve and within two minutes a characteristic kick and chase by Bishop resulted in an obstruction on the little half-back from which Keegan landed an equalising penalty goal. After 57 minutes Britain took the lead with another Keegan goal but Barnes levelled the scores with his second penalty in the 62nd minute.

Twelve minutes from time Britain unfolded a movement which almost won the game. Left-winger Wriglesworth raced across the face of the home defence to puncture the line on the far right before sending out a pass to Burgess who would surely have scored had the transfer not been too hot to handle. Australia escaped by the skin of their teeth and responded with a barrage on the Lions' line, Walsh almost struggling over. Four minutes from time the pressure finally told when Hardisty, Brooke and Wriglesworth were ruled off-side and Barnes landed the most vital goal of his test career, a comparatively simple shot from just outside the "25". For Barnes it was a gloriously fitting finale to his international career which ended with this stormy test.

The test was the first to end try-less since Britain's 4-0 victory at Belle Vue, Manchester in 1933 and only the third in the history of Ashes conflict. The 45,000 fans had little to applaud save some wonderful tackling by the British for whom Watson, Robinson and Myler performed wonders.

TEST MATCH 72

AT SYDNEY CRICKET GROUND – 23 July, 1966
AUSTRALIA 19 GREAT BRITAIN 14 (HT 8-2)

LH Johns (Canterbury) 2G	K Gowers (Swinton) 4G
KJ Irvine (Norths) 3T	W Burgess (Barrow)
P Dimond (Wests)	I Brooke (Bradford N)
JW Greaves (Canterbury)	A Buckley (Swinton)
JC King (St. George) T	G Wriglesworth (Leeds)
JW Gleeson (Brothers, Brisbane)	A Hardisty (Castleford) 2T
WJ Smith (St. George)	T Bishop (St. Helens)
NR Kelly (Wests)	JB Edgar (Workington T) capt
IJ Walsh (St. George) capt	PJ Flanagan (Hull KR)
J Wittenberg (Theodore)	CH Watson (St. Helens)
M Veivers (Manly)	J Mantle (St. Helens)
† AH Beetson (Balmain)	W Ramsey (Hunslet)
RJ Lynch (Parramatta) T	D Robinson (Swinton)
SUB G Banks (South Newcastle) DNP	SUB WR Aspinall (Warrington) DNP
SUB RN Thornett (Parramatta) for Beetson	SUB W Bryant (Castleford) for Mantle

Referee - C Pearce (NSW)   Crowd - 63,503   Gate - $59,347
Scoring - 0-2 3-2 8-2 8-7 11-7 11-9 16-9 16-14 19-14

Australia retained the Ashes after a game full of incident. Britain had every right to feel aggrieved at the dismissal in the 46th minute of fiery prop Cliff Watson who was alleged to have kicked at the equally fiery Australian centre Peter Dimond, particularly as Dimond had already been lectured thrice by the referee. The burden of playing a man short for almost half the match ultimately proved too much for the Lions who must have experienced a feeling of *déjà vu* when recalling the events of the previous test. In the final analysis Australia scored five tries to two which was perhaps a truer reflection of their superiority than the score-line indicated.
The first half saw Australia gain an early ascendancy although it was Britain who struck the first blow after only three minutes when Gowers kicked a penalty. By the half-hour the home team led by 8-2, however, following two tries inspired by debutant second-rower Arthur Beetson. The first resulted from a stolen ball and went to winger Ken Irvine who thus scored his tenth try in tests against the Britons to pass the record aggregate of tries in Ashes games formerly held by Billy Boston. The second was registered on the opposite flank when Beetson kicked through from half-way to allow King to chase, gather and touch down. Johns converted and an all-ticket, sell-out crowd settled back to await an avalanche of points from the home side. They were even more confident of Australia's success when Watson was dismissed only six minutes into the second half but the set-back seemed to spur the Lions who quickly got back into the game with a superb interception try from Hardisty who flashed unerringly onto Lynch's pass to Johns to leave everyone in his slipstream. Gowers' improvement brought Britain to within a point of Australia but fate turned its face from the Lions in the 57th minute. Johns broke clear of the British defence but was caught from behind by Brooke and threw to Irvine who appeared to spill the ball forwards but was allowed to regather and dive over for a highly contentious try. Gowers pulled back two points for the Lions with a penalty and then Australia crossed again when Gleeson got Lynch over. This time the referee had spotted a knock-on and ruled no-try. It hardly mattered, however, as shortly afterwards Lynch again crashed over for a legitimate try and a fine conversion from Johns seemed to have put the game out of Britain's reach at 16-9. Twelve minutes from time, however, Britain hauled themselves back into contention. Once again Hardisty did the trick, punting past the home defence and racing after the ball only to be unceremoniously chopped down from behind by a desperate fullback. The referee awarded a penalty try. Gowers converted and was promptly made to take the kick again as a player had moved. The result was the same but Gowers got only two points for his two successful kicks.
Four minutes later the destiny of the Ashes was settled as Johns, feinting hither and thither, slashed through the British ranks to send Irvine careering in for his hat-trick, a feat which remarkably was not emulated for another twenty years. Even more remarkably Irvine thus became the first and only player in Ashes history to score three tries in a test in his own country.
The game ended riotously as Lions loose-forward Dave Robinson was felled precipitating a brawl as the final bell rang out.

Headingley, first test, 1967. British scrum-half Tommy Bishop meets Noel Kelly head on.
Bill Holliday and 'Flash' Flanagan race to cover.

Headingley, first test, 1967. Graeme Langlands crosses for a try before Roger Millward can challenge him.

TEST MATCH 73

AT HEADINGLEY, LEEDS – 21 October, 1967
GREAT BRITAIN 16 AUSTRALIA 11 (HT 7-7)

A Keegan (Hull)	LH Johns (Canterbury)
† CC Young (HUll KR) T	JN McDonald (Toowoomba)
I Brooke (Wakefield T)	GF Langlands (St. George) T,4G
† MJ Price (Rochdale H)	RW Gasnier (St. George) capt
W Burgess (Barrow)	JC King (St. George)
R Millward (Hull KR) T,3G	JW Gleeson (Brothers, Brisbane)
T Bishop (St. Helens) G	WJ Smith (St. George)
W Holliday (Hull KR) capt G	PM Gallagher (Brothers, Brisbane)
PJ Flanagan (Hull KR)	NR Kelly (Wests)
CH Watson (St. Helens)	† DP Manteit (Brothers, Brisbane)
RA Irving (Oldham)	RJ Lynch (Parramatta)
J Mantle (St. Helens)	EW Rasmussen (St. George)
D Robinson (Swinton)	JW Raper (St. George)
SUB G Jordan (Featherstone R) DNP	SUB AR Branson (Nowra) DNP
SUB GT Rees (St. Helens) DNP	SUB EA Walters (Souths) DNP

Referee - GF Lindop (Wakefield)   Crowd - 22,293   Gate - £7,811
Scoring - 2-0 7-0 7-5 7-7 12-7 12-9 14-9 16-9 16-11

Australia had a man sent off, saw captain Reg Gasnier limp off at the close with a cracked bone in his leg and played for the last half hour with Johnny Raper in concussion after suffering a depressed fracture of the jaw. Yet the game was not unduly rough and there was no quibbling that the better team won a thoroughly entertaining encounter. Unfortunately Gasnier's injury marked the end of a glorious test career during which he had proved himself to be one of his country's greatest champions.

Apart from a second minute penalty attempt by Millward which quirkily veered past the post when apparently on target, Australia dominated the first fifteen minutes. Keegan was forced to hurriedly fly-hack the ball into touch as McDonald hared on to a shrewd kick from Gasnier and Johns failed with a drop at goal before the Kangaroos suffered a major disappointment. Gasnier intercepted Bishop's lofted pass, bolted into space and sent King scorching over only to have the referee rule a forward pass. More pressure resulted only in two failures at goal by Langlands before Britain began to turn the game. Young was downed two yards short after a 40 yards run by Brooke and then Burgess was ruled off-side after touching down a cute kick by Bishop. However, it was the cheeky Bishop who put the first points on the board in the 21st minute with a neat drop-goal. Two minutes later Britain produced a fine try covering 70 yards begun by Holliday's pass to Brooke who beat Gasnier before timing his pass perfectly for Young to sprint 45 yards for the try, which Millward improved. Australia hit back within six minutes as a long kick by Johns set up the position from which Gleeson made an incisive diagonal run before Langlands crossed for a try which he converted himself. Two minutes later Langlands levelled the scores with a penalty incurred by Price's off-side.

Four minutes after the break Britain regained the initiative. Mantle foraged successfully for a loose ball, stepped out of King's tackle and gave an awful pass to Millward, who not only managed to hang on to it but immediately got into his stride, cut inside Gasnier and baffled Langlands before crossing near the posts. "The Dodger" also added the goal. Soon afterwards Langlands kicked a penalty, the ball striking the post at the right angle for the Kangaroos. In the 49th minute Gallagher fouled Bishop and Millward kicked the resultant penalty. Raper then received his injury in assisting in a double tackle on Keegan but by this stage the British forwards were well on top, Irving and Mantle running particularly well and Holliday setting a fine example as leader of the pack, whilst the home half-backs were outplaying Gleeson and Smith and linking well with their three-quarters.

Three minutes from time Millward was heavily tackled by debutant prop Dennis Manteit who was sent off for his indiscretion. His crime was doubly punished when Holliday smacked over the penalty to place Britain beyond reach although Langlands replied with a penalty in injury time, thereby scoring all his side's eleven points.

It was beginning to appear that Australia would never lay their Headingley hoodoo - nine tests at Leeds had reaped nine defeats for the Kangaroos over the last 46 years.

TEST MATCH 74

AT WHITE CITY STADIUM, LONDON – 3 November, 1967
GREAT BRITAIN 11 AUSTRALIA 17 (HT 2-2)

A Keegan (Hull)	LH Johns (Canterbury)
CC Young (Hull KR)	JW Greaves (Canterbury)
I Brooke (Wakefield T)	GF Langlands (St. George) T,4G
N Fox (Wakefield T) 3G	JN McDonald (Toowoomba)
† WR Francis (Wigan)	JC King (St. George) T
R Millward (Hull KR)	† AR Branson (Nowra)
T Bishop (St. Helens) T,G	JW Gleeson (Brothers, Brisbane)
W Holliday (Hull KR) capt	PM Gallagher (Brothers, Brisbane) capt
PJ Flanagan (Hull KR)	NR Kelly (Wests)
CH Watson (St. Helens)	† NJ Gallagher (Bundaberg)
RA Irving (Oldham)	RJ Lynch (Parramatta)
J Mantle (St. Helens)	EW Rasmussen (St. George)
† F Foster (Hull KR)	† RJ Coote (Souths) T
SUB MJ Price (Rochdale H) DNP	SUB KJ Irvine (Norths) DNP
SUB D Robinson (Swinton) DNP	SUB DP Manteit (Brothers, Brisbane) DNP

Referee - GF Lindop (Wakefield)   Crowd - 17,445   Gate - £8,859

Scoring - 0-2 2-2 7-2 7-4 7-7 9-7 9-9 9-14 11-14 11-17

One down in the rubber, having also lost four of their eight other fixtures and lacking the services of that great St. George triumvirate of Reg Gasnier, Billy Smith and Johnny Raper, it hardly seemed likely that the Kangaroos would perform any better than at Leeds. Yet, sterlingly led by third-choice captain Peter Gallagher, Australia upset all predictions and fully merited their hard-won victory in a very intense but orderly test.

The first half was a try-less affair as handling errors and steadfast defences held sway. Langlands gave the Kangaroos a brief lead by landing a penalty but after twenty minutes Bishop popped over a drop goal from twenty yards, having already rattled the woodwork with a previous attempt. Both sides missed chances in the opening half with the best falling to Australia when a fine break by Langlands came to grief as Gleeson was unable to hold the scoring pass as he approached the posts.

The second half was fifteen minutes old before a try did finally materialise as Britain's centre Brooke made a burst deep into Australian territory before being scythed down by the fast-covering Coote. The ball was moved quickly to the left of the posts where Bishop was heavily tackled but had the presence of mind to play the ball to himself and dive for the touch-down. Fox added the goal and Britain led 7-2. Instead of being down-hearted the Kangaroos came back stronger. On the hour Bishop conceded a penalty at a scrum close to the British line and Langlands kicked a simple goal and a couple of minutes later Australia were on level terms. Branson, a highly successful debutant, was the architect making the gap before giving a delicious short pass to Langlands to drive slant-wise through a broken defence to score at the posts. To everyone's amazement Langlands made a hash of the conversion and a gilt-edged opportunity to take the lead was thrown away. The miss assumed greater proportions as within two minutes Fox landed a penalty to restore the advantage to Britain.

The last quarter of an hour, however, saw the Kangaroos emerge the stronger. Thirteen minutes remained when a Langlands penalty hit the mark to level the scores and in the 70th minute the crucial points fell to Australia. Johns, a towering figure at full-back, kicked high and deep into the British "25" where Keegan failed to gather but the danger seemed to have passed as Holliday brought the ball away in a clearing run to the "25" before sending out a pass to Brooke. The pass could have been better for it struck the centre on the shoulder and fell behind him whereupon King swooped, brilliantly gathered and swept over for the try. King's control of the ball had been remarkable as conditions by this stage were far from ideal as steady rain fell. Langlands' conversion gave Australia a five points advantage but with five minutes remaining a Fox penalty reduced the arrears to three. Australia had the last word, however, in the 78th minute when Coote crashed over at the corner for a try which the British claimed had not been properly touched down.

Australia had been the better team all-round, notably superior in support play and giving nothing away in defence. Ron Coote, at the beginning of a superb test career, was a revelation with his speed about the field, whilst Langlands, Johns and Peter Gallagher all played prominent roles. In an out-gunned British pack Irving never gave up but far and away the best Briton was little Tommy Bishop whose tackling was prodigious.

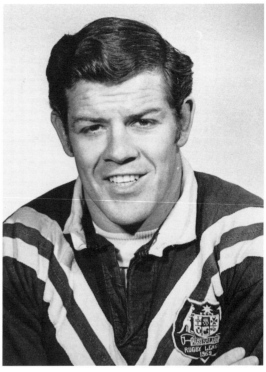

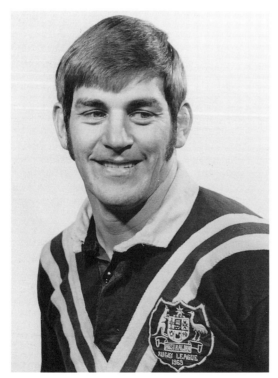

Four prominent Australian Ashes players.
Top: Ron Coote and Bob McCarthy
Bottom: Elwyn Walters and Billy Smith

TEST MATCH 75

AT STATION ROAD, SWINTON – 9 December, 1967
GREAT BRITAIN 3 AUSTRALIA 11 (HT 0-3)

A Keegan (Hull)	LH Johns (Canterbury)
CC Young (Hull KR)	JN McDonald (Toowoomba)
I Brooke (Wakefield T)	GF Langlands (St. George) G
MJ Price (Rochdale H) T	JW Greaves (Canterbury)
G Jordan (Featherstone R)	JC King (St. George) T
R Millward (Hull KR)	JW Gleeson (Brothers, Brisbane)
T Bishop (St. Helens)	WJ Smith (St. George)
W Holliday (Hull KR) capt	PM Gallagher (Brothers, Brisbane)
PJ Flanagan (Hull KR)	NR Kelly (Wests)
CH Watson (St. Helens)	DP Manteit (Brothers, Brisbane)
RA Irving (Oldham)	RJ Coote (Souths) T
† RA Valentine (Huddersfield)	EW Rasmussen (St. George)
D Robinson (Swinton)	JW Raper (St. George) capt
† SUB A Burwell (Hull KR) for Young	SUB AR Branson(Nowra) T for Gleeson
SUB CW Renilson (Halifax) for Watson	SUB RJ Lynch (Parramatta) DNP

Referee - GF Lindop (Wakefield)   Crowd - 13,615   Gate - £5,045
Scoring - 0-3 0-8 0-11 3-11

Disregarding treacherous arctic-like conditions, the Kangaroos tackled Great Britain to distraction to become the first Australian team to retain the Ashes in England and the first to win three Ashes series in succession. In circumstances which should surely have favoured the home XIII, the Kangaroos gave Britain an object lesson in resolute defence, slavishly supported the ball-carrier and reduced the British pack to a shambles. Johnny Raper, playing in his last test against the Poms and sporting a corset to support a back injury, led from the front and can rarely have commanded such a willing crew. Britain had their fair share of the play but lacked the driving commitment of the kamikaze Kangaroos who took the chances that fell to them with relish whilst Britain squandered theirs.

Snow began to fall as Holliday won the toss and elected to take advantage of the elements, which became increasingly hostile as the first half progressed. The first threat came from Australia as Langlands chased and collected Smith's kick but fell to a tackle by Jordan a few yards from the line. For the next fifteen minutes Great Britain applied continuous pressure. Millward missed a 30 yard penalty and then Brooke ran well and fed Price who kicked on only for Johns to push the ball out of play. Then a Bishop-inspired move saw Millward almost dribble over but King saved the situation. It was a bolt from the blue when after seventeen minutes of dour defending Australia posted the first try. The ball was fanned from wing to wing and only brave tackling by Keegan on both wingers saved the line but there was no stopping Coote who capitalised on good approach work by Raper and Gallagher to storm over wide out. Langlands missed the goal on a day which was hardly ideal for the kicker's art.

After 24 minutes Britain lost Young injured and three minutes later Gleeson was led off with a broken jaw. Almost immediately Britain exploited the disorganisation in the tourists' ranks as Bishop, Valentine and Price whipped the ball wide to Jordan who gleefully rammed the ball down just inside the flag. The joy was short-lived, however, as the touch-judge ruled that the winger had stepped into touch, a decision which was hotly disputed. The game warmed up considerably and Manteit, Irving and Raper were cautioned before the half-time whistle blew. It was increasingly obvious that Australia were gaining the ascendancy as their forwards, notably Coote and Rasmussen, were running hard and often.

With the elements in their favour and a 3-0 lead, Australia had the game in their grasp and eight minutes after the interval substitute stand-off Branson scored a lovely solo try beating three men, including the redoubtable Keegan, Britain's star-man on the day, as he swept 30 yards over the bone-jarring surface. Langlands kicked the only goal of the match and the Kangaroos' 8-0 lead seemed mountainous. Four minutes later Australia prised open the British defence for another try. Raper, Branson and Gallagher did the damage before Gallagher's long pass found King five yards from the line with no one to beat. Britain replied in the 64th minute with a try by Price, brilliantly engineered by Millward, and the game ended on a sour note when Kelly was sent off for a high tackle on Bishop as the scrum-half chased his own kick through.

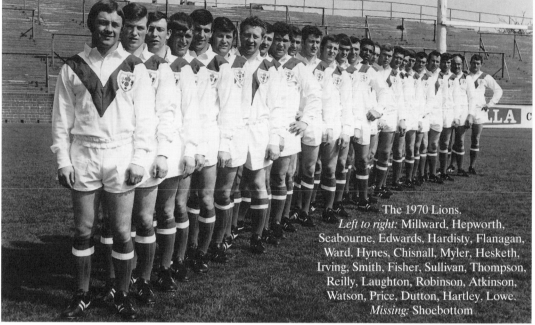

The 1970 Lions.
Left to right: Millward, Hepworth, Seabourne, Edwards, Hardisty, Flanagan, Ward, Hynes, Chisnall, Myler, Hesketh. Irving, Smith, Fisher, Sullivan, Thompson, Reilly, Laughton, Robinson, Atkinson, Watson, Price, Dutton, Hartley, Lowe. *Missing:* Shoebottom

Sydney, second test, 1970. Two of the hardest players in the history of the game clash.
John Sattler wraps himself round Mal Reilly's legs.

TEST MATCH 76

AT LANG PARK, BRISBANE – 6 June, 1970
AUSTRALIA 37 GREAT BRITAIN 15 (HT 13-5)

GF Langlands (St. George) capt 9G	†TG Price (Bradford N) 3G
JC King (St. George) 2T	CA Sullivan (Hull)
JN McDonald (Manly) T	F Myler (St. Helens) capt
†JE Brass (Easts)	MD Shoebottom (Leeds)
J Cootes (Wests, Newcastle)	JB Atkinson (Leeds)
†PF Hawthorne (St. George) 2G	A Hardisty (Castleford)
WJ Smith (St. George)	K Hepworth (Castleford)
J Wittenberg (St. George)	†D Chisnall (Leigh)
EA Walters (Souths)	PJ Flanagan (Hull KR) T
†J Morgan (Easts) 2T	CH Watson (St. Helens) T
AH Beetson (Balmain)	D Robinson (Wigan)
RJ Lynch (Parramatta)	†CD Laughton (Wigan) T
RJ Coote (Souths)	†MJ Reilly (Castleford)
SUB R Thompson (Wests, Brisbane) DNP	SUB R Millward (Hull KR) DNP
SUB C Weiss (Bundaberg) for Lynch	SUB RA Irving (Oldham) for Robinson

Referee - D Lancashire (NSW)   Crowd - 42,807 Gate - $47,608
Scoring - 2-0 4-0 6-0 11-0 11-5 13-5 18-5 23-5 23-8 23-10 28-10 30-10 30-15 32-15 37-15

Having swept like a whirlwind through Queensland in running up 165 points in the first five games of their tour, Britain entered the first test as clear favourites but emerged from the wreckage thoroughly chastened. Australia's forwards were complete masters of the match, comprehensively outplaying their counterparts and dictating that the ball should be kept from the wings. Beetson was in particularly magnificent form and orchestrated his fellow packmen to perfection with his judicious distribution whilst Jim Morgan at prop had a truly memorable test debut in scoring twice as well as collecting a broken nose. Several of the Lions hardly played upto test match standards and only Reilly, Watson and Hepworth caused the Australians any palpitations.

The opening half was a heated affair but between the fisticuffs Australia soon established their superiority. Within six minutes Australia led 4-0 by courtesy of two penalties kicked by Langlands, the second of which enabled him to break Jim Sullivan's points aggregate record (62) for Anglo-Australian tests. By the end of the game Langlands' record had stretched to 77 points and by kicking nine goals he had broken Australia's record in tests against Britain set by Noel Pidding in 1954.

A third penalty to the captain gave Australia a six points cushion after nineteen minutes and three minutes later Morgan intercepted an ill-conceived pass by Flanagan to crash over wide out. A fine goal from Langlands took Australia into a commanding 11-0 lead. In the 29th minute Britain at last woke up when Watson ran twenty yards unchallenged to score a try converted by Price. On the stroke of half-time Hawthorne dropped a goal to send Australia ahead by eight points.

Almost immediately after the resumption Hawthorne struck again, this time cleverly chipping over the British defence where Flanagan failed to retrieve the ball. McDonald, less profligate, was there in a trice and danced round Price for a converted try which knocked the stuffing out of the tiring Lions, who must have been thoroughly disheartened a couple of minutes later when Atkinson stormed 40 yards to touch down only to be recalled for having stepped into touch. After 52 minutes Britain's cause was lost as King finished an Australian attack with a try, again converted. Six minutes later Flanagan replied with a well-worked try and in the 61st minute a goal by Price reduced the arrears to thirteen points. Morgan's second try (65 minutes), Langlands' conversion and a 67th minute drop-goal from Hawthorne stretched the home lead to 30-10. A minute later Laughton scored for the Lions and Price converted but a Langlands penalty (75 minutes) and his conversion of King's second try two minutes from time firmly put the Lions in their place.

The 1970 series was notable in that it was the only one to be played under the four-tackles rule. All subsequent series have been contested under the six-tackles rule, a rule which coincidentally has proved an insuperable obstacle to the British in Ashes series since its inception.

TEST MATCH 77

AT SYDNEY CRICKET GROUND – 20 June, 1970
AUSTRALIA 7 GREAT BRITAIN 28 (HT 2-11)

† R Laird (Mackay)	D Edwards (Castleford)
JC King (St. George) T	† MA Smith (Leeds)
JN McDonald (Manly) G	† S Hynes (Leeds) G
JE Brass (Easts)	F Myler (St. Helens) capt
J Cootes (Wests, Newcastle)	JB Atkinson (Leeds) T
PF Hawthorne (St. George) G	R Millward (Hull KR) 2T,7G
WJ Smith (St. George)	K Hepworth (Castleford)
J Wittenberg (St. George)	D Hartley (Castleford)
B Fitzsimmons (Townsville)	† A Fisher (Bradford N) T
JW Sattler (Souths) capt	CH Watson (St. Helens)
RJ Coote (Souths)	CD Laughton (Wigan)
AH Beetson (Balmain)	† J Thompson (Featherstone R)
C Weiss (Bundaberg)	MJ Reilly (Castleford)
SUB R Fulton (Manly) DNP	SUB MD Shoebottom (Leeds) for Edwards
SUB R Costello (Canterbury) DNP	SUB RA Irving (Oldham) DNP

Referee - D Lancashire (NSW)   Crowd - 60,962   Gate $56,703
Scoring - 0-5 0-7 0-9 2-9 2-11 2-13 4-13 4-18 4-23 4-28 7-28

In a startling reversal of roles from the Brisbane test, Great Britain hammered, sometimes almost literally, Australia to abject defeat. The home team, lacking the injured Langlands, Lynch, Morgan and Walters, gave a lifeless, unimaginative display and at no stage threatened to overtake the lead quickly established by a resolute, hard-tackling and abrasive Lions XIII. Whilst the game never reached great heights Great Britain had every reason to be pleased with their performance especially as they had played a man short for the last 24 minutes following the dismissal of Hynes. What good football there was was entirely played by Britain and in little Roger Millward they had the undoubted hero of the day. The tiny stand-off had a field day and his twenty points equalled the series' record set by Langlands (1963) and Lewis Jones (1954). Apart from his creativity and opportunism in the open, Millward's goal-kicking was infallible, all seven attempts bisecting the posts. He was ably abetted by a tremendously vigorous pack, every member of which excelled. In contrast the Australian pack was innocuous with only the indomitable Coote adding to his laurels.

From the word "go" Britain were on top. Three minutes into the match Reilly put up a tantalising high kick which bounced badly for Laird and there was Millward haring over for a try to which he added the goal. Four minutes later he banged over a 40 yard penalty and in the twelfth minute he sent a 30 yard drop-goal flying between the posts. Australia were clearly rattled and unable to penetrate a dreadnought defence. Their solitary reward during the first half was a 30 yard penalty goal kicked by McDonald in the 27th minute but this was cancelled out three minutes later when that man Millward landed his fourth goal and the Lions went in at the break 11-2 ahead.

Following the restart Australia exerted pressure but both McDonald and Cootes failed with penalty kicks and their exertions came to nought. In the 53rd minute Hynes landed a lovely 35 yard drop-goal but three minutes later the hero turned villain as Mr. Lancashire sent him off for kicking, unsuccessfully, at Beetson, who had just done the Leeds centre considerable facial harm with a late tackle. Two minutes elapsed before Australia scored through a Hawthorne drop-goal but so dominant were the Lions forwards that a guileless home side failed utterly to utilise their numerical advantage, even though they enjoyed a greater share of scrum possession and a penalty count of 12-5 in their favour.

Down to twelve men Britain still contrived to run in three converted tries between the 59th and 76th minutes. The first fell like a gift from the gods as Beetson, having an off-day, allowed the ball to run loose enabling Atkinson to gather and claim a simple try. Millward's second try in the 75th minute was followed a minute later by an extraordinary interception try by hooker Tony Fisher whose one good leg seemed to be all he needed as he hobbled 30 yards for the touch-down.

An ignominious defeat was made fractionally more palatable when King scored an opportunist try two minutes before the end. The match concluded with mayhem on "The Hill" as fights and rioting broke out amongst spectators much the worse for drink and perhaps fuming at the mauling given to their idols.

THE ASHES OF DEFEAT

Great Britain skipper Frank Myler triumphantly bears the "Ashes" cup aloft as team mates chair him in a victory lap of the Sydney Cricket Ground after the tourists' great third Test win.

RUGBY LEAGUE WORLD, August, 1970 Page 35

According to Australia's *Rugby League World* magazine, 1970 represented THE ASHES OF DEFEAT.
A British perspective would indicate THE ASHES OF VICTORY!

TEST MATCH 78

AT SYDNEY CRICKET GROUND – 4 July, 1970
AUSTRALIA 17 GREAT BRITAIN 21 (HT 10-15)

†A McKean (Easts) 7G	MD Shoebottom (Leeds)
JN McDonald (Manly)	MA Smith (Leeds)
R Fulton (Manly)	S Hynes (Leeds) T
JE Brass (Easts)	F Myler (St. Helens) capt
JC King (St. George)	JB Atkinson (Leeds) 2T
PF Hawthorne (St. George) capt	R Millward (Hull KR) T,3G
†R Grant (Souths)	K Hepworth (Castleford)
J Morgan (Easts)	D Hartley (Castleford) T
EA Walters (Souths)	A Fisher (Bradford N)
AH Beetson (Balmain)	CH Watson (St. Helens)
R McCarthy (Souths) T	CD Laughton (Wigan)
R Costello (Canterbury)	J Thompson (Featherstone R)
RJ Coote (Souths)	MJ Reilly (Castleford)
SUB G Lye (Parramatta) DNP	SUB A Hardisty (Castleford) DNP
SUB C Weiss (Bundaberg) DNP	SUB RA Irving (Oldham) DNP

Referee - D Lancashire (NSW)   Crowd - 61,258   Gate - $57,008
Scoring - 2-0 4-0 4-2 6-2 6-7 6-10 6-15 8-15 10-15 12-15 12-18 14-18 17-18 17-21

Despite the score-line there was only one team in this fierce encounter. The four point margin was an insult to the effort and skill of the Lions and a gross exaggeration of Australia's contribution. Five tries to one tells its own story yet, thanks to a miraculous display of goal-kicking from debutant full-back McKean, Britain found themselves staring defeat in the face with only four minutes left. Australia, strangely bereft of attacking ideas and tactically bankrupt, had at last scored a try - on the day, characteristically scrambled - which brought them, more by luck than management, to within a solitary point of the Lions at 17-18. Amidst seething tension McKean took the touch-line conversion which, seemingly laden with justice, failed to find its mark and Britain had won the Ashes for the first time since 1962.

There was still time for three of the greatest Britons to conjure up a stunning *coup de grâce* in the 78th minute. Reilly put Laughton through a gap for the second-rower to burst into the open before linking with Millward who scampered 40 yards to score at the corner, thereby quashing any false hopes nurtured in Australian breasts.

Australia had begun well enough and after eleven minutes led 6-2, McKean potting penalties, all for off-side, in the second, sixth and eleventh minutes, the latter a beauty off the touch-line. In reply Millward had kicked a goal after nine minutes following a scrum infringement. In the twelfth minute, however, the Lions gained a lead they were not to relinquish when Hartley charged down McKean's attempted clearance, gathered and plunged over between the sticks. Millward converted. Eight minutes went by before Britain struck again, Atkinson romping away for a try after intercepting a careless high pass by Beetson. A third try within the space of ten minutes followed as Reilly, a veritable scourge to the green and golds, astutely grubber-kicked for Hynes to score a cleverly worked try, to which Millward added the goal. Further goals to McKean after 24 and 29 minutes wondrously kept Australia in the match and at half-time they trailed by only five points.

Eleven minutes into the second session McKean landed a 45 yard goal but two minutes later a pulverising burst by Shoebottom shredded the home defence and Atkinson was up in support to take the scoring pass. On the hour the inevitable happened as Beetson was dismissed for punching at Watson in a tackle. He had already been cautioned, as had Grant and no fewer than six Lions. Four minutes after the prop's departure McKean landed a massive 50 yard goal to set up the thrilling finale which so nearly robbed Britain of the game and the series.

Frank Myler's 1970 Lions were the last British side to win the Ashes. It would have been rank injustice if McKean's conversion had succeeded for despite the awful hiding in the first test no one seriously doubted that Great Britain had proved much the better combination. That defeat in the first test had been the only one conceded in the whole tour of Australia and New Zealand, making the 1970 Lions the most successful in playing terms of all British touring teams.

Wembley, first test, 1973.
Top: Ken Maddison shatters the British defence. Fellow second-rower Bob McCarthy leaps to follow him.
Bottom: Great Britain hooker Colin Clarke scores his team's second try.

TEST MATCH 79

AT WEMBLEY STADIUM, LONDON – 3 November, 1973
GREAT BRITAIN 21 AUSTRALIA 12 (HT 4-2)

HP Charlton (Salford)	GF Langlands (St. George) capt 3G
CA Sullivan (Hull) capt	R Branighan (Manly) T
S Hynes (Leeds)	R Fulton (Manly) T
C Hesketh (Salford)	G Starling (Balmain)
JB Atkinson (Leeds)	E Goodwin (St. George)
† D Topliss (Wakefield T)	T Pickup (Norths)
S Nash (Featherstone R) DG	T Raudonikis (Wests)
TA Clawson (Oldham) 4G	R O'Reilly (Parramatta)
C Clarke (Wigan) T	EA Walters (Souths)
B Lockwood (Castleford) T	AH Beetson (Easts)
P Lowe (Hull KR) 2T	R McCarthy (Souths)
G Nicholls (St. Helens)	† K Maddison (Cronulla)
R Batten (Leeds)	P Sait (Souths)
SUB D Eckersley (St. Helens) DNP	SUB MW Cronin (Gerringong) DNP
SUB J Mantle (St. Helens) DNP	SUB T Randall (Manly) DNP

Referee - WH Thompson (Huddersfield)   Crowd - 9,874   Gate - £10,581
Scoring - 3-0 3-2 4-2 9-2 14-2 14-7 14-12 16-12 21-12

At Australia's insistence the venue of this test match was moved from Wigan to Wembley. Live television coverage kept the attendance down to paltry proportions but those who did attend saw a magnificent contest worthy of its grandiose setting. Played at a furious pace and in a sporting manner, except for one notable indiscretion by the steely Raudonikis, the test was an eloquent advertisement for the game.

Great Britain never surrendered the lead taken as early as the fourth minute, looked home and dry with a twelve points advantage after 50 minutes but were stunned mid-way through the second half as the Kangaroos blasted back to within two points after scoring ten points in the space of four minutes. There were towering performances from Phil Lowe, Terry Clawson and debutant David Topliss on the British side whilst in Bobby Fulton the Kangaroos had the game's finest three-quarter and in Arthur Beetson an inspirational forward. Overall, however, Britain displayed the more cohesive team work and reaped a just reward.

From the outset Australia's defence seemed uncertain and they were fortunate not to be five points down within the first minute as Clawson, Lowe, Batten and Hynes collaborated sweetly to send Sullivan racing away only to see the winger throw an uncatchable pass to Charlton who must have scored under the posts. A few minutes later, however, there was no let-off for Australia as Charlton, Hynes and Hesketh handled before Lockwood found the gap to send Lowe speeding irresistibly to the line. For the first fifteen minutes it was all Great Britain but gradually Australia came into the game. Only two fine tackles by Atkinson on Starling and Fulton prevented tries and McCarthy actually crossed after good work by Goodwin but was recalled for a forward pass. The pressure paid off in the 29th minute when Langlands kicked a penalty. A drop-goal by Nash ten minutes later completed the first half scoring.

Within ten minutes of the resumption Britain's morale was sky-high as they ripped the Aussie defence to shreds with two well-conceived tries. With a mesmeric sleight of hand Ray Batten "showed" the Australians the ball and persuaded them to look long enough to allow Clarke to storm on to it for a try converted by Clawson. Seven minutes later Nicholls and Topliss combined superbly to get Lockwood in under the posts for another try converted by Clawson. In the process of scoring Lockwood was laid out by Raudonikis - senseless action in more ways than one!

If Britain thought they could relax they were badly mistaken. After 56 minutes Pickup, Sait and Starling combined well before Beetson expertly held off a clutch of tacklers to enable Branighan to score at the flag. Langlands converted magnificently. Another four minutes and the game was poised on a knife-edge. Pickup lofted a high punt to the home line where Hynes and Fulton joined in aerial combat. Hynes fluffed the ball but Fulton did not and dropped out of the sky for the try, improved by Langlands. In the 65th minute Raudonikis stole the ball and Clawson potted the resulting penalty but it was not until the 72nd minute that British palpitations subsided at which point Topliss carved out an opening for Lowe to thunder 30 yards for the clinching try. Clawson's goal was just a little icing on the cake.

TEST MATCH 80

AT HEADINGLEY, LEEDS – 24 November, 1973
GREAT BRITAIN 6 AUSTRALIA 14 (HT 6-4)

HP Charlton (Salford)	†G Eadie (Manly) 5G
CA Sullivan (Hull) capt	L Williamson (Newtown)
S Hynes (Leeds)	G Starling (Balmain)
C Hesketh (Salford)	R Branighan (Manly)
JB Atkinson (Leeds)	†D Waite (Wests, Wollongong)
D Topliss (Wakefield T)	R Fulton (Manly) DG
S Nash (Featherstone R)	T Raudonikis (Wests)
TA Clawson (Oldham) 3G	R O'Reilly (Parramatta)
C Clarke (Wigan)	EA Walters (Souths)
B Lockwood (Castleford)	AH Beetson (Easts)
P Lowe (Hull KR)	R McCarthy (Souths) capt T
J Mantle (St. Helens)	G Stevens (Souths)
R Batten (Leeds)	P Sait (Souths)
†SUB D Eckersley (St. Helens) for Topliss	SUB D Ward (Wests, Newcastle) DNP
SUB CJ Dixon (Salford) for Mantle	SUB K Maddison (Cronulla) for McCarthy

Referee - WH Thompson (Huddersfield)   Crowd - 16,674   Gate - £11,878.90

Scoring - 2-0 4-0 4-2 4-4 6-4 6-9 6-11 6-12 6-14

Historically Headingley held no hope for Australia whose dismal record in test matches there was played nine, lost nine. However, there was a precedent for Australia of victory over Great Britain at Leeds for three years earlier in a brutal World Cup Final seven of the current Kangaroos had helped Australia to a momentous, almost murderous, triumph. The Headingley test of 1973 did not degenerate to the depths of that 1970 debacle but it was a rugged affair, replete with relentless, even reckless, tackling. Gone was the breathtaking movement of the Wembley test and sustained open play was at a premium. Only one try was scored and that was hotly disputed. Yet there was no doubting that Australia won worthily.

A gale force wind blew throughout the match and when McCarthy elected to play into it there were mutterings about his sanity. Events proved his judgement correct but he must have wondered if he had done the right thing as Australia went four points behind within eight minutes. Only four minutes had elapsed when O'Reilly fouled Topliss and Clawson used the wind as his ally to land a 52 yard goal followed by another successful shot in the eighth minute after Beetson had impeded Lockwood at a play-the-ball. A similar offence on Starling five minutes later enabled Graham Eadie, a nineteen-year-old prodigy, to pull back two points. The game was remarkable in that every kick at goal was successful even under such blustery conditions. After half an hour Australia levelled when Mantle's high tackle on McCarthy gave Eadie simple retribution but two minutes later Clawson restored Britain's lead with a forty-yarder following a scrum offence. However, things began to look ominous as Australia took the game to Britain. McCarthy (twice), Stevens and Raudonikis were all stopped feet from the line and Fulton actually crossed but lost the ball in Batten's tackle. The home side had never looked like scoring a try and a mere two points advantage and the gale to face did not augur well.

By the time the second half was seven minutes old Britain's worst fears were realised and the game was decided. Three minutes into the half O'Reilly's hefty charge opened the British defence and there was McCarthy striding away some thirty yards from the line. Two yards short Charlton seemed to have held him but the big man's momentum allowed him to slide over. Eadie's goal made it 9-6 and Britain had a mountain to climb but not the equipment necessary. McCarthy had dislocated his collar-bone in touching down and took no further part in the tour. In the 47th minute Lockwood was sent off for a late tackle on Fulton and Britain's position was hopeless although with twelve men they prevented any further Australian tries thanks to Clarke's fine hooking and the injection of substitutes Eckersley and Dixon. Britain persisted in tackling high and paid the penalty in a literal sense in the 68th minute, Eadie landing a 45 yard goal. Two minutes later Fulton popped over a drop-goal and Eadie's fifth goal shortly afterwards brought the final score to 14-6, a score-line which flattered the losers.

Australia had learned their lessons from Wembley. Britain's reliance on Lowe had been noted and he was met by droves of tacklers every time he had the ball, whilst Fulton's move to stand-off was a master-stroke. O'Reilly, Beetson and McCarthy ruled the forward exchanges to the extent that the home backs, Nash and Charlton apart, were mere shadows of the Wembley wizards.

TEST MATCH 81

AT WILDERSPOOL, WARRINGTON – 1 December, 1973
GREAT BRITAIN 5 AUSTRALIA 15 (HT 2-12)

HP Charlton (Salford)	G Eadie (Manly)
MA Smith (Leeds)	L Williamson (Newtown)
S Hynes (Leeds)	G Starling (Balmain) T
C Hesketh (Salford)	R Branighan (Manly)
CA Sullivan (Hull) capt	D Waite (Wests, Wollongong)
D Eckersley (St. Helens)	R Fulton (Manly) T
R Millward (Hull KR) T,G	T Raudonikis (Wests) capt
TA Clawson (Oldham)	R O'Reilly (Parramatta)
C Clarke (Wigan)	EA Walters (Souths) T
M Harrison (Hull)	AH Beetson (Easts)
P Lowe (Hull KR)	K Maddison (Cronulla) 2T
G Nicholls (St. Helens)	G Stevens (Souths)
CD Laughton (Widnes)	P Sait (Souths)
SUB D Watkins (Salford) for Millward	SUB T Pickup (Norths) for Eadie
SUB CJ Dixon (Salford) for Clawson	SUB J Lang (Easts, Brisbane) DNP

Referee - WH Thompson (Huddersfield)   Crowd - 10,019   Gate - £6,419.50
Scoring - 0-3 0-6 2-6 2-9 2-12 5-12 5-15

Eighteen tons of straw had been laid to protect the Wilderspool pitch and had the game been anything other than an Ashes decider there is little doubt that it would never have taken place. Arctic cold had frozen the surface and left icy patches and tractor tyres had bequeathed a legacy of solid jagged ruts. It was a masochist's dream! The fact that Australia won so convincingly was perhaps perversely a reflection of their unfamiliarity with such alien conditions. There was a widespread impression that many of the British players, knowing full well the perils of playing on such a dangerous surface, were something less than whole-hearted in their approach. The Kangaroos, wisely commissioning rubber studs which gave them a better footing, simply played as they might on a rock-hard pitch back home and made mince-meat of their opponents to win the Ashes for the third time in a row in England.

Australia got off to a flying start. Clawson had possession near the left touch-line at half-way when he tried to short-pass inside to Eckersley. Fulton, playing in the town of his birth, became the happiest if most unpopular of Warringtonians, as he stole in for the interception to streak unchallenged for a try at the corner. Twelve minutes later Branighan was almost over at the corner, the ball was brought back inside and Raudonikis, Australia's third captain in the series, sent Maddison crashing over. Quarter of an hour gone and Australia led 6-0. Millward kicked a penalty after nineteen minutes but there was little respite for Britain as the kamikaze Kangaroos tackled and ran with incredible commitment. Twenty-nine minutes had elapsed when Eadie made a terrific burst from his own line to develop a passage of play which ended with Maddison, unstoppable on the day, slashing clean through three tackles in a twenty yard dash to the line for a sensational try. Minutes later Raudonikis was stopped in the last stride by Charlton after a 35 yard surge and two minutes before half-time the Kangaroos struck again as Maddison sent out a long pass to Eadie on the burst for the full-back to send Starling over.

Five minutes after the break British aspirations rose momentarily as splendid handling and support between Hesketh, Dixon and Lowe enabled Millward to scoot over for a finely worked try. The Australians simply came back stronger and it took two courageous tackles by Millward on the rampaging Stevens and Maddison, who were reducing the home forwards to anonymity, to keep the line intact. A try had to come and in the 52nd minute it did. A furious raid featuring some inspired handling from Branighan, Eadie and Beetson ended in Walters crossing for the final try. It was just as well that Eadie and Branighan could not land a goal from their seven opportunities or the home side would have been swamped. Only Millward and Laughton made any impression on the Kangaroos who played as if they were totally impervious to the numbing conditions. There could be no excuses for Britain who had a scrum advantage of 16-8 and a penalty count of 7-4 in their favour. They simply had no answer to the power and guile of man-of-the-series Arthur Beetson and his fearless pack. Tommy Raudonikis was a real thorn in the British side, constantly breaking from the rucks and providing an ideal link between pack and backs.

Big Jim Mills, a Lion in 1974 and 1979, lets an opponent know he's about!

Wembley, first test, 1973. Great Britain prop Brian Lockwood canters over for a try.

TEST MATCH 82

AT LANG PARK, BRISBANE – 15 June, 1974
AUSTRALIA 12 GREAT BRITAIN 6 (HT 7-2)

GF Langlands (St. George) capt 4G	HP Charlton (Salford)
D Waite (Cronulla)	D Redfearn (Bradford N)
R Fulton (Manly) DG	D Watkins (Salford) G
MW Cronin (Gerringong)	C Hesketh (Salford) capt
† W Orr (Wests, Brisbane) T	† JC Bevan (Warrington)
† G Richardson (Wests, Brisbane)	R Millward (Hull KR)
T Raudonikis (Wests)	S Nash (Featherstone R)
R O'Reilly (Parramatta)	TA Clawson (Oldham) 2G
EA Walters (Easts)	JH Bridges (Featherstone R)
AH Beetson (Easts)	† J Mills (Widnes)
P Sait (Souths)	CJ Dixon (Salford)
† R Higgs (Nambour)	J Thompson (Featherstone R)
RJ Coote (Easts)	G Nicholls (St. Helens)
SUB R Branighan (Manly) DNP	SUB D Eckersley (St. Helens) for Bridges
SUB J Lang (Easts, Brisbane) DNP	SUB JD Gray (Wigan) for Nicholls

Referee - D Lancashire (Toowoomba)   Crowd - 30,280   Gate - $56,155
Scoring - 2-0 2-2 4-2 7-2 7-4 9-4 11-4 11-6 12-6

Australia proved the better of two thoroughly unimaginative sides to win a drab, lacklustre and pedestrian match which fell far short of the standards expected of an Anglo-Australian test, either in terms of entertainment or intensity. It was hardly the best of fare to set before Prime Minister Gough Whitlam, the first holder of that office to attend a test match in Queensland.

Australia never trailed yet could only score a solitary try whilst Britain hardly ever threatened to cross the Australian line and on those rare occasions when they did create chances they were accompanied by bad luck at best and ineptitude at worst.

After three minutes Britain fell behind when Langlands kicked a penalty following an infringement by Nicholls but three minutes later Clawson equalised with a goal from 40 yards for a scrum offence. The game meandered aimlessly, devoid of incident, until a well-judged kick from Nicholls caused a few palpitations. The ball came to earth over the Australian line where Waite and Langlands decided it would run dead. Instead it mischievously sat up offering the chasing Bevan and Hesketh hope of a touchdown but trickled out of play just before they arrived. Fulton raised Australian hopes when he raced through and chipped over the defence but was pole-axed by Nicholls. Langlands exacted retribution by landing the resultant penalty and a minute before the interval the Australian lead was extended when a copy-book try issued to debutant winger Warren Orr after an orthodox chain passing movement in which half-a-dozen players handled. It was the only successful movement of the match.

Eight minutes into the second period the Lions reduced the Australian lead to 7-4 when Clawson landed a massive goal from over 50 yards and for a while Britain held the upper hand. Australia were next to score, however, Langlands kicking his third penalty-goal after Fulton had been fouled by Dixon and in the 61st minute, following the first scrum of the half, he potted a fourth to stretch Australia's advantage to 11-4. It was then that Britain came nearest to scoring a try. Thompson did well to unleash Millward whose pass to Nash saw the scrum-half diving to touch down under the posts only to lose the ball in a marvellous last-ditch tackle by Ron Coote. There was a small consolation in the 64th minute when Watkins kicked a simple goal following a scrum infringement. There was a scare for Australia when Hesketh, now operating at loose-forward because of injuries to Bridges, Nicholls and Redfearn, got Charlton away almost from the British line. The speedy full-back easily got past Langlands and appeared to have a clear field but was grounded by Bob Fulton at half-way. It was Fulton who put the issue beyond doubt by dropping a goal four minutes from time.

Beetson, Coote and O'Reilly foraged hard for the winners but lacked support and the Australian backs barely saw the ball despite an equal share of possession, stand-off Richardson receiving hardly any passes from his scrum-half. For the Lions only Nash and Millward shone - in defence, a damning indictment of the forward effort.

TEST MATCH 83

AT SYDNEY CRICKET GROUND – 6 July, 1974
AUSTRALIA 11 GREAT BRITAIN 16 (HT 3-10)

G Eadie (Manly)	HP Charlton (Salford)
D Waite (Cronulla)	† LP Dyl (Leeds)
R Fulton (Manly) T	D Eckersley (St. Helens)
MW Cronin (Gerringong) G	C Hesketh (Salford) capt
W Orr (Wests, Brisbane)	R Millward (Hull KR)
G Richardson (Wests, Brisbane)	K Gill (Salford) T
T Raudonikis (Wests)	S Nash (Featherstone R)
R O'Reilly (Parramatta)	J Mills (Widnes)
J Lang (Easts, Brisbane) T	JD Gray (Wigan) 3G,DG
AH Beetson (Easts) capt	J Thompson (Featherstone R)
P Sait (Souths)	CJ Dixon (Salford) T
G Stevens (Souths)	† E Chisnall (St. Helens) T
RJ Coote (Easts) T	G Nicholls (St. Helens)
SUB R Branighan (Manly) for Eadie	SUB A Bates (Dewsbury) DNP
SUB R McCarthy (Souths) for O'Reilly	† SUB S Norton (Castleford) for Gray

Referee - K Page (NSW) Crowd - 48,006 Gate - $83,095
Scoring - 3-0 3-5 3-10 3-15 3-16 6-16 11-16

Following their powder-puff performance at Brisbane no one outside the British party believed in the miracle of a Lions victory but a patched-up, make-shift, injury-ridden Great Britain shook the Rugby League world rigid with a display of skill and spirit to rank with the "Rorke's Drift Test" of 1914 and the Brisbane epic of 1958. Dyl, Eckersley, Millward and Thompson were all conscripts to their positions and in John Gray Britain fielded a third choice hooker who only a year before had been playing Rugby Union.

If Australia were suffering from complacency they must have felt justified when in the eighth minute from a close-in scrum Raudonikis served Fulton who skirted the rising packs on the blind-side, found a non-existent cover and touched down at his leisure. It seemed like Brisbane revisited but Britain's genteel approach dramatically altered. Three minutes after Fulton's score Jim Mills flattened Aussie tackling-machine Gary Stevens and lit the fuse for a monumental blow-up at a scrum in the fourteenth minute. When the dust settled John Gray was taken off having been kicked in the face. He returned, five stitches in his forehead now swathed in bandages and one eye rapidly closing. Britain played for twelve minutes short-handed during which time Australia, with almost total possession, must have sensed it was not to be their day as Britain refused to budge an inch. Gray returned to play the game of his life and when he was led off for good in the 75th minute with a dislocated finger his side was safe at 16-6.

In a devastating period of eight minutes either side of the half-time hooter Great Britain masterfully contrived to score three tries behind the sticks, all converted by Gray, thereby rocketing from 0-3 down to a 15-3 lead. All were the results of clever combination and clinical finishing. In the 36th minute Nicholls stormed through the middle off a pass from Gill and fed Nash who calmly turned the ball the other way for Eric Chisnall to mark his test debut with a superb try. Three minutes later Gray created a gap for Chisnall to exploit. Hesketh shot up in support and Dixon took the final pass to touch down. Any plans Australia had for a second half rally were scuppered in the 44th minute as Britain's half-backs worked a hypnotic scissors move, Gill ghosting untouched through a static defence. Gray, exacting full retribution for his injuries, dropped a neat goal in the 51st minute and the tries scored by Lang (70 minutes) and Coote (76 minutes), the latter converted by Cronin, were merely a face-saving exercise.

The Lions' forwards rose to great heights as they harried, covered and contested every inch, orchestrated expertly by Nash and Gill and ably supported by their unlikely-looking three-quarters. Australia's play was unimaginative and lethargic, only beginning to liven up when Bob McCarthy substituted for O'Reilly, playing his final test, in the 52nd minute. They were unlucky to lose Graham Eadie after half an hour when the full-back broke his nose in a collision with David Waite but nothing should detract from one of the gutsiest performances of a British XIII in modern times.

TEST MATCH 84

AT SYDNEY CRICKET GROUND – 20 July, 1974
AUSTRALIA 22 GREAT BRITAIN 18 (HT 10-16)

GF Langlands (St. George) capt T,5G	HP Charlton (Salford)
L Williamson (Newtown) T	†MCR Richards (Salford) T
R Fulton (Manly)	LP Dyl (Leeds) T
MW Cronin (Gerringong)	C Hesketh (Salford) capt
R Branighan (Manly)	JC Bevan (Warrington)
T Pickup (Norths)	K Gill (Salford)
T Raudonikis (Wests)	S Nash (Featherstone R)
AH Beetson (Easts)	TA Clawson (Oldham)
R Turner (Cronulla)	JD Gray (Wigan) 6G
J O'Neill (Manly)	J Thompson (Featherstone R)
G Stevens (Souths)	CJ Dixon (Salford)
R McCarthy (Souths) T	E Chisnall (St. Helens)
RJ Coote (Easts) T	G Nicholls (St. Helens)
SUB W Orr (Wests, Brisbane) DNP	SUB R Millward (Hull KR) for Gill
SUB P Sait (Souths) DNP	†SUB P Rose (Hull KR) for Dixon

Referee - K Page (NSW) Crowd - 55,505 Gate - $91,225
Scoring - 3-0 3-5 5-5 5-7 10-7 10-9 10-11 10-16 13-16 15-16 17-16 22-16 22-18

The 1974 series was perhaps the most fluctuating of all Ashes series and the final test saw the pendulum of fortune swinging more violently than ever. Britain, favourites before the first test, labelled no-hopers after it, risen from the dead to glory in the second test, now entered the deciding test with soaring spirits and at least an even chance, though it was not general knowledge that five of their number played with the aid of pain-killing injections.

At half-time the Lions led 16-10 despite having to face a strong wind and the Ashes looked to be within their grasp but in a fast, entertaining match Australia again upset the odds coming back like champions as British fitness and stamina gave out. The teams were never separated by more than six points and the lead changed hands on no fewer than five occasions.

Two men gave outstanding performances. John Gray landed six goals from six attempts in one of the most majestic displays of place-kicking ever seen on the SCG. Gray also won the scrums and played like a demon in the loose but the darling of the crowd was Graeme Langlands, playing in his twelfth and final test against Britain. His thirteen points brought his total in Ashes tests to 104, a record unsurpassed until 1992. It was no wonder he was chaired from the field in triumph at the close. It was also a test finale for fellow greats McCarthy and Coote as well as O'Neill, Williamson and Pickup.

Australia led after nine minutes, Williamson slipping an outside pass to Langlands for "Changa" to skirt the touch-line before passing back inside to Williamson who touched down. Nine minutes later Charlton made a telling break which ended in Hesketh being grounded just short but from the play-the-ball Dyl forced his way over for a converted try. Langlands and Gray in turn landed penalties before disaster struck the Lions in the 27th minute. Gill, this time much subdued by tight marking, passed straight to McCarthy for a gift try improved by Langlands and Australia led 10-7. Two monster penalties by Gray edged the Lions ahead and in the 39th minute Gray kicked high to Branighan who spilled the ball. Richards was up in a flash and toed the ball forward inches inside the touch-line to score at the flag. Gray, kicking into a roaring wind, converted with aplomb.

Within eighteen minutes of the restart the game had turned upside-down as the Lions pack faded. In the 48th minute Beetson and Coote displayed consummate skill and timing to send Langlands diving in at the corner and eight minutes later "Changa" landed a penalty to bring up his Ashes century of points. Another penalty goal to Langlands put Australia into the lead and in the 58th minute came the killer score. Fulton broke away beautifully and worked a sweet scissors with Cronin who sent Coote racing over wide out for the best try of the match. Langlands kicked a fine goal and the only further score was a 72nd minute penalty goal to Gray.

Australia had now won five of the last six series. It was going to be a long time before Britain mounted a serious challenge to the supremacy of the green and gold ....

TEST MATCH 85

AT CENTRAL PARK, WIGAN – 21 October, 1978
GREAT BRITAIN 9 AUSTRALIA 15 (HT 6-6)

GA Fairbairn (Wigan) 3G	G Eadie (Manly)
S Wright (Widnes)	K Boustead (Innisfail) T
† E Hughes (Widnes)	SF Rogers (Cronulla)
† E Cunningham (St. Helens)	MW Cronin (Parramatta) 4G
JC Bevan (Warrington) T	C Anderson (Canterbury)
R Millward (Hull KR) capt	R Fulton (Easts) capt T,DG
S Nash (Salford)	T Raudonikis (Wests)
J Thompson (Bradford N)	G Olling (Parramatta)
DJ Ward (Leeds)	M Krilich (Manly)
P Rose (Hull KR)	C Young (St. George)
G Nicholls (St. Helens)	† GM Gerard (Parramatta)
L Casey (Hull KR)	RW Reddy (St. George)
S Norton (Hull)	RA Price (Parramatta)
SUB JS Holmes (Leeds) for Cunningham	SUB AS Thompson (Manly) DNP
SUB PG Hogan (Barrow) for Casey	SUB S Kneen (Cronulla) DNP

Referee - R Campbell (Widnes) Crowd - 17,644 Gate - £21,300

Scoring - 0-2 0-4 2-4 4-4 6-4 6-6 6-7 9-7 9-10 9-15

In a test full of niggliness and tension the play never rose to great heights, defences being so dominant that the first try did not arrive until quarter of an hour before the final whistle. The turning point of the game occurred after 55 minutes when the rival scrum-halves, Raudonikis and Nash, were sent off for fighting. Nash, the lynch-pin of the home team, was missed more than his opponent but all things considered Australia were the better side, having more to offer on attack and finishing the stronger. The niggles spilled over into the post-match recriminations as Britain accused two of the Australians of biting whilst the Kangaroos complained about their opponents' head-hunting. Certainly it was not a game for the faint-hearts. Nash suffered a broken nose and Millward was concussed, whilst a British forward was clearly seen to have kicked Ray Price on the head.

The first half was eminently forgettable with all the scoring confined to penalty goals. Britain did well to recover from going four points down in the first eight minutes to level at 6-6 by the break though they never looked like scoring a try in the first 40 minutes. The greasy turf militated against open play and what chances there were fell to Australia. Great tackling by Jimmy Thompson, playing his 21st and final test, and Nash, who saved two tries in stopping Cronin and Raudonikis, was all that kept Britain in touch.

Following the dismissal of the half-backs Australia began to stretch the home defence to its limit. Rogers broke through deep in his own half and served Reddy who made a 30 yard cross-field run to release Anderson. Anderson left the defence behind as he shot from half-way for the touch-down only to be recalled, much to his disgust, for a forward pass. Still Australia would not be deterred and Reddy, the best forward on the field, drove deep into the British "25" from where Fulton coolly dropped a goal to put the Kangaroos 7-6 up after 62 minutes. Four minutes later Cronin threw a bad pass on the half-way line. Bevan got a foot to it and gave chase. Hacking on once more he found himself in a desperate race with Eadie and as the ball crossed the Australian goal-line the pair dived in unison but it was Bevan who got the vital touch and improbably Britain took the lead.

Intead of thoroughly demoralising the Kangaroos the score seemed to rejuvenate them for in the 70th minute Rogers and Gerard cracked the defence for Reddy and Cronin to send Boustead flying past the remnants of opposition for a try which broke the hearts of the home XIII. Five minutes from time Eadie steamrollered through before feeding Fulton who forced his way over despite the resistance of three tacklers. Cronin's conversion put the game out of Britain's reach. It was fitting that Fulton should score the winning try as he had been the major source of trouble to the British side, bombarding them with pin-point high kicks, organising the back play and generally looking the likeliest man to produce something special in a grim, uncompromising encounter.

Top: Sydney, second test, 1974. The scourge of many Great Britain XIIIs, Bob Fulton loses the ball.
Rival hookers John Gray and Johnny Lang await the outcome.
Bottom: Odsal, second test, 1978. Aussie centre Steve Rogers tries to foil a kick by Roger Millward whilst
John Joyner prepares to chase.

TEST MATCH 86

AT ODSAL STADIUM, BRADFORD – 5 November, 1978
GREAT BRITAIN 18 AUSTRALIA 14 (HT 11-4)

GA Fairbairn (Wigan) 6G	G Eadie (Manly)
S Wright (Widnes) 2T	K Boustead (Innisfail)
† JD Joyner (Castleford)	SF Rogers (Cronulla) T,2G
LP Dyl (Leeds)	MW Cronin (Parramatta) 2G
JB Atkinson (Leeds)	C Anderson (Canterbury)
R Millward (Hull KR) capt	R Fulton (Easts) capt
S Nash (Salford)	T Raudonikis (Wests)
J Mills (Widnes)	G Olling (Parramatta)
A Fisher (Bradford N)	M Krilich (Manly)
B Lockwood (Hull KR)	C Young (St. George)
G Nicholls (St. Helens)	GM Gerard (Parramatta)
P Lowe (Hull KR)	RW Reddy (St. George)
S Norton (Hull)	RA Price (Parramatta) T
SUB JS Holmes (Leeds) for Millward	† SUB AS Thompson (Manly) for Cronin
SUB P Rose (Hull KR) for Norton	SUB LW Boyd (Manly) for Gerard

Referee - MJ Naughton (Widnes)   Crowd - 26,447   Gate £27,258
Scoring - 0-2 2-2 4-2 4-4 6-4 11-4 13-4 18-4 18-9 18-11 18-14

For the first time in England an Anglo-Australian test match was played on a Sunday and despite live television coverage of the entire game Odsal housed the largest crowd for five years at a Rugby League match outside Wembley. Most of the spectators undoubtedly expected to see the super-fit Kangaroos clinch the Ashes, especially as Great Britain had selected a team rather unkindly dubbed as a "Dad's Army" outfit with a front row carrying a combined age of 101 years. Much to the delight of the British fans and the chagrin of the Aussies it was the display of the geriatric Mills, Fisher and Lockwood which formed the basis for a remarkable British victory. Lockwood, a veteran of the Sydney Premiership, played a masterfully controlled game, directing operations astutely and making play for his supports. He was unquestionably the man Australia feared and he was singled out for severe treatment. Two of the goals kicked by Fairbairn were from penalties awarded for vicious fouls on Lockwood. Fisher, at 35, played a remarkable game, winning the scrums, covering relentlessly and driving hard at the set-pieces. Mills was simply the "Big Jim" Mills fans either loved or hated, prepared to take on the entire Kangaroo pack and thereby distract them from playing too much football.

The first half was almost a replica of the try-less affair at Wigan with just three penalties to Fairbairn against a couple by Cronin before Britain struck dramatically and crucially just before the hooter went. George Nicholls, who had a storming match, crashed down the centre-field before slipping a pass to Millward who made ground quickly and was then engulfed in an avalanche of Australian tacklers but not before he had put in a wickedly precise kick to the left corner flag. The ball came to rest in the in-goal area and Stuart Wright outpaced the cover for a beautifully worked try. Fairbairn's kick from the touch-line sneaked over and Britain had a grip on the game. Millward's reward for his artistry was a calf injury which ended his involvement in the match. Fortunately, his replacement John Holmes took over where Millward left off, combining to good effect with Nash, again the best back on view, and his three-quarters.

A penalty goal by Fairbairn put Britain further ahead five minutes after the break and Australia were unable to counter an inspired home XIII who sealed the game after 69 minutes with a gem of a try. Again it was Nicholls who did the initial damage in puncturing the defence. Joyner took his pass and swerved sinuously in and out of tacklers before firing out a basketball pass to Wright who flew over at the flag. Another superb conversion by Fairbairn gave Britain an unassailable 18-4 lead. It was fortunate, however, that there were only ten minutes left to play for inevitably the Kangaroos' fitness began to tell. Five minutes from time Fulton put up a bomb which Fairbairn dropped over his line for Price to grab a fortuitous try. Two minutes later Fulton was obstructed and Rogers kicked the resultant penalty and on the stroke of time Raudonikis and Reddy combined to send Rogers over at the corner.

Eighty minutes elapsed not a second too soon for a breathless Britain. Their victory was well merited. Skill tempered with steel had overcome fitness fuelled with fury. Few could imagine that Britain would not beat Australia again for ten years, skill and steel being in short supply in the interim.

TEST MATCH 87

AT HEADINGLEY, LEEDS – 18 November, 1978
GREAT BRITAIN 6 AUSTRALIA 23 (HT 0-19)

GA Fairbairn (Wigan)	G Eadie (Manly)
S Wright (Widnes)	K Boustead (Innisfail)
JD Joyner (Castleford)	SF Rogers (Cronulla)
JC Bevan (Warrington) T	MW Cronin (Parramatta) 5G
JB Atkinson (Leeds)	C Anderson (Canterbury)
R Millward (Hull KR) capt T	R Fulton (Easts) capt DG
S Nash (Salford)	T Raudonikis (Wests) T
J Mills (Widnes)	C Young (St. George)
A Fisher (Bradford N)	GC Peponis (Canterbury) T
† V Farrar (Hull)	R Morris (Easts, Brisbane)
G Nicholls (St. Helens)	GM Gerard (Parramatta) T
P Lowe (Hull KR)	LW Boyd (Wests) T
S Norton (Hull)	RA Price (Parramatta)
SUB JS Holmes (Leeds) for Atkinson	SUB AS Thompson (Manly) for Rogers
SUB P Rose (Hull KR) for Fisher	SUB I Thomson (Manly) for Boyd

Referee - MJ Naughton (Widnes)   Crowd - 29,627   Gate - £34,864
Scoring - 0-2 0-4 0-9 0-14 0-19 0-20 3-20 6-20 6-23

Australia won their third successive Ashes series with a display of power and discipline which completely demoralised Great Britain who at no time threatened to wrest the lead from Australia, taken as early as the third minute. The home team had overwhelming possession, having an advantage in the scrums of 13-6 and a penalty count of 15-9 in their favour. They were, however, bereft of strength, imagination and resolution. In the end they were so thoroughly frustrated that some of their number resorted to tactics which brought no credit to themselves or their country.

With only three minutes gone Fisher was penalised for stiff-arming Fulton and Cronin banged over a goal from 30 yards. It was the type of tackle all too prevalent from the British XIII on the day. In the thirteenth minute Fulton kicked high, Fairbairn knocked the ball forward and Millward picked up in an off-side position, enabling Cronin to pot a simple penalty. Eight minutes later Fulton kicked deep to set up the position from which Peponis cheekily bored through for a try from a play-the-ball. Cronin's conversion emphasized the cost to Britain of three missed penalties by Fairbairn, whose kicking in this test was the antithesis of his great marksmanship at Odsal.

Britain then laid siege to the Australian line for the best part of quarter of an hour without gaining any tangible reward but in the process lost the services of John Atkinson who was stretchered off with a knee injury after half an hour. Having absorbed all that Britain could throw at them the Kangaroos bounced back to destroy any thoughts of victory the home team harboured with a devastating burst of scoring in the last 60 seconds of the half. Raudonikis, adjudged the man of the match, opened up a gap to send Boyd tearing in from the "25" and was again the architect in the move which ended in Gerard careering 40 yards for a breath-taking touch-down. Both tries were goaled by Cronin and Australia had effectively won the match and the Ashes.

A minute after the resumption Fulton dropped a goal which struck the upright but it was no more than he deserved as he led his men to victory in sterling style. Australia appeared to ease off a little having established a twenty points cushion and Britain took advantage to stage a brief rally scoring two tries within four minutes. Millward claimed the first after racing over from Lowe's pass in the 54th minute. Fairbairn, luck having deserted him completely, saw his kick hit the post and bounce the wrong way. Joyner and Holmes then combined well to send Bevan plunging in at the corner. The six points, however, were merely flea-bites to the Kangaroos. Eadie, a huge success, crossed but his claim for a try was rejected because of a forward pass. Raudonikis made no mistake after 62 minutes, charging round the blind-side of a scrum and contemptuously shrugging off Norton to score a try which was a just reward for a performance equally as aggressive but markedly more constructive than in the previous tests. He had been merely the best of a team of totally committed footballers whereas Britain could not claim to have had a solitary player who enhanced his reputation.

TEST MATCH 88

AT LANG PARK, BRISBANE – 16 June, 1979
AUSTRALIA 35 GREAT BRITAIN 0 (HT 16-0)

G Eadie (Manly)	† J Woods (Leigh)
K Boustead (Easts) 2T	† D Barends (Bradford N)
SF Rogers (Cronulla)	JD Joyner (Castleford)
MW Cronin (Parramatta) 10G	E Hughes (Widnes)
† LJ Corowa (Balmain) T	† R Mathias (St. Helens)
AS Thompson (Manly)	JS Holmes (Leeds)
T Raudonikis (Wests)	† G Stephens (Castleford)
C Young (St. George)	J Mills (Widnes)
GC Peponis (Canterbury) capt	DJ Ward (Leeds)
R Morris (Balmain)	† T Skerrett (Wakefield T)
LW Boyd (Wests)	CD Laughton (Widnes) capt
RW Reddy (St. George)	G Nicholls (St. Helens)
RA Price (Parramatta) 2T	S Norton (Hull)
SUB A McMahon (Balmain) DNP	† SUB S Evans (Featherstone R) for Joyner
SUB R Brown (Wests) DNP	SUB PG Hogan (Hull KR) for Mills

Referee - E Ward (Queensland)   Crowd - 23,051   Gate - $121,092
Scoring - 2-0 5-0 7-0 9-0 14-0 16-0 21-0 26-0 31-0 33-0 35-0

Hammered at Headingley in 1978, humiliated at Brisbane in 1979, the British Lion had a distinctly sheepish look after this latest *débâcle* which represented the biggest test defeat once-Great Britain had suffered in Australia. It was also the first time Britain had been nilled in a test in Australia and the first time a test Down-Under had been played under flood-lights. Most onlookers thought that Britain would have been better playing in the dark - at least their embarrassment at such a shoddy show would have been covered.
Without detracting too much from a super Australian performance there was no escaping from the fact that Britain were simply too bad to be true. They appeared to have no mastery of the game's basic skills and their handling and support play were abysmal. Most importantly their tackling was terrible. When it was not sloppy it was crude. Ray Price's comment on this aspect of the British play was terse but true - *I just kept ducking.* Another critic remarked, *Boustead bobbed and weaved under arms hung out like lines of washing.*
At best the British played two-man rugby whilst Australia, supremely fit and confident, ran like stags, tackled like demons and backed each other up in droves. Mick Cronin kicked goals from all over the park, landing ten out of eleven attempts to equal Lewis Jones' record for Anglo-Australian tests set a quarter of a century earlier. His twenty points also equalled the record shared by Jones, Langlands and Millward. For Jim Mills, said by one observer to *have undergone a personality change,* and Doug Laughton it was a very inauspicious good-bye to test football.
The nightmare began for Britain after three minutes when Cronin hammered a 40 yard penalty over the bar. The first try unfolded after nine minutes. Peponis and Boyd made the initial incisions before orthodox cross-field passing enabled Boustead to cross unmolested wide out. Cronin missed the conversion, his solitary failure, but landed a penalty eight minutes later. In a rare British attack Holmes and Joyner got Barends over but the try was disallowed and Australia compounded the Lions' misery when Rogers received a palpably forward pass from Peponis before putting Boustead over by the flag. Cronin's touch-line kick was a beauty and his magic boot provided another two points from a penalty before the half-time hooter allowed the tourists some respite.
Britain could do nothing right. In the 47th minute Nicholls at last penetrated the home defence with a powerful burst before passing to Norton who in turn tried to serve Mathias some 50 yards from Australia's line. The pass never reached the wing as Eadie intercepted and thundered away down the touch-line before passing inside for Australia to swing the ball along the line in style until Rogers gave the final scoring pass to Corowa. It was a magnificent effort, fit for a match much better than this. Price, the outstanding figure of the match, scored two tries, one straight from a scrum, before Australia eased up and the last scores of the massacre were two Cronin penalties. The final indignity befell Britain when debutant forward, Trevor Skerrett, the defensive bastion of the British pack, was sent off four minutes from time.

Sydney, second test, 1979. *Top:* Rival centres John Joyner (GB) and Mick Cronin brace themselves to clash. Rod Reddy looms in the background. *Bottom:* Lions captain George Nicholls steps through Rod Morris' tackle. Len Casey watches the action.

TEST MATCH 89

AT SYDNEY CRICKET GROUND – 30 June, 1979
AUSTRALIA 24 GREAT BRITAIN 16 (HT 17-4)

G Eadie (Manly)	GA Fairbairn (Wigan)
K Boustead (Easts)	D Barends (Bradford N)
SF Rogers (Cronulla) T	JD Joyner (Castleford) T
MW Cronin (Parramatta) 2T,6G	J Woods (Leigh) 5G
LJ Corowa (Balmain)	E Hughes (Widnes) T
AS Thompson (Manly)	JS Holmes (Leeds)
T Raudonikis (Wests)	G Stephens (Castleford)
C Young (St. George)	G Nicholls (St. Helens) capt
GC Peponis (Canterbury) capt	DJ Ward (Leeds)
R Morris (Balmain)	T Skerrett (Wakefield T)
LW Boyd (Wests)	L Casey (Bradford N)
RW Reddy (St. George) T	†J Grayshon (Bradford N)
RA Price (Parramatta)	†M Adams (Widnes)
SUB A McMahon (Balmain) DNP	SUB S Evans (Featherstone R) for Holmes
SUB R Brown (Wests) DNP	†SUB D Watkinson (Hull KR) for Skerrett

Referee - G Hartley (NSW)   Crowd - 26,387   Gate - $77,955

Scoring - 0-2 2-2 7-2 12-2 17-2 17-4 17-9 17-14 19-14 22-14 22-16 24-16

Half an hour into this test match Australia seemed to have retained the Ashes having established a lead of fifteen points and Britain were on course for a hiding worse than that received at Lang Park. A second half revival, however, had these extraordinary green and golds looking a little pale as for the first and only time in the series the Lions roared, albeit briefly.

The match had begun quite well for Great Britain who took a tenth minute lead from a penalty goal by Woods and they were further heartened when Fairbairn pulled off a superb tackle on Corowa as the winger looked set to score. Things soon began to go wrong, however, as Cronin landed a simple penalty in the seventeenth minute after Casey had strayed off-side at a drop-out. Then the Australians cut loose to shred the Lions' defence for three tries within ten minutes, all converted by Cronin. After 23 minutes Reddy and Eadie linked to allow Rogers to scorch round Fairbairn on a 30 yard dash to the line. Five minutes later Cronin must have thought it was Christmas as he tore 35 yards straight from a scrum as the British defence stood and bathed in his slipstream. Four minutes later he was over again although this time luck played the biggest part as a kick by Thompson cannoned off a prostrate Lion in the in-goal area and Cronin simply had to fall on the ball. Britain's reply was a solitary penalty goal.

After half-time the crowd sat back expecting Australia to run riot. Instead they found they had something akin to a real test match to watch as Britain, playing with spirit and a new sense of urgency, pulled back to 17-14 within ten minutes of the restart. Two minutes into the half Stephens and Holmes performed a run-around move on half-way. Casey took the ball on and linked with Nicholls. Nicholls found Joyner in support on the "25" and the centre left Corowa and Eadie floundering with a blistering burst to the line. Woods converted and eight minutes later added the goal to a fine opportunist try by Hughes. Australia were attacking on the Lions' "25" when Boustead lost the ball allowing Hughes to hack on over 70 yards before beating Eadie to the touch-down. For a time it appeared that the impossible was about to become reality but Australia shook off their torpor to reassert their authority. A scrum offence enabled Cronin to land his fifth goal before criminally bad defence allowed Reddy to score the try that sealed the match and retained the Ashes. There was no danger as Reddy received a pass on the tourists' "25". The lanky second-row stopped dead and so did the British defenders at which point Reddy suddenly bolted like a startled hare for the corner flag to score a remarkable try without a finger being laid on him. Woods, in wonderful kicking form, pulled back another two points with a 45 yard penalty but Cronin's sixth goal in the 64th minute brought the scoring to a close.

Thus for the first time since 1920 Australia had won the first two tests of a series on their home soil. Mick Cronin's eighteen points enabled him to pass Graeme Langlands' record of 35 points in the 1963 series in England but the real stars of the game had been the rampaging Price and Reddy whilst Morris, Young and Raudonikis had mounted a blockade of the middle with their powerful defence and brought off vital tackles at critical times to nip the British revival in the bud.

TEST MATCH 90

AT SYDNEY CRICKET GROUND – 14 July, 1979
AUSTRALIA 28 GREAT BRITAIN 2 (HT 9-0)

G Eadie (Manly) T	GA Fairbairn (Wigan) G
C Anderson (Canterbury)	S Evans (Featherstone R)
SF Rogers (Cronulla)	JD Joyner (Castleford)
MW Cronin (Parramatta) 8G	J Woods (Leigh)
T Fahey (Souths)	E Hughes (Widnes)
AS Thompson (Manly)	D Topliss (Wakefield T)
T Raudonikis (Wests)	†A Redfearn (Bradford N)
C Young (St. George)	G Nicholls (St. Helens) capt
GC Peponis (Canterbury) capt	DJ Ward (Leeds)
R Morris (Balmain)	L Casey (Bradford N)
LW Boyd (Wests) T	PG Hogan (Hull KR)
RW Reddy (St. George) T	J Grayshon (Bradford N)
RA Price (Parramatta) T	S Norton (Hull)
SUB A McMahon (Balmain) DNP	SUB JS Holmes (Leeds) for Topliss
SUB R Brown (Wests) DNP	SUB M Adams (Widnes) for Casey

Referee - E Ward (Queensland) Crowd - 16,854 Gate - $38,095
Scoring - 2-0 4-0 7-0 9-0 14-0 17-0 17-2 22-2 24-2 26-2 28-2

For Australia the third test represented an unprecedented triumph - their first whitewash of Great Britain in a series, a record number of points in a series (87 - four more than the 1963 Kangaroos), a try tally of 13-2 and for Mick Cronin an individual record for any series of 24 goals and 54 points. For Britain the series was an unmitigated disaster, a recurring nightmare with no redeeming feature and, if anything, their performance in this final test was worse than in the shambles at Brisbane. Once again the tackling was at best slipshod and at worst dangerously illegal and on attack there was simply nothing to offer. The pack was hopelessly outgunned and Australia's "25" seemed to be a no-go area. By the time the third test took place the Australian public had realised that the Lions were simply no opposition for their heroes and responded by their absence, the attendance being the lowest yet for a Lions test in Australia.

Inside ten minutes Cronin had kicked Australia into a 4-0 lead but somehow Britain kept their line intact until the nineteenth minute when Fairbairn missed a tackle on Price in mid-field, an error which led to Rogers sending Eadie, playing in his last test, strolling over on the right. A penalty to Cronin after 31 minutes sent Australia in at half-time with a 9-0 advantage and never a glimmer of a try from the tourists. Five minutes after the break Britain found themselves in the virgin territory of the home "25" where Hughes, possibly from the shock, put down Norton's pass. Australia immediately went to the other end where Young contemptuously brushed off two tackles before sending the supporting Price over for a try converted as usual by Cronin. The try was soon followed by a brawl but Australia concentrated on playing football as Britain's niggling increased. After 51 minutes Redfearn needlessly kicked away possession for Reddy to respond by toying with some slap-dash tackling before providing Boyd with a try-scoring pass. Fairbairn spared Great Britain the indignity of a second nilling by landing a goal after 56 minutes but then lost possession in the shadow of his own goal for Young to loft a high pass to Reddy who crossed unhindered at the corner. The touch-line conversion was no obstacle to Cronin and Australia led 22-2.

There followed a rash of off the ball incidents culminating in the dismissal of Norton in the 68th minute following a clash with Rogers. Britain's discomfort was made complete by the addition of three Cronin penalty goals. Australia's superiority was such that the game appeared dull and tame but it was hardly the fault of the victors that the opposition just fell down and died.

Incredible though it seemed in 1979 worse was to follow for the British in 1982 ....

"THE INVINCIBLES"

BACK ROW (left to right): John Ribot, Paul McCabe, Gene Miles, Don McKinnon, Ian Schubert, Eric Grothe, John Muggleton, Craig Young, Greg Brentnall. MIDDLE ROW: Frank Stanton (coach), Mal Meninga, Rod Morris, Rohan Hancock, Rod Reddy, Les Boyd, Ray Brown, Greg Conescu, Ray Price, Brett Kenny, Wayne Pearce. FRONT ROW: Alf Richards (trainer), Chris Anderson, Steve Mortimer, Steve Ella, Steve Rogers, Frank Farrington (manager), Max Krilich (captain), Tom Drysdale (manager), Wally Lewis, Peter Sterling, Kerry Boustead, Mark Murray, Dr Bill Monaghan.

The 1982 Kangaroos

TEST MATCH 91

AT BOOTHFERRY PARK, HULL – 30 October, 1982
GREAT BRITAIN 4 AUSTRALIA 40 (HT 4-10)

GA Fairbairn (Hull KR)	GF Brentnall (Canterbury)
DL Drummond (Leigh)	K Boustead (Easts) T
E Hughes (Widnes)	MN Meninga (Souths, Brisbane) T,8G
LP Dyl (Leeds)	SF Rogers (St. George)
S Evans (Hull)	† E Grothe (Parramatta) T
J Woods (Leigh)	BE Kenny (Parramatta) T
S Nash (Salford) capt	† PJ Sterling (Parramatta)
J Grayshon (Bradford N)	C Young (St. George)
DJ Ward (Leeds)	M Krilich (Manly) capt
T Skerrett (Hull)	LW Boyd (Manly) T
L Gorley (Widnes)	† WJ Pearce (Balmain) T
† L Crooks (Hull) 2G	RW Reddy (St. George) T
S Norton (Hull)	RA Price (Parramatta) T
SUB K Kelly (Warrington) DNP	SUB SJ Ella (Parramatta) DNP
† SUB D Heron (Leeds) for Crooks	SUB J Muggleton (Parramatta) DNP

Referee - J Rascagneres (France)   Crowd - 26,771   Gate - £65,254
Scoring - 2-0 2-2 2-5 2-10 4-10 4-15 4-20 4-25 4-30 4-35 4-40

Max Krilich's Kangaroos of 1982 were arguably the greatest international combination either code of rugby has produced in any era. All the superlatives which rained upon them barely did them justice. They were the true *non pareils*. Even allowing for the paucity of the opposition afforded them by Great Britain, those privileged to have witnessed the complete and utter annihilation of their antagonists were acutely aware that as rugby teams go Australia 1982 were as near to perfection as makes no difference.

Great Britain were given a lesson in absolutely everything. The only thing that Australia were unable to teach was how to be good losers. They had no experience to pass on in that respect. Great Britain must have felt like a single Roman cohort being ordered to stop Attila and his Huns. It simply could not be done.

For four minutes Britain actually led, Crooks having landed a penalty in the second minute which was cancelled out when Meninga responded with one after six minutes. Somehow Britain contrived to keep in the game for the first twenty minutes but it was like Canute thinking he could hold back the sea. The first wave to crash through the British defence, such as it was, came in the mighty shape of Mal Meninga who finished a movement begun by Young and Pearce with a hand-off on Dyl not unlike a horizontal steam-piston. The crowd positively shuddered. The conversion proved too much for Meninga but it was to be his last failure at goal in the match. The second try arrived in the 26th minute, Pearce opening the way for Boyd to score wide out on the right. After 33 minutes Crooks landed a second penalty and, although Britain went in only 10-4 down at the interval, not even the mothers of the British XIII believed these Kangaroos could be tied down.

The second half was a procession, a master class, as Australia went through their party pieces. Tries came at regular intervals to Grothe (43 minutes), Price (54), Boustead (57), Kenny (59), Pearce (64) and Reddy (79), all converted by Meninga. Each bore the hall-mark of confidence in the Aussies' ablity to do the basic things well and the difficult things superbly. Such was the all-round excellence of the team that the eight tries were scored by eight different players with no fewer than four of them falling to members of a supremely robust, mobile and athletic pack. Wayne Pearce, the youngest of the Australians, was adjudged man of the match for a display of forward skills which belied his age and defied description. There were towering performances too from Krilich and Young. Indeed at times Australia looked as if they were playing a different game to Britain, which in essence, of course, they were.

Just how a team having the advantage of a 21-7 penalty count could contrive to lose by 40-4 was an indication of the unbridgeable gap between the two sides. For Steve Nash, captain and best performer for Britain in his 24th test, Les Dyl, Eric Hughes, David Ward, Les Gorley and Steve Norton there would be no more test matches. Even if they had not gone out on top they had certainly gone out against the best. Someone else could play at King Canute.

TEST MATCH 92

AT CENTRAL PARK, WIGAN – 20 November, 1982
GREAT BRITAIN 6 AUSTRALIA 27 (HT 6-15)

†K Mumby (Bradford N) 3G	GF Brentnall (Canterbury)
DL Drummond (Leigh)	K Boustead (Easts)
M Smith (Hull KR)	MN Meninga (Souths, Brisbane) T,6G
†DR Stephenson (Wigan)	SF Rogers (St. George) T
HC Gill (Wigan)	E Grothe (Parramatta) T
JS Holmes (Leeds)	BE Kenny (Parramatta)
K Kelly (Warrington)	PJ Sterling (Parramatta) T
J Grayshon (Bradford N) capt	C Young (St. George)
†J Dalgreen (Fulham)	M Krilich (Manly) capt
T Skerrett (Hull)	LW Boyd (Manly)
†WR Eccles (Warrington)	WJ Pearce (Balmain)
†C Burton (Hull KR)	RW Reddy (St. George)
D Heron (Leeds)	RA Price (Parramatta) T
SUB J Woods (Leigh) for Holmes	SUB WJ Lewis (Valleys) for Grothe
†SUB A Rathbone (Bradford N) for Burton	†SUB R Brown (Manly) for Reddy

Referee - J Rascagneres (France)   Crowd - 23,216   Gate - £50,108
Scoring - 0-2 2-2 2-7 2-12 2-15 4-15 6-15 6-17 6-22 6-27

In 1929 Great Britain lost the first test at Hull by 31-8, made ten changes and went on to win the Ashes. In 1982 following another first test hiding on Humberside Great Britain again made ten changes. This time it made no difference. Indeed it is perhaps not too far fetched to say that had the selectors merely added another ten men to the thirteen who had played in the previous test, Great Britain would have still lacked the wit and the will to lick the legion of super-heroes which composed the 1982 Australian test XIII.

True, the score-line was more acceptable this time and, true, the British performance with a younger side was marginally better than in the first test. Yet Australia still won as they pleased, still pulverised the opposition and still sent the crowd into raptures over their magical manoeuvres and virtuoso performers. Moreover they did it, much to Britain's embarrassment, with only twelve men from the 34th minute when Boyd, their only concession to indiscipline, was sent off for kicking, albeit in retaliation at a prostrate Dalgreen.

As in the first test Britain resisted for the first quarter, in their limited fashion, holding the Kangaroos to 2-2 until the dam burst in the 19th minute. By the 26th minute the score had leapt to 15-2 as three rapid-fire tries were posted. Relentless pressure and some fine approach work by Sterling opened the way for Price to dive over for the opening touch-down. Meninga converted this try and another five minutes later when left-winger Grothe initiated a movement from a play-the-ball on the opposite flank which concluded when Meninga sent Sterling over near the posts. The third try in this devastating seven minute blast was a tremendous individual effort from Grothe, whose pace and strength made a mockery of the British defence. A brace of penalty goals in the 30th and 35th minutes constituted Britain's innocuous response. The kicker, Mumby, was one man who had the necessary spirit and expertise to resist the green and gold onslaught, never putting a foot wrong and saving at least three tries with model tackles. For most of the time, unfortunately, he ploughed a lonely furrow.

If there were hopes that Australia might tire through depleted numbers as the game wore on they were completely unfounded. Australia were so busy entertaining an enthralled audience that Britain were permitted only one excursion to their "25" and that was fruitless. A penalty goal by Meninga in the 42nd minute was followed twelve minutes later by a try and conversion to bring his points tally to a far from unlucky thirteen. The score was stunningly simple as Sterling combined with Lewis for the substitute stand-off to hurl a pass fully 25 yards to Meninga who rumbled over at the flag. The touch-line conversion was a mere bagatelle to the huge Queenslander. A final try was recorded nine minutes from time when Kenny judiciously served Rogers for the centre to expose poor covering in his passage to the line. Meninga's conversion was academic.

Loose-forward Ray Price was officially named man of the match but the award could have gone just as deservedly to Craig Young, so powerful and purposeful at prop, or to the captain, Krilich, a magnificent organiser from the rucks, or to the young-bloods Sterling, Kenny or Pearce, or simply to any one of a dozen glorious green and golds.

TEST MATCH 93

AT HEADINGLEY, LEEDS – 28 November, 1982
GREAT BRITAIN 8 AUSTRALIA 32 (HT 4-6)

GA Fairbairn (Hull KR)
DL Drummond (Leigh)
DR Stephenson (Wigan)
M Smith (Hull KR)
S Evans (Hull) T
D Topliss (Hull) capt
A Gregory (Widnes)
† M O'Neill (Widnes)
† BD Noble (Bradford N)
P Rose (Hull)
P Smith (Featherstone R)
L Crooks (Hull) 2G,DG
† M Crane (Hull)
SUB J Woods (Leigh) DNP
† SUB N Courtney (Warrington) for O'Neill

GF Brentnall (Canterbury)
K Boustead (Easts) T
MN Meninga (Souths, Brisbane) 7G
SF Rogers (St. George) T
J Ribot (Manly) T
BE Kenny (Parramatta) T
PJ Sterling (Parramatta)
LW Boyd (Manly)
M Krilich (Manly) capt T
R Morris (Wynnum-Manly)
P McCabe (Manly)
RW Reddy (St. George)
WJ Pearce (Balmain) T
SUB WJ Lewis (Valleys) for Ribot
SUB R Brown (Manly) for Boyd

Referee - J Rascagneres (France)   Crowd - 17,318   Gate - £41,150
Scoring - 0-2 2-2 2-4 2-6 4-6 5-6 5-9 5-14 8-14 8-17 8-22 8-27 8-32

In the end Australia won in a canter but for the first 50 minutes of a bruising encounter they at least had to raise a sweat as a doggedly belligerent British XIII fully tested the mettle of their awesome opponents. The ferocity of the exchanges was reflected in the dismissal of Lee Crooks in the 53rd minute and in the sin-binning of Australians Boyd and Brentnall and Britons Crane and Rose.

The first half was remarkably even and the only points came from penalties kicked by Meninga in the 10th, 25th and 35th minutes and by Crooks in the 12th and 38th. Simmering animosity erupted into a full-scale brawl on the stroke of half-time following the felling of Topliss, Britain's third captain of the series, by Boyd and the second half was opened by Monsieur Rascagneres' ceremonial dispatch of Boyd and Crane to the sin-bin for their part in the unseemly fracas ten minutes earlier.

Six minutes into the second session Crooks dropped a delightful goal from 30 yards and the Kangaroos' lead seemed precarious but, like the champions that they were, Australia began to turn the screw. Fifty minutes had passed when Pearce broke through, swept disdainfully past Evans and fed Reddy who was quick to put Ribot over at the corner. There was no conversion but three minutes later Meninga improved a splendid try. Pearce was again the instigator, breaking a double tackle on halfway before handing on to Kenny who subtly turned the ball inside to the supporting Krilich who shot 35 yards to the posts as the cover converged too late. In the aftermath of the try Crooks was sent off for punching and five minutes later Rose and Brentnall had an altercation which ended in the sin-bin. Down to eleven men against twelve and 14-5 in arrears, Great Britain confounded the odds by scoring their first try in four tests against Australia. The score, after 65 minutes, followed unusually intense British pressure as the ball was swept from right of the posts to the left wing. A superb long pass from Crane allowed Stephenson to serve Evans who was able to beat the cover to score at the flag. It was, however, Britain's last act of defiance.

The last ten minutes saw the Kangaroos put on an exhibition of rugby which provided a fitting finale to a record-breaking tour and encapsulated all the elements of a team at peak performance. First to touch down was Boustead who took a masterful reverse pass from Kenny following a lightning foray down the right flank. Four minutes later Boustead provided the final pass for Rogers to storm over and in the 76th minute Pearce scored a gem of a try as the Kangaroos rolled like thunder over their crestfallen opponents. From a play-the-ball Meninga fed Lewis who picked out Kenny with an amazingly long pass. Kenny worked his way inside before releasing Pearce who rounded Smith and streaked away to the posts. Even then the Kangaroos were not finished for Lewis created an opening for Kenny to snake his way down the centre of the field for a final scintillating score. Meninga converted the final three tries and during those last frenetic ten minutes Australia had scored eighteen points and Britain had not touched the ball save to kick off.

Australia thus completed their first clean sweep of a series in Britain and in the process scored a record 99 points whilst Meninga's personal contribution of 48 points was a record for an Anglo-Australian series in Great Britain.

Top: Hull, first test, 1982. Kangaroo loose-forward Ray Price disposes of a challenge by prop Jeff Grayshon.
Bottom: Headingley, third test, 1982. Referee Julian Rascagneres hits a flash point as Les Boyd hovers over Britain's captain David Topliss. Rod Reddy and Mick Crane (13) prepare to join the fray.

TEST MATCH 94

AT SYDNEY CRICKET GROUND – 9 June, 1984
AUSTRALIA 25 GREAT BRITAIN 8 (HT 8-2)

† GG Jack (Balmain)	M Burke (Widnes) 2G
K Boustead (Manly) T	DL Drummond (Leigh)
G Miles (Wynnum-Manly)	GE Schofield (Hull) T
BE Kenny (Parramatta)	K Mumby (Bradford N)
† R Conlon (Canterbury) 4G	EC Hanley (Bradford N)
WJ Lewis (Wynnum-Manly) capt T,DG	D Foy (Oldham)
MW Murray (Redcliffe) T	† NA Holding (St. Helens)
D Brown (Manly)	L Crooks (Hull)
† GJ Conescu (Gladstone Brothers)	BD Noble (Bradford N) capt
† GI Dowling (Wynnum-Manly)	AI Goodway (Oldham)
WJ Pearce (Balmain)	C Burton (Hull KR)
† B Niebling (Redcliffe)	M Worrall (Oldham)
RA Price (Parramatta) T	M Adams (Widnes)
SUB C Young (St. George) for Brown	SUB JP Lydon (Widnes) for Holding
SUB C Close (Manly) DNP	SUB D Hobbs (Featherstone R) for Crooks

Referee - R Shrimpton (New Zealand)   Crowd - 30,190   Gate - $201,000
Scoring - 2-0 8-0 8-2 12-2 12-8 18-8 19-8 25-8

Despite losing by seventeen points, conceding four tries to one, having a man sent off and clearly being inferior to their opponents both the British and Australian press welcomed a much more virile performance than of yore from an unusually youthful Lions XIII. The Lions certainly bared their teeth more threateningly than in any test since Odsal, 1978 and there was plenty of fight and fire from them in a game which, whilst on the whole scrappy and penalty-strewn, was a real test. Even allowing for Britain's much improved showing Australia, admittedly but a shadow of the 1982 Invincibles, still proved too powerful, too cohesive and too talented. They never lost the lead, taken as early as the eleventh minute, and made light of an adverse penalty count of 9-19. In Wally Lewis, Ray Price and Wayne Pearce they had dominating figures whom the Lions just could not match.

The opening exchanges were grim and after three minutes the first scrum broke up and was replaced by an all-in brawl, resulting in cautions for Brown, Crooks and Goodway. Eight minutes later Conlon opened the scoring for Australia with a penalty goal. Britain were unfortunate to lose live-wire scrum-half Holding with a knee injury after twenty minutes and before he could be replaced they found themselves eight points down. Lewis was the creator and executioner, first breaking past Worrall before parting to Pearce whose return pass enabled the Australian captain to slither over beneath the bar. Conlon's conversion was a formality. Limpet-like Britain stuck to their task and five minutes before the break reduced their arrears when Burke landed a goal.

Twelve minutes into the second half Hanley dropped a high kick, Australia secured and quickly spread the ball wide via Kenny and Pearce to Price who crashed over to push Australia into a 12-2 lead. Five minutes later Crooks and Dowling were ordered to the sin-bin and on the hour Great Britain made everyone sit up when they conjured a magical try. Inside his own half Lydon made a little room for Drummond, who displayed exceptional pace and elusiveness in beating four tacklers as he raced down the middle. Schofield, now at scrum-half for the departed Holding, was up in support to take Drummond's pass and dive over near the posts for a score which brought the house down. Burke converted and Britain were back in the game with a vengeance, only to be slapped back down again within two minutes. Lack of concentration allowed Lewis to send Kenny skipping round Adams before Boustead finished the move by crossing at the corner and unforgivably being unhindered in racing along the in-goal area to touch down under the posts for an easily converted try.

Five minutes from time Lewis stretched Australia's lead to 19-8 with a dropped goal and with two minutes remaining Australia's wining margin was given a flattering proportion when Murray scored direct from a scrum after shaking off some sloppy tackling. Conlon kicked the goal but the game ended on a sour note as Hobbs, a 72nd minute substitute, was sent off for a nasty foul on Conescu who was stretchered off.

An eighth successive victory for Australia over the old enemy had been no real surprise but at least Britain had indicated that they would no longer go like lambs to slaughter.

TEST MATCH 95

AT LANG PARK, BRISBANE – 26 June, 1984
AUSTRALIA 18 GREAT BRITAIN 6 (HT 6-0)

GG Jack (Balmain)	M Burke (Widnes) G
K Boustead (Manly)	DL Drummond (Leigh)
G Miles (Wynnum-Manly)	GE Schofield (Hull) T
MN Meninga (Souths, Brisbane) T,3G	K Mumby (Bradford N)
E Grothe (Parramatta) T	EC Hanley (Bradford N)
WJ Lewis (Wynnum-Manly) capt	A Myler (Widnes)
MW Murray (Redcliffe)	NA Holding (St. Helens)
D Brown (Manly)	Keith Rayne (Leeds)
GJ Conescu (Gladstone Brothers)	BD Noble (Bradford N) capt
GI Dowling (Wynnum-Manly)	L Crooks (Hull)
P Vautin (Manly)	C Burton (Hull KR)
B Niebling (Redcliffe)	AI Goodway (Oldham)
WJ Pearce (Balmain) T	M Worrall (Oldham)
SUB SC Mortimer (Canterbury) for Murray	SUB A Gregory (Widnes) for Burke
SUB WJ Fullerton-Smith (Redcliffe) for Brown	SUB M Adams (Widnes) for Crooks

Referee - R Shrimpton (New Zealand)   Crowd - 26,534   Gate - $159,749
Scoring - 2-0 6-0 8-0 14-0 14-6 18-6

Played under floodlights on a Tuesday evening, this second test produced a fast and furious match brimful of incident, error and endeavour. A classic it may not have been but it was a contest worthy of the Ashes tradition as Britain fought tooth and nail to contain a much heftier and more powerful Australian XIII. Unfortunately, it also contained a number of unsavoury incidents which culminated in a very heated final ten minutes during which the British captain Noble sustained a broken nose and the Australian second-rower Vautin a fractured cheek-bone. Wally Lewis, so influential as the Australian pivot, was subjected to some shamefully rough treatment to which he understandably responded in kind, although it was unfortunate that Rayne was twice banished to the sin-bin for fouls on Lewis which had clearly been committed by other players.

Aided by a significant scrummaging superiority in the first half-hour, Australia had most of the early play but a combination of tenacious tackling and faulty handling enabled the Lions to withstand all efforts to cross their line and all the home side could glean from their pressure was a Meninga penalty goal. Britain were unlucky to see Burke strike a post with a penalty and on one occasion were desperately close to scoring when, following good play by Myler and Burke, Hanley was just crowded out at the corner by Boustead and Jack. Britain were equally relieved when Grothe, all power and purpose, was grounded by three men five yards short but in the 36th minute they could not restrain the giant winger who raced over from 30 yards after Miles had squeezed out a pass when seemingly held by a trio of tacklers.

In the 48th minute Worrall went off-side and Meninga stretched the home lead to 8-0. Nine minutes later it was 14-0 as Pearce scattered the defence in an irresistible 30 yard surge to score near the posts, enabling Meninga to land his third goal. Britain struck back gloriously with a try to rank with the greatest of test tries. The move began on the right flank deep in British territory as Myler and Adams created some day-light for Schofield to pierce the defence, career upfield, exchange passes with Drummond, link with the rampaging Goodway and receive the ball a third time before accelerating away from Boustead to score at the left corner. It was fitting that such a regal try should be crowned by Burke's splendid touch-line conversion.

It was to be the only British score, however, as Australia reasserted themselves with a final try after 69 minutes. Britain won a scrum near their own line but failed to secure possession. Murray was not so wasteful and served Meninga on the blind-side. On the burst and from such a short distance Meninga was unstoppable and made light work of the attempted tackles.

Despite the creditable performance of the British side there was no denying the superiority of the men in green and gold whose victory had given them the Ashes for the sixth successive series. It was beginning to look as if they would never relinquish them.

TEST MATCH 96

AT SYDNEY CRICKET GROUND – 7 July, 1984
AUSTRALIA 20 GREAT BRITAIN 7 (HT 8-7)

GG Jack (Balmain) T	M Burke (Widnes) G
K Boustead (Manly)	DL Drummond (Leigh)
G Miles (Wynnum-Manly)	GE Schofield (Hull)
MN Meninga (Souths, Brisbane) 4G	K Mumby (Bradford N)
E Grothe (Parramatta) T	EC Hanley (Bradford N) T
WJ Lewis (Wynnum-Manly) capt	A Myler (Widnes)
SC Mortimer (Canterbury)	NA Holding (St. Helens) DG
B Niebling (Redcliffe)	D Hobbs (Featherstone R)
GJ Conescu (Gladstone Brothers) T	BD Noble (Bradford N) capt
GI Dowling (Wynnum-Manly)	† BG Case (Wigan)
WJ Pearce (Balmain)	C Burton (Hull KR)
WJ Fullerton-Smith (Redcliffe)	AI Goodway (Oldham)
RA Price (Parramatta)	M Adams (Widnes)
SUB BE Kenny(Parramatta) for Miles	SUB M Smith (Hull KR) DNP
SUB D Brown (Manly) for Fullerton-Smith	SUB Keith Rayne (Leeds) DNP

Referee - A Drake (New Zealand)   Crowd - 18,756   Gate - $140,852

Scoring - 2-0 2-6 2-7 4-7 8-7 14-7 20-7

By their own high standards Australia played poorly but were still much too good for a Great Britain team which at one stage held the lead for almost quarter of an hour - something which had not occurred for 519 minutes of Ashes conflict, back in that first catastrophic test of 1982. During those fifteen minutes there was real hope that a victory could at long last be won but Australia, even on this anaemic showing, had enough in reserve to complete their third consecutive series whitewash and register a tenth straight win over the Poms.

The game, following the fireworks at Brisbane, was surprisingly tame and lacklustre and was far from the blood-bath many critics were forecasting. Australia completely dominated the first quarter and it was not until 23 minutes had elapsed that the Lions managed to cross the centre-line. Even so all Australia had to show for their pains was a fifteenth minute penalty goal kicked by a strangely subdued Meninga, who had fluffed two very simple chances in the fifth and sixth minutes. It took a shock try by Britain to put some sparkle into the play as Australia suddenly found themselves 6-2 down after 25 minutes. Stand-off Myler began the scoring movement when he made a beautiful run past three Australians before being halted at half-way. A quick play-the-ball and Schofield fed Hanley who had come in from the wing. Quickly into his stride Hanley bumped off Lewis and Niebling and set a direct course for the posts 40 yards away. He was not to be denied despite the frantic efforts of both Australian wingers to cut him off and Burke landed the simple conversion. Britain carried the game to their opponents and when Holding impudently dropped a goal in the 33rd minute Australia sensed an upset and hit back hard. Meninga pulled back two points when the Lions were caught off-side and two minutes before half-time they grabbed the lead with a typical barnstorming try from Grothe who received the ball near touch and ten yards out. It seemed impossible to score but Grothe somehow managed to dispose of Schofield and then drove straight through a determined tackle by Burke for a stunning try.

The second half saw Australia pin the British inside their own "25" for long periods but their only rewards were two tries scored in the 53rd and 73rd minutes, both converted by Meninga. The first should certainly have been prevented but Conescu made light of the tackles of Burke and Myler as he cheekily scored from the acting half-back position. The second, scored by full-back Jack, was the culmination of a 40 yard passing bout involving Mortimer, Jack, Pearce and Boustead but the final pass seemed to many to have been forward.

This test was an undistinguished game for one of the most distinguished of modern Australian footballers to bow out of the international arena but loose-forward Ray Price no doubt cherishes the memory of yet another victory over the old enemy and his triumphal chairing from the field at the game's conclusion.

TEST MATCH 97

AT OLD TRAFFORD, MANCHESTER – 25 October, 1986
GREAT BRITAIN 16 AUSTRALIA 38 (HT 0-16)

JP Lydon (Wigan) T	GG Jack (Balmain) T
A Marchant (Castleford)	L Kiss (Norths)
GE Schofield (Hull) 2T	BE Kenny (Parramatta)
EC Hanley (Wigan)	G Miles (Wynnum-Manly) 3T
HC Gill (Wigan) G	MD O'Connor (St. George) 3T,5G
A Myler (Widnes)	WJ Lewis (Wynnum-Manly) capt
JD Fox (Featherstone R)	PJ Sterling (Parramatta)
KA Ward (Castleford)	GI Dowling (Wynnum-Manly)
D Watkinson (Hull KR) capt	R Simmons (Penrith)
J Fieldhouse (Widnes)	SD Roach (Balmain)
I Potter (Wigan)	N Cleal (Manly)
L Crooks (Hull) G	B Niebling (Redcliffe)
AI Goodway (Wigan)	RF Lindner (Wynnum-Manly)
SUB S Edwards (Wigan) DNP	SUB MN Meninga (Canberra) for Kiss
SUB A Platt (St. Helens) DNP	SUB TJ Lamb (Canterbury) for Lindner

Referee - J Rascagneres (France)   Crowd - 50,583   Gate - £251,061
Scoring - 0-4 0-8 0-10 0-14 0-16 2-16 6-16 10-16 10-22 10-26 10-32 10-38 16-38

Britain entered the 1986 Ashes series in an optimistic mood. In the intervening two years since the last series vast amounts of time, money and effort had gone into the preparation of the national team. A record crowd for a test match in Britain assembled at historic Old Trafford anticipating at the very least a close run thing. Teeming autumnal rain seemed to betoken the gods' favour. In the event any indication of a British improvement was a mirage.

Australia for the eleventh successive time proved much too direct, physical and tactically in control to brook any threat to their superiority. Britain scored three tries, a feat they last achieved in Sydney in 1974. Australia scored seven and could have had a few more. The Australian left-wing partnership, Gene Miles and Michael O'Connor, had a field day, becoming the first pair of players to score a try-hat-trick in an Ashes test. O'Connor, moreover, booted five goals to aggregate a record 22 points.

Britain held out for the first nine minutes but were then taken apart when Lewis and Kenny sent Miles in for his first try. Twelve minutes later Lewis and Miles combined to send O'Connor through Marchant's tackle for a try near the flag. By half-time the Kangaroos led 16-0 as O'Connor snaffled another eight points, landing penalty goals in the 25th and 36th minutes and finishing off a Sterling-Kenny-Miles extravaganza on 32 minutes.

The early period of the second half presented Great Britain with the incentive to make a match of it as Australian concentration briefly evaporated. Six minutes into the half Crooks, recently returned from the sin-bin, landed a penalty after an obstruction by Kenny. In the 50th minute Crooks provided Schofield with the opportunity to dance round Jack for a try but struck the post with his conversion attempt. Four minutes later the crowd erupted as Myler and Goodway released Lydon on an astonishing 70 yard run down the left flank. A dummy and a dash of acceleration disposed of Gary Jack's challenge as Lydon became the first British full-back to score a try in an Ashes test.

At 10-16 Britain suddenly threatened an upset but within two minutes had tossed their chance away. An horrendous mistake by Henderson Gill from the kick-off gifted possession to the Kangaroos. Lewis swept through the mid-field, took a late tackle for which Lydon was sin-binned, and put Miles over under the posts. O'Connor converted and Britain were about to be put to the sword, despite Roach's dispatch to the sin-bin. Between the 64th and 76th minute the Kangaroos rattled up three tries and stretched their lead to 38-10. Exquisite centre play by Kenny and Miles presented O'Connor with his third try and when Myler spilled the ball in front of the posts Miles disdainfully strolled through from the play-the-ball for his own hat-trick. O'Connor kicked the goal and added another when Australia scored a try bordering on sheer perfection after Sterling's cross-kick was gathered by Jack before it hit the ground.

A minute from time Britain made the score vaguely respectable when Crooks, the best home forward on view, made a try for Schofield which was improved by Gill. As had become usual over the past decade, it was far too little far too late. Almost as the game concluded Maurice Bamford, the British coach, stunned everyone by announcing the same British squad would face Lewis's Unbeatables at Elland Road in the second test. Discretion used to be the better part of valour. Bamford, loyal to his toenails, turned that proverb on its head.

The 1986 "UNBEATABLES"
Back: Meninga, Hasler, Jack, Kiss, Shearer, Bella, Langmack, Mortimer, Alexander, Folkes, Kenny, Miles
Middle: Monaghan, Davidson, Niebling, Cleal, Dunn, Furner, Lindner, Roach,
Dowling, Daley, Sironen, Brittan
Front: Lamb, O'Connor, Sterling, Treichel, Lewis, Fleming, Simmons, Belcher, Elias

Old Trafford, first test, 1986.
Garry Jack fails to stop Joe Lydon from becoming the first British full-back to score a try in an Ashes test.

TEST MATCH 98

AT ELLAND ROAD, LEEDS – 8 November, 1986
GREAT BRITAIN 4 AUSTRALIA 34 (HT 0-12)

JP Lydon (Wigan)	GG Jack (Balmain) 2T
† BD Ledger (St. Helens)	D Shearer (Manly)
GE Schofield (Hull) T	BE Kenny (Parramatta) T
A Marchant (Castleford)	G Miles (Wynnum-Manly)
HC Gill (Wigan)	MD O'Connor (St. George) T,5G
A Myler (Widnes)	WJ Lewis (Wynnum-Manly) capt T
JD Fox (Featherstone R)	PJ Sterling (Parramatta)
KA Ward (Castleford)	GI Dowling (Wynnum-Manly)
D Watkinson (Hull KR) capt	R Simmons (Penrith)
J Fieldhouse (St. Helens)	P Dunn (Canterbury)
I Potter (Wigan)	N Cleal (Manly)
L Crooks (Hull)	B Niebling (Redcliffe)
AI Goodway (Wigan)	RF Lindner (Wynnum-Manly) T
SUB S Edwards (Wigan) for Myler	SUB TJ Lamb (Canterbury) for Sterling
SUB A Platt (St. Helens) for Watkinson	SUB MN Meninga (Canberra) for Niebling

Referee - J Rascagneres (France)   Crowd - 30,808   Gate - £140,609

Scoring   0-2 0-8 0-12 0-18 0-24 0-28 0-34 4-34

In perfect conditions Australia were given a fright for half-an-hour but then proceeded to play on a different planet to an error-ridden, self-destructive Great Britain XIII who thus surrendered the Ashes for the seventh consecutive series.

Michael O'Connor took up where he left off at Old Trafford by booting the Kangaroos into a third minute lead when Crooks was penalised for an obstruction. For the next 25 minutes Britain took the game to Australia but failed to take any of the chances that fell to them. Myler was almost over, only a last-gasp ankle tap from Lewis preventing a try and the chance to equalise was passed up in the 20th minute when Britain futilely chose to run an eminently kickable penalty. Most agonisingly of all, however, was the failure to profit from a magnificent run by Myler. The stand-off sliced through to the Australian "25" and with only Jack to beat and Schofield in a perfect scoring position elected to kick. The ball and Britain's best and last chance sailed dead.

Sterling and Lewis now took the test by the scruff of the neck and wrung the life out of the hapless British. On the 28th minute the outstanding second-rower Noel Cleal shrugged off Platt and Lydon before presenting the fast-supporting Lindner with an easy touchdown at the posts. O'Connor's goal made it 8-0 and it was the dashing winger who extended Australia's lead to twelve points after 33 minutes. Britain's cover was non-existent as Sterling shot out a wayward pass to the flank. O'Connor snapped the ball up in his own half, shot forward and punted past a static Lydon to win a one-man race for the try. His failure to add the conversion was neither here nor there in the context of what would follow in the second half.

Britain had already lost their skipper David Watkinson with a shin injury after 20 minutes. The second half saw Britain leaderless and clueless. The Australian half-backs were controlling everything and after 47 minutes they effectively sealed the game and the series when Sterling's pass sent Lewis sidestepping past a posse of defenders for a try under the bar. O'Connor tagged on the goal as he did three minutes later when Cleal's shattering break opened up the defence for Jack to score.

Jack repeated the dose in the 57th minute. Lewis robbed Myler of the ball before Dowling and, inevitably, Sterling sent the full-back over for his second try. Myler's misery came to an end as he limped off on the hour to be replaced by Shaun Edwards. By now Australia were in full flow and with ten minutes remaining Kenny initiated and finished a sublime movement involving Shearer and Jack. O'Connor's fifth goal left Britain 34 points in arrears. Britain had hardly raised a worthwhile attack throughout the second half but as spectators streamed away in embarrassment at their team's performance O'Connor and Jack magnanimously contrived to allow Schofield to profit from a rare blunder with a try three minutes from time.

Before the 1986 test series began many pundits believed that Max Krilich's Invincibles of 1982 would prove incomparable. Wally Lewis's 1986 Unbeatables were proving that theory decidedly shaky.

TEST MATCH 99

AT CENTRAL PARK, WIGAN – 22 November, 1986
GREAT BRITAIN 15 AUSTRALIA 24 (HT 6-12)

JP Lydon (Wigan) 2G	GG Jack (Balmain)
HC Gill (Wigan) G	D Shearer (Manly) T
GE Schofield (Hull) 2T,DG	BE Kenny (Parramatta)
DR Stephenson (Wigan)	G Miles (Wynnum-Manly) T
J Basnett (Widnes)	MD O'Connor (St. George) 4G
A Myler (Widnes)	WJ Lewis (Wynnum-Manly) capt T
A Gregory (Warrington)	PJ Sterling (Parramatta)
KA Ward (Castleford)	GI Dowling (Wynnum-Manly)
D Watkinson (Hull KR) capt	R Simmons (Penrith)
L Crooks (Hull)	P Dunn (Canterbury)
AI Goodway (Wigan)	MN Meninga (Canberra)
C Burton (Hull KR)	B Niebling (Redcliffe)
H Pinner (Widnes)	RF Lindner (Wynnum-Manly) T
SUB S Edwards (Wigan) DNP	SUB TJ Lamb(Canterbury) for Meninga
SUB I Potter (Wigan) for Burton	† SUB L Davidson (Souths) for Dunn

Referee - J Rascagneres (France)   Crowd - 20,169   Gate - £74,288
Scoring - 0-6 0-12 6-12 12-12 12-18 14-18 15-18 15-24

Australia were pushed to their limits by Great Britain for the first time for eight years and did not seal their victory until the dying minutes of a gripping and controversial match. The referee Julien Rascagneres had given every satisfaction in the first two tests but was destined to become the villain of this particular piece. The Kangaroos began at a blistering pace forcing Britain into early mistakes and taking the lead after only two minutes. There was a storm of indignation from the crowd and the British players after Simmons, Sterling and Lewis enabled Dowling to send Miles over for the opening score. Only Monsieur Rascagneres appeared to believe that Dowling's pass had not been feet if not yards forward. O'Connor added insult to injury by kicking the conversion.

Australia accepted the windfall with relish and subjected Britain to heavy pressure, Jack and Dunn going close to tries and O'Connor firing wide a penalty, before doubling their lead in the 21st minute. Again a combination of Sterling, Lewis and Dowling did the damage allowing Lindner to storm through an inviting gap to score another converted try. At this point Britain might have been excused for losing interest but instead produced a startling comeback.

Basnett was almost in at the corner as Gregory and Pinner inspired Britain to heights few thought they could reach. Australia were rattled and appearing to commit fouls which the referee failed to punish much to the annoyance of the assembled multitudes. The pressure told after 27 minutes when Pinner's astute pass launched Myler on an incisive run into the Australian "25" where he drew Jack before looping an overhead pass to Schofield who raced for the touchdown. Gill added the goal and improbably Britain went in at the break only 12-6 down.

Six minutes into the second half Britain were level as Pinner, Crooks and Stephenson combined to put the predatory Schofield over for his second try of the game and his fifth of the series. Schofield thus became the first man to score a try in each test in an Ashes series since Ken Irvine in 1963. Lydon's conversion gave Britain a parity which lasted a mere eleven minutes. After 52 minutes Burton was ordered to the sin-bin for a high tackle on Dunn, a fate Lewis was fortunate not to share following his retaliation on Burton. Five minutes later Burton's indiscretion caught up with Britain as, a man short, they struggled to cover a run down the wing by Shearer. On reaching the British "25" Shearer kicked ahead and was tackled from behind by Basnett. It was clearly an obstruction but there was little possibility of Shearer or any other Kangaroo scoring. The referee thought otherwise, however, and awarded a penalty try under the posts which O'Connor duly improved.

Despite this mortifying decision Britain stuck manfully to their task. A penalty goal by Lydon after 62 minutes and a drop goal by Schofield after 69 minutes dragged the Kangaroos back into trouble at 15-18. Yet it was the Kangaroo captain Wally Lewis, subdued by his customary high standards, who killed stone-dead the possibility of a miraculous home victory seven minutes from the final hooter when he supported a superb break by Simmons to jink through a bewildered defence to score at the goal. O'Connor's conversion gave him his 44th point of the series, a total bettered only by Mick Cronin and Mal Meninga.

Brett Kenny played his eighth and final Ashes test. He had never been on the losing side.

TEST MATCH 100

AT SYDNEY FOOTBALL STADIUM – 11 June, 1988
AUSTRALIA 17 GREAT BRITAIN 6 (HT 0-6)

GG Jack (Balmain)	PJP Loughlin (St. Helens) G
A Ettingshausen (Cronulla)	P Ford (Bradford N)
MD O'Connor (Manly) 2G	GE Schofield (Leeds)
† P Jackson (Canberra) 2T	DR Stephenson (Leeds)
† A Currie (Canterbury)	MN Offiah (Widnes)
WJ Lewis (Brisbane B) capt DG	DJ Hulme (Widnes)
PJ Sterling (Parramatta)	A Gregory (Wigan)
† P Daley (Manly)	KA Ward (Castleford)
GJ Conescu (Brisbane B)	K Beardmore (Castleford)
† S Backo (Canberra) T	PA Dixon (Halifax)
P Vautin (Manly)	A Platt (St. Helens)
WJ Fullerton-Smith (St.George)	MK Gregory (Warrington)
RF Lindner (Parramatta)	EC Hanley (Wigan) capt T
† SUB G Belcher (Canberra) for Sterling	SUB HC Gill (Wigan) for Loughlin
SUB S Folkes (Canterbury) for Vautin	SUB RC Powell (Leeds) for M Gregory

Referee - F Desplas (France) Crowd - 24,202 Gate $346,751

Scoring - 0-2 0-6 6-6 12-6 13-6 17-6

In 1988 Australia celebrated her bicentenniel with rare gusto. The Australian Rugby League, however, failed lamentably to promote this 100th Ashes test as a celebration of Rugby League. Perhaps there were mitigating factors. After all Britain had now lost thirteen straight tests to Australia and few observers regarded Britain's abysmal defeats against Northern Division (12-36) and Manly (0-30) in the run-up to the test as auguries of a competitive encounter. In the event the test was a fine contest, Britain exceeded all expectations and yet ultimately Australia overpowered their opponents.

The first half was a revelation as far as Britain were concerned. Their tackling was potent enough to prevent Australia gaining any fluency as Ward, the Lions' outstanding player, Dixon and Platt fuelled a smothering forward barrage. At half-time Britain were in the novel situation of leading, something which had not happened since Odsal 1978. Moreover, it could have been better had Loughlin's goal-kicking been better and had some chances been exploited.

As it was, the Lions were grateful to take a twelfth minute lead when Loughlin's penalty goal punished Phil Daley's high tackle on Beardmore. Britain finally broke down the Australian defence two minutes before the interval when a beautiful long pass from Gregory to Hulme set Hanley in motion just outside the home "25". The loose-forward offered a hint of a dummy causing Jackson to overshoot, crabbed right, fended off Sterling's flying tackle and arrowed over in the corner for a magnificent try.

At 6-0 and the possibility that Australia's mainspring Peter Sterling might not appear for the second half having had a shoulder joint put out in the 39th minute, the omens looked good for Britain. It was not to be, however. Sterling reappeared, Australia got their act together and gradually ground Britain down. Britain held out for the first ten minutes of the half but then succumbed to a desperately lucky try as Sterling, on the sixth tackle and a few yards from the Lions' line, completely miscued a grubber kick only to make a silk purse from a sow's ear by grabbing a wicked bounce and putting Backo over. O'Connor's goal levelled the scores. Loughlin should have kicked Britain back into the lead but failed to land a simple penalty. In the 62nd minute Australia took the lead for the first time when Peter Jackson raced over on the right after Sterling's superb pass had made the opening. Britain's claims that Lindner had obstructed during the movement were waived away as O'Connor potted the conversion. The disappointment was compounded when a tremendous effort from the belligerent Ward sent Gregory scampering over only for Ward's pass to be ruled forward. Gregory's petulance at the decision did nothing to help the British cause as the resultant penalty transferred the pressure from the Australian to the British defence.

With the Australian half-backs at last playing with their customary authority the game was whisked irretrievably away from the Lions. First Lewis imperiously dropped a 25-yard goal on 69 minutes and then with seven minutes remaining the *coup de grâce* was delivered when a brilliant movement, conceived on the right flank and sustained inevitably by Lewis and Sterling down the middle, ended in a try on the left flank by Jackson, a delighted two-try debutant.

TEST MATCH 101

AT LANG PARK, BRISBANE – 28 June, 1988
AUSTRALIA 34 GREAT BRITAIN 14 (HT 18-4)

GG Jack (Balmain)	PJP Loughlin (St. Helens) 3G
A Ettingshausen (Cronulla) T	HC Gill (Wigan)
MD O'Connor (Manly) T,5G	P Ford (Bradford N) T
P Jackson (Canberra) T	EC Hanley (Wigan) capt
A Currie (Canterbury)	MN Offiah (Widnes) T
WJ Lewis (Brisbane B) capt T	DJ Hulme (Widnes)
PJ Sterling (Parramatta)	A Gregory (Wigan)
P Daley (Manly)	KA Ward (Castleford)
GJ Conescu (Brisbane B)	K Beardmore (Castleford)
S Backo (Canberra) T	R Powell (Leeds)
P Vautin (Manly)	A Platt (St. Helens)
WJ Fullerton-Smith (St. George)	PA Dixon (Halifax)
WJ Pearce (Balmain) T	MK Gregory (Warrington)
SUB G Belcher (Canberra) for Ettingshausen	† SUB D Wright (Widnes) for Ford
SUB RF Lindner (Parramatta) for Conescu	† SUB P Hulme (Widnes) for Platt

Referee - F Desplas (France)   Crowd - 27,103   Gate - $295,439
Scoring - 0-2 6-2 6-4 8-4 14-4 18-4 18-10 24-10 28-10 34-10 34-14

Australia took the lessons of the first test to heart and pressured the Lions relentlessly from the outset. All the promise exhibited by Great Britain in that earlier encounter counted for nothing as they gave a display of alarming ineptitude, characterised by high and sloppy tackling, inane field-kicking, careless handling and dreadful indiscipline. Australia's dominance was as complete as that displayed by the 1982 and 1986 Kangaroos.

Britain started well enough, Gill making a lively burst before Loughlin gave them a third minute lead with a penalty goal after Lewis's high tackle on David Hulme. Three minutes later a hopelessly bungled tackle by Ford on O'Connor allowed the Australian winger to sidestep through for a try he converted himself. Loughlin reduced the deficit to two points in the 14th minute with a penalty after Lewis had held down a British attacker in the tackle. O'Connor responded with a penalty for off-side three minutes later and in the 20th minute Lewis, far and away the best man on the pitch, grubber kicked through, deftly regathered and put Jackson over for a try, again goaled by O'Connor. Just before the break Lewis handled twice in a splendid movement which sent Ettingshausen sweeping past Offiah to score at the corner.

Eight minutes into the second half Britain pulled back to 18-10 with a long-distance try inspired by Hanley whose devastating dummy and break from his own half scattered the Australian defence. His inside pass to Ford sent the centre scorching to the posts for a try converted by Loughlin. The rally ended there, however. Perhaps the distraction of a 50th minute set-to and the loss of second-rower Andy Platt with a broken wrist were contributory factors but it was more likely that a combination of British lack of concentration and Australia's superior teamwork resulted in the home team running away with the match and the Ashes.

Three tries within the space of ten minutes rocketed Australia from a precarious 18-10 advantage to an unassailable 34-10 lead and plunged the Lions into an ever-deepening despair. In the 59th minute, after a prolonged siege of the British line, fearsome prop Sam Backo bashed his way over at the posts for O'Connor to kick an easy conversion. Seven minutes later Wayne Pearce took advantage of Britain's defensive frailty on the left wing to go over at the flag whilst in the 69th minute a ravishing movement involving Jackson, Sterling, Pearce and Lindner ended in Lewis capping a virtuoso performance with a try under the bar, again converted by O'Connor.

Six minutes from time Andy Gregory was sin-binned for an asssault on Ettingshausen's head which would have done credit to Charles I's executioner. It came as something of a surprise that Britain still had enough resolve to score a spectacular try after 77 minutes when Offiah launched himself on a 60 yard run through Belcher's tackle and left Jack for dead in claiming a try which made the crowd wonder how much more damage he could do if Britain ever managed to get him into the game with any regularity.

Australia had now won fifteen straight tests against the British, had not lost to them for a decade and had held the Ashes for fifteen years. Would it ever end?

TEST MATCH 102

AT SYDNEY FOOTBALL STADIUM – 9 July, 1988
AUSTRALIA 12 GREAT BRITAIN 26 (HT 0-10)

GG Jack (Balmain)	P Ford (Bradford N) T
A Ettingshausen (Cronulla)	HC Gill (Wigan) 2T
MD O'Connor (Manly) 2G	DR Stephenson (Leeds)
P Jackson (Canberra)	PJP Loughlin (St. Helens) 3G
A Currie (Canterbury)	MN Offiah (Widnes) T
WJ Lewis (Brisbane B) capt T	DJ Hulme (Widnes)
PJ Sterling (Parramatta)	A Gregory (Wigan)
† M Bella (Norths)	KA Ward (Castleford)
GJ Conescu (Brisbane B)	P Hulme (Widnes)
S Backo (Canberra) T	H Waddell (Oldham)
P Vautin (Manly)	R Powell (Leeds)
WJ Fullerton-Smith (St. George)	MK Gregory (Warrington) T
WJ Pearce (Balmain)	EC Hanley (Wigan) capt
SUB G Belcher (Canberra) for Sterling	SUB D Wright (Widnes) DNP
SUB RF Lindner (Parramatta) for Fullerton-Smith	SUB BG Case (Wigan) for Waddell

Referee - F Desplas (France) Crowd - 15,994 Gate - $167,914
Scoring - 0-4 0-10 6-10 6-16 12-16 12-20 12-26

The smallest crowd to attend an Ashes test in Australia was a telling indictment of Britain's inability to compete with the wearers of the green and gold. The series was dead, Britain were fielding a make-shift, patched-up team and top Australian official Bob Abbott had declared that promoting a dead horse was easier than promoting the Lions. After 80 minutes the dead British horse had stomped all over Australia's thoroughbreds and kicked Ashes football back into life. Moreover Britain's victory was achieved in the grand manner. The thousand or so British fans in the SFS and the millions viewing the telecast back in Britain could scarcely believe their eyes as the Lions gave a performance bordering on the miraculous.

Britain were denied a try in the first five minutes when the referee disallowed a touchdown by Ford before being subjected to a tremendous battering by the Australian attack. They survived, however, and took the lead in the 16th minute when Andy Gregory worked a run-around with Kevin Ward to send Offiah haring in for the first try. Four minutes later Gregory was first to a loose ball on the home "25" to launch Ford on a an incredibly serpentine yet swift dash past Bella, Backo, Currie and Sterling. The make-do full-back touched down under the posts, Loughlin converted and the Lions led 10-0.

Sterling had to retire hurt seven minutes before half-time, an unfortunate finale to a wonderful test career, but the writing was already on the wall even though Hanley was grounded a yard short just before the break. The first 20 minutes of the second half were a grim test of Britain's resolve. In the 42nd minute Lewis, playing his eleventh and final Ashes test, displayed brute strength for a change to shake off three tacklers as he forced the ball down under the posts for a try converted by O'Connor. Six minutes later Britain answered those who doubted their staying power when Andy Gregory conjured up another try. Kicking to the Australian in-goal he caused such confusion that Belcher and Jack collided allowing Gill to touch down. Loughlin's conversion restored Britain's ten point lead. Australia roared back into the game on 61 minutes when Sam Backo bullocked through Loughlin's challenge to score his third try of the series. Backo thus became the first forward to score a try in each test in an Ashes series. O'Connor's goal brought Australia to 12-16, the closest they would come to taking the lead.

Britain's response, three minutes later, was stunning. Hemmed in their own "25", the Lions worked the ball to Loughlin who burst through two defenders, shot into open space down the right flank, hit the half-way line and parted to Henderson Gill who screamed along the touch-line for 40 yards before diving in at the corner. If that was not enough to depress the Australian challenge, the next try certainly was. Seventy-one minutes had elapsed when Andy Gregory, playing the game of his life, cheekily took on the Australian defence a mere fifteen yards from his own line. A feint, a mad ten-yard dash and he had opened up the defensive line. Mike Gregory took his short pass and took off for the goal posts 75 yards away. Offiah accompanied him all the way, insurance if the chasing Lewis and Pearce should overtake the flying second-rower. No chance. Gregory left them all in his wake to score the try that symbolically restored the pride to British Rugby League. Loughlin kicked the goal and a decade of misery and humiliation had ended for the Brits. Hallelujah!

TEST MATCH 103

AT WEMBLEY STADIUM, LONDON – 27 October, 1990
GREAT BRITAIN 19 AUSTRALIA 12 (HT 2-2)

SR Hampson (Wigan)	G Belcher (Canberra)
BP Eastwood (Hull) 2T,3G	M Hancock (Brisbane B)
DA Powell (Sheffield E)	MN Meninga (Canberra) capt T,2G
C Gibson (Leeds)	M McGaw (Cronulla) T
MN Offiah (Widnes) T	A Ettingshausen (Cronulla)
GE Schofield (Leeds) DG	†R Stuart (Canberra)
A Gregory (Wigan)	AJ Langer (Brisbane B)
†K Harrison (Hull)	SD Roach (Balmain)
L Jackson (Hull)	Kd Walters (Brisbane B)
PA Dixon (Leeds)	M Bella (Manly)
DC Betts (Wigan)	PI Sironen (Balmain)
RC Powell (Leeds)	†J Cartwright (Penrith)
EC Hanley (Wigan) capt	RF Lindner (Wests)
SUB K Fairbank (Bradford N) for Harrison	SUB D Shearer (Brisbane B) for Hancock
SUB KA Ward (St. Helens) for RC Powell	SUB G Alexander (Penrith) for Langer
SUB S Edwards (Wigan) DNP	SUB GP Lazarus (Canberra) for Bella
SUB DJ Hulme (Widnes) DNP	SUB D Hasler (Manly) for Cartwright

Referee - A Sablayrolles (France)   Crowd - 54,569   Gate - £553,757
Scoring - 2-0 2-2 6-2 6-6 12-6 13-6 13-12 17-12 19-12

A record crowd for a test match in Britain witnessed a dramatic, action-packed game which, following directly on the Lions' epic victory in the previous test at Sydney two years earlier, confirmed that Ashes tests were once again truly competitive. Britain, spurred by a strangely emotional and patriotic crowd, capitalised on the chances which were presented and finished worthy winners. The Kangaroos, possibly overawed by the pomp and circumstance engendered by Wembley, could not impose their customary stranglehold on the opposing pack and were compelled to make uncharacteristic errors which cost them the test.

The first half was a furious affair which failed to yield a solitary try. Eastwood, one of the British heroes of the day, rattled the post with a first minute penalty as Britain took the game to the Australians. Ten minutes later Meninga fired wide a penalty and then Gregory failed with a drop goal for Britain. The deadlock was broken in the 21st minute when Eastwood landed a penalty after Lindner infringed at the play-the-ball. Britain held that slender 2-0 lead until the 37th minute when Hampson lashed out with his foot in a tackle by Kerrod Walters. Meninga equalised by kicking the ensuing penalty.

The second half was much more open and eventful. Three minutes had passed when, Ellery Hanley, the match's towering figure, smashed through the Australian defence, chipped delicately over Belcher, regathered and headed for the line only to be overwhelmed just short. A quick play-the-ball completely messed up Australia's defence and enabled Jackson to send Eastwood burrowing through two hapless tacklers for the game's first try. Nine minutes later it was back to square one when McGaw sent Meninga through a crumbling defence to score wide out.

Britain regained the lead after 56 minutes when Hanley struck once more. Hoisting a high kick, the British captain followed up and crashed into Belcher as he took the falling ball. The impact jarred the ball loose and Offiah was there in a flash, scooping it up and diving over close to the posts. Eastwood kicked the goal and Australia trailed 6-12 which became 6-13 when Schofield popped over a simple drop goal in the 63rd minute. The Kangaroos were far from finished, however, and had reduced the deficit to a solitary point within four minutes. A magnificent effort covering half the length of the field by Mark McGaw began with him evading Offiah and Gregory as he swept down the right touch-line. Gibson seemed to have effected a good tackle on him around the "25" but as Hampson came into complete the job the two Brits appeared to knock each other off the tackle and McGaw strode away majestically to score wide out. Meninga's fine conversion set the game on a knife-edge.

A mere ten minutes remained when Britain struck the crucial blow. For a third time it was a kick in broken play which undid the Kangaroos. This time Schofield broke in mid-field and lobbed a little kick over the defence for Daryl Powell to gather, take Ettingshausen's tackle and send out a perfect pass to Eastwood who scooted over near the flag. The winger missed the conversion but sealed a famous British victory when he landed a difficult penalty two minutes from time after Hanley had been obstructed chasing another dangerous kick-through. Great Britain had not won the first test in an Ashes series since 1973. Perhaps it was not merely coincidental that the previous occasion was also at nerve-jarring Wembley.

Wembley, first test, 1990. Michael Hancock fractures the British line. Darryl Powell (3), Lee Jackson, Karl Harrison, Roy Powell and Paul Dixon are left behind.

TEST MATCH 104

AT OLD TRAFFORD, MANCHESTER – 10 November, 1990
GREAT BRITAIN 10 AUSTRALIA 14 (HT 2-4)

SR Hampson (Wigan)	G Belcher (Canberra)
BP Eastwood (Hull) G	A Ettingshausen (Cronulla)
DA Powell (Sheffield E)	MN Meninga (Canberra) capt T,G
C Gibson (Leeds)	LW Daley (Canberra)
MN Offiah (Widnes)	D Shearer (Brisbane B) T
GE Schofield (Leeds)	†C Lyons (Manly) T
A Gregory (Wigan)	R Stuart (Canberra)
K Harrison (Hull)	SD Roach (Balmain)
L Jackson (Hull)	CP Elias (Balmain)
A Platt (Wigan)	GP Lazarus (Canberra)
DC Betts (Wigan)	PI Sironen (Balmain)
PA Dixon (Leeds) T	RF Lindner (Wests)
EC Hanley (Wigan) capt	B Mackay (St. George)
SUB PJP Loughlin (St. Helens) T for Offiah	SUB G Alexander (Penrith) DNP
SUB KA Ward (St. Helens) for Harrison	SUB D Hasler (Manly) DNP
SUB DJ Hulme (Widnes) DNP	SUB M Sargent (Newcastle) DNP
SUB RC Powell (Leeds) DNP	SUB J Cartwright (Penrith) DNP

Referee - A Sablayrolles (France)   Crowd - 46,615   Gate - £381,000
Scoring - 0-4 2-4 6-4 6-10 10-10 10-14

Australia deserved to square the series in an epic encounter at Old Trafford. They were demonstrably the better team but had to wait until the dying seconds of injury time to shake off and finally subdue a magnificently dogged challenge from a fired-up Great Britain. Both sides would probably have settled for the 10-10 draw which had loomed likely from the 70th minute try by Loughlin which had brought Britain level. Test matches are never settled by compromise, however, and Australia had the nerve and killer instinct which divides winners and losers.

The first half resembled the opening half at Wembley. Again only two scores accrued from forty minutes of the most intense football imaginable. At half-time the Kangaroos held a 4-2 lead despite having spent most of the game in their own territory and Britain were left rueing four abortive drop goal attempts when other ploys may have been more profitable. It was decidedly against the run of play that Australia scored the first points after 24 minutes. Cliff Lyons, making a notable test debut, initiated a movement which sliced the British defence alarmingly easily. Stuart backed up his half-back partner and lobbed the ball to the onrushing Shearer who swept down the flank past Hanley and Schofield for a classic winger's try which Meninga failed to convert. Eight minutes later a penalty goal by Eastwood proved to be the only other score of the half.

If Britain had dominated the first half, Australia certainly made up for that in the second. Even so, it was Great Britain who registered the next try twelve minutes into the half. It was a short range affair conceived by Schofield whose short ball was taken on the burst by Dixon, an explosive second-rower, who blasted through a combined Belcher-Meninga tackle to plant the ball down over the line. Britain's 6-4 lead lasted only four minutes before the Kangaroos conjured up a try fit to win any match. The ball travelled fifty yards and through a dozen pairs of hands before Ettingshausen punted perfectly infield for Lyons to touch down. This magical try, converted by Meninga, could reasonably have been expected to totally deflate the British effort. Instead the home team clung like limpets to the increasingly confident Kangaroos and though the game seemed destined to slip away from them, the Kangaroo half-back Ricky Stuart suddenly turned benefactor. Breaking down the right side of the field Stuart appeared to have opened up the British defence only to throw a pass which was too close to the long arm of Paul Loughlin who momentarily juggled with the capricious ball before racing 50 yards to the Australian goal-line. His touchdown could have been nearer the posts but the kick was still relatively simple. Eastwood, hero-turned-villain, missed the goal and the test was tied.

Stuart, so nearly the man who could have lost the Ashes, was presented with a last second chance to redeem his sin. Running the ball out from his own "25", he dummied past Jackson and launched into a 50 yard arcing run to the right flank hotly pursued by several defenders and Ettingshausen and Meninga. On reaching the home "25" Meninga, summoning up astonishing speed, forced Gibson out of his path and accepted Stuart's pass to dive over for the match-winning try. It was a truly stunning end to one of modern test history's most thrilling encounters.

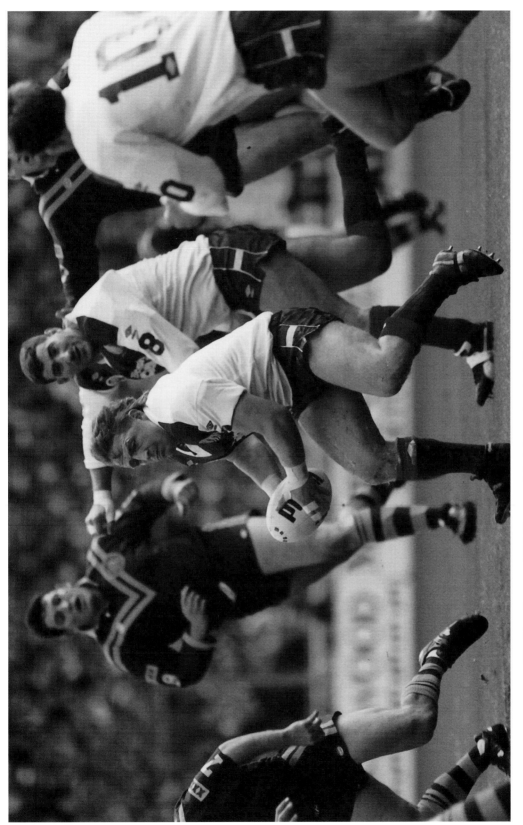

Wembley, first test, 1990. Veteran of six Ashes series, Andy Gregory prepares to feed Paul Dixon.

Old Trafford, second test, 1990. Great Britain captain Ellery Hanley is confronted by Laurie Daley.

TEST MATCH 105

AT ELLAND ROAD, LEEDS – 24 November, 1990
GREAT BRITAIN 0 AUSTRALIA 14 (HT 0-4)

SR Hampson (Wigan)	G Belcher (Canberra)
BP Eastwood (Hull)	A Ettingshausen (Cronulla) T
DA Powell (Sheffield E)	MN Meninga (Canberra) capt T,G
C Gibson (Leeds)	LW Daley (Canberra)
MN Offiah (Widnes)	D Shearer (Brisbane B)
GE Schofield (Leeds)	C Lyons (Manly)
A Gregory (Wigan)	R Stuart (Canberra)
K Harrison (Hull)	SD Roach (Balmain)
L Jackson (Hull)	CP Elias (Balmain) T
A Platt (Wigan)	GP Lazarus (Canberra)
DC Betts (Wigan)	PI Sironen (Balmain)
PA Dixon (Leeds)	RF Lindner (Wests)
EC Hanley (Wigan) capt	B Mackay (St. George)
SUB J Davies (Widnes) for Gibson	SUB G Alexander (Penrith) for Shearer
SUB MK Gregory (Warrington) for Dixon	SUB D Hasler (Manly) for Mackay
SUB RC Powell (Leeds) for Harrison	†SUB M Sargent (Newcastle K) for Lazarus
SUB DJ Hulme (Widnes) DNP	SUB D Gillespie (Canterbury) for Sironen

Referee - A Sablayrolles (France)   Crowd - 32,500   Gate - £239,000
Scoring - 0-4 0-10 0-14

For the first time since 1978 the third test was to be the Ashes decider. The previous two matches had been high quality thrillers. This test was a disappointment in that despite Britain's valiant efforts there was only one team in it from beginning to end and that was Australia. The conditions were appalling, torrential rain and gusting winds never ceasing. Australia played the perfect game under the circumstances, making a minimum of mistakes, trusting to their superb defence and taking the chances which came their way. Britain, on the other hand, wasted possession, failed to mount any real attacking threat and found their tacticians at the scrum-base, Hanley, Gregory and Schofield, securely shackled.

The first half produced just one score and luck certainly favoured the Kangaroos when it came. British centre Carl Gibson was injured in the eighth minute and as the home team tried forlornly to get substitute Jonathan Davies on to the pitch Australia ruthlessly exploited their numerical advantage. Sensing Britain's weakness, Australia worked an overlap culminating in Ricky Stuart slinging a monster pass out to Ettingshausen who beat the cover to plunge over at the corner. Australia should have extended their lead to 6-0 just prior to the interval but Meninga failed with an eminently kickable penalty. Britain had produced only a couple of half-chances for Davies and Betts in the first half which the Kangaroos had been quick to kill.

In the second half Australia strangled the life out of Britain. The crucial score came ten minutes into the half and again Stuart was the architect. Stuart took the ball close to the play-the-ball, noticed that Schofield was hell-bent on intercepting but shot his pass quickly enough to evade the British stand-off's straining fingers. The ball reached Lyons who hit the gap, made ground and nonchanantly dropped the ball over his shoulder into the hands of the rampaging Meninga who drove unmolested to the line for a try which he converted himself. Meninga thus became the first Australian captain to score a try in each test of an Ashes series.

Nine minutes from time the Kangaroos wrapped up the game when Laurie Daley took off from dummy-half in his own half and unleashed Ettingshausen on a run almost to the line before Davies tackled him. The resultant disarray at the play-the-ball was exploited clinically by the splendid Kangaroo hooker Benny Elias who romped over at the corner for the try, despite the discomfort of broken ribs and a battery of pain-killing injections.

So miserly had the Australian defence been that Britain had not even had a shot at goal and Britain's nilling had been their first at home for 60 years. The series as a whole, however, had been rivetting. The aggregate attendance of 133,684 was a record for a series in England and Ashes football had again reached a pinnacle.

TEST MATCH 106

AT SYDNEY FOOTBALL STADIUM – 12 June, 1992
AUSTRALIA 22 GREAT BRITAIN 6 (HT 8-2)

A Ettingshausen (Cronulla)	G Steadman (Castleford)
RJ Wishart (Illawarra) 3G	P Newlove (Featherstone R)
MN Meninga (Canberra) capt 2T	DA Powell (Sheffield E)
LW Daley (Canberra)	PJP Loughlin (St. Helens)
M Hancock (Brisbane B) T	MN Offiah (Wigan)
P Jackson (Norths)	GE Schofield (Leeds) capt
AJ Langer (Brisbane B)	A Gregory (Wigan)
GP Lazarus (Brisbane B)	K Skerrett (Wigan)
S Walters (Canberra)	M Dermott (Wigan)
†PW Harragon (Newcastle K)	L Crooks (Castleford) G
PI Sironen (Balmain) T	DC Betts (Wigan)
RF Lindner (Wests)	A Platt (Wigan)
B Clyde (Canberra)	P Clarke (Wigan)
SUB Kv Walters (Brisbane B) for Jackson	SUB JP Lydon (Wigan) T for Loughlin
SUB B Fittler (Penrith) for Lindner	SUB S Edwards (Wigan) for Newlove
SUB D Gillespie (Wests) for Lazarus	SUB MG Jackson (Wakefield T) for Dermott
SUB B Mackay (St. George) for Sironen	SUB I Lucas (Wigan) for Skerrett

Referee - D Hale (New Zealand)   Crowd - 40,141   Gate - $820,427
Scoring - 2-0 8-0 8-2 12-2 18-2 18-6 22-6

The Ashes series of 1992 was the first entirely played under floodlights, each test being staged on a Friday night. The fact that Australians now regarded Anglo-Australian tests as highly as they had two decades earlier was witnessed in the capacity crowds for all three matches.

Australia found themselves on the rack as the Lions strove to play an open game in order to utilise the blistering pace of Martin Offiah. It took two wonderful tackles from Andrew Ettingshausen to thwart menacing runs by Offiah in the third and 23rd minute, the latter after the winger had stood up Wishart and dashed 70 yards. Britain certainly had the better of the first quarter although Andy Gregory found himself in the sin-bin after nine minutes following a high tackle on Jackson. Gregory was making history by figuring in his sixth Ashes series, a feat achieved previously only by Graeme Langlands. Gregory was playing against Australia for the tenth and final time and his third tour was shortly to end prematurely in injury.

It was completely against the run of play that Australia took the lead after 26 minutes when Wishart kicked a penalty after Daley had old-manned the referee at a play-the-ball. Two minutes later the home team bagged an absolutely magnificent try. From a play-the-ball on their own "25" Australia took the ball via half-a-dozen passes to half-way where Meninga bounced Schofield from his path and passed to Gillespie. Ettingshausen and Jackson carried the movement on before Meninga rejoined the action to sweep through Crooks' challenge to score a truly memorable try ten yards from the right corner-flag. Wishart hit a fine goal and Australia led 8-0 having endured most of the pressure. All Britain had to show for a stupendous effort was a 39th minute penalty from Crooks.

The second half saw Australia gain the ascendancy, manfully though the Lions resisted. Meninga more or less settled the game in the 49th minute. The ball was shifted from the left to the right flank allowing Daley to step inside Britain's defence on the "25" and serve Meninga who sent Clyde cruising through three tackles before returning the ball to Meninga who crunched through Steadman's challenge to score at the flag. In the 64th minute Britain cracked again. Gillespie had been prevented from scoring only by colliding with the goal-post and intense pressure finally resulted in a try by Sironen. The huge forward must have been surprised that the British defenders were so keen to take his dummy and allow him to plunge over under the bar without hindrance. Wishart converted. Six minutes later Harragon hit Lucas in a horrendous tackle which virtually finished the British prop's playing career. The referee failed even to award a penalty.

Nine minutes from time Schofield found a chink for Lydon to kick through from ten yards and beat Hancock to the touchdown at the corner but Hancock cancelled out this score within five minutes as he dotted down at the opposite corner after fine play from Langer, Daley and Clyde. Australia finished good winners but the score hardly did the Lions justice.

TEST MATCH 107

AT PRINCES PARK, MELBOURNE – 26 June, 1992
AUSTRALIA 10 GREAT BRITAIN 33 (HT 0-22)

A Ettingshausen (Cronulla)	G Steadman (Castleford) T
RJ Wishart (Illawarra)	BP Eastwood (Hull) 6G
MN Meninga (Canberra) capt G	DA Powell (Sheffield E)
LW Daley (Canberra)	P Newlove (Featherstone R) T
M Hancock (Brisbane B)	MN Offiah (Wigan) T
P Jackson (Norths)	GE Schofield (Leeds) capt T,DG
AJ Langer (Brisbane B)	S Edwards (Wigan)
D Gillespie (Wests)	K Skerrett (Wigan)
S Walters (Canberra)	M Dermott (Wigan)
PW Harragon (Newcastle K)	A Platt (Wigan)
PI Sironen (Balmain)	DC Betts (Wigan)
RF Lindner (Wests) T	† W McGinty (Wigan)
B Clyde (Canberra)	P Clarke (Wigan) T
SUB C Johns (Brisbane B) T for Wishart	SUB GJ Connolly (St. Helens) for Newlove
SUB Kv Walters (Brisbane B) for Jackson	SUB JP Lydon (Wigan) for Powell
SUB B Mackay (St. George) for Harragon	SUB K Harrison (Halifax) for Skerrett
SUB GP Lazarus (Brisbane B) for Sironen	SUB P Hulme (Widnes) for McGinty

Referee - D Hale (New Zealand)   Crowd - 30,257   Gate - $716,728
Scoring - 0-2 0-4 0-10 0-16 0-22 0-23 6-23 10-23 10-29 10-33

For the first time in Ashes history an Australian venue other than Brisbane or Sydney staged a test. Melbourne's Princes Park was packed to the rafters to witness an astounding humiliation of Australia. So severe was the shock to the Australian management and press corps that no excuse was left unused - the hostility of the crowd, including upwards of 8,000 British tour followers, the unfamiliarity of the Australian players with Melbourne, the wet weather and even the length of the grass were blamed. The truth was that Britain played out of their skins and on the day the Australians, uncharacteristically slipshod, simply could not cope.

Britain began at breakneck pace, Schofield sending Offiah on a 50 yard dash, quickly followed by an Edwards chip and chase which was scrambled away at the corner. The pressure on Australia was reflected in their concession of penalty goals to Paul Eastwood after six and eleven minutes, both for off-side at rucks. After 18 minutes the Lions scored the first try when from a play-the-ball 15 yards out Powell sent Clarke dummying through a gap provided by Harragon and Sironen to allow Eastwood an easy conversion. Over a quarter of the game had gone before Australia exerted any real pressure but the Lions tacklers were like bees swarming and Australia cracked alarmingly again on the half-hour. Dermott began the move which saw Edwards step inside Sironen around half-way and direct a kick to the home in-goal just to the left of the posts. Offiah was first there but overshot only for Newlove to finish the job. Eastwood landed his fourth goal. Four minutes later he kicked his fifth following a cheeky try by Schofield whose little kick and chase from 15 yards had Ettingshausen floundering hopelessly on the greasy surface. Incredibly Britain went in for the break 22 points clear.

Australia came out fighting and within three minutes Ettingshausen had a try disallowed after Newlove forced him to lose the ball over the line. Nine minutes into the half Schofield eased Britain further ahead with a 20 yard drop goal but then Australia, inspired by substitute Kevin Walters, produced a period of sustained pressure which yielded ten points and breathed life back into the game. In the 56th minute Bob Lindner forced the ball down after being apparently held on his back. Meninga converted and four minutes later Langer and Walters sent out long passes which opened the way for Johns to race 20 yards for a try and the score was 23-10.

Eight minutes from time the Lions reasserted their dominance when Steadman dashed 30 yards down the left wing blind-side of the defence to dive low past Ettingshausen for a superb try which the immaculate Eastwood goaled from the touch-line. In the last minute Schofield broke from his own half, chipped yet again, regathered and slung the ball to Offiah who outran Ettingshausen and Hancock to score at the corner. Britain's 23 points winning margin equalled their record 40-17 victory in the third test of 1958. Much of the credit was due to a magnificent pack, culled, uniquely in test history, from one club, Wigan.

TEST MATCH 108

AT LANG PARK, BRISBANE – 3 July, 1992
AUSTRALIA 16 GREAT BRITAIN 10 (HT 8-4)

A Ettingshausen (Cronulla)
WJ Carne (Brisbane B)
B Fittler (Penrith)
MN Meninga (Canberra) capt T,4G
M Hancock (Brisbane B)
LW Daley (Canberra) T
AJ Langer (Brisbane B)
GP Lazarus (Brisbane B)
S Walters (Canberra)
PW Harragon (Newcastle K)
PI Sironen (Balmain)
RF Lindner (Wests)
B Clyde (Canberra)
SUB Kv Walters (Brisbane B) for Ettingshausen
SUB C Johns (Brisbane B) for Carne
SUB D Gillespie (Wests) for Sironen
SUB J Cartwright (Penrith) for Lindner

G Steadman (Castleford)
BP Eastwood (Hull) 3G
DA Powell (Sheffield E)
P Newlove (Featherstone R)
MN Offiah (Wigan) T
GE Schofield (Leeds) capt
S Edwards (Wigan)
K Skerrett (Wigan)
M Dermott (Wigan)
A Platt (Wigan)
DC Betts (Wigan)
W McGinty (Wigan)
P Clarke (Wigan)
SUB GJ Connolly (St. Helens) for Newlove
SUB JP Lydon (Wigan) for Schofield
SUB P Hulme (Widnes) for McGinty
SUB K Harrison (Halifax) for Skerrett

Referee - D Hale (New Zealand)   Crowd - 32,313   Gate - $624,807
Scoring - 2-0 2-2 4-2 4-4 6-4 8-4 12-4 16-4 16-10

An Ashes decider on a warm, humid night in Brisbane with an excitable crowd, almost a third of which were visiting Britons, provided an ideal scenario for a classic test match. Unfortunately, the game did not live upto expectations as Australia won the match and their tenth consecutive Ashes series much more comfortably than the final score suggested.

For one man, however, the game was a major triumph. Mal Meninga, whose solitary goal at Melbourne had taken him past Neil Fox's all-comers record of 228 points in tests, became Australia's most capped test player having represented his country 37 times, thereby eclipsing Reg Gasnier's record established a quarter century earlier. Meninga was also equalling Keith Holman's record of appearing in 14 Ashes tests and by the end of the game he had smashed Graeme Langlands' record 104 points scored in Anglo-Australian tests. By the final hooter Mighty Mal had bagged 108 points against Britain and 242 points in all tests and looked good for many more.

The first half was very desultory. True, the ball moved from end to end, as it invariably does in the modern, kick-dominated game but it was largely a scrappy, error-ridden affair, uncomfortably like a Rugby Union international. All the first half scoring consisted of penalty goals. Meninga potted the first after five minutes when Edwards got involved in a silly fracas with Carne at a ruck under the posts. Seven minutes later Eastwood levelled only for Meninga to restore Australia's advantage in the 17th minute when Dermott obstructed Daley under the sticks as he chased a kick through. Within five minutes the scores were locked when Eastwood punished Lindner's lying-on at a tackle. It was Meninga's turn again on 27 minutes when Skerrett obstructed Langer and bang on half-time the Australian captain landed his fourth goal after Dermott's truculence at Steve Walters' raking the ball from him at a play-the-ball.

Australia dominated the second period, which was marginally more entertaining than the first. Bradley Clyde was first to threaten with a good, mazy run as pressure built on the Lions. In the 47th minute Fittler provided the spark for the opening try when he broke the Lions' defence ten yards out and whipped out a less than perfect pass which Daley picked off his boots to take two tacklers over the line for a try which Meninga could not convert.

It was inevitable and fitting that Meninga should wrap up the test and the Ashes when he claimed the second green and gold try in the 55th minute. Fittler took the ball at a ruck on the Lions' "25" and served Daley who grubber-kicked exquisitely to the right wing where Meninga scooped it up, went through Betts and Edwards and planted the ball one-handed on the goal-line.

Britain had dropped far too much ball, missed far too many tackles and taken too many wrong options, yet with five minutes remaining they suddenly found themselves back in the game. Australia were camped on the British "25" when Dermott charged into Meninga who spilled the ball. Offiah hacked it on, took a benign bounce at half-way and cantered to the posts for Eastwood to convert. Australia's defence was too disciplined to make another mistake, however, and Britain returned home minus the Ashes, as usual.

Elland Road, third test, 1994. Britain's full-back Gary Connolly struggles to shake off Kangaroo winger Rod Wishart.

Elland Road, third test, 1994. Full-back Brett Mullins moves in to help bring down British centre Paul Newlove.

TEST MATCH 109

AT WEMBLEY STADIUM, LONDON – 22 October, 1994
GREAT BRITAIN 8 AUSTRALIA 4 (HT 6-0)

J Davies (Warrington) T,G	BW Mullins (Canberra)
JT Robinson (Wigan)	A Ettingshausen (Cronulla)
GJ Connolly (Wigan)	MN Meninga (Canberra) capt
A Hunte (St. Helens)	S Renouf (Brisbane B) T
MN Offiah (Wigan)	† WJ Sailor (Brisbane B)
DA Powell (Sheffield E)	LW Daley (Canberra)
S Edwards (Wigan) capt	AJ Langer (Brisbane B)
K Harrison (Halifax)	I Roberts (Manly)
L Jackson (Sheffield E)	S Walters (Canberra)
CM Joynt (St. Helens)	PW Harragon (Newcastle K)
DC Betts (Wigan)	PI Sironen (Balmain)
A Farrell (Wigan)	B Clyde (Canberra)
P Clarke (Wigan)	B Fittler (Penrith)
SUB: R Goulding (St. Helens) G for Farrell	SUB: R Stuart (Canberra) for Daley
SUB: AG Bateman (Warrington) for Davies	† SUB: D Furner (Canberra) for Clyde
† SUB: B McDermott (Wigan) for Powell	† SUB: D Pay (Canterbury) for Sironen
† SUB: M Cassidy (Wigan) for Harrison	SUB: T Brasher (Balmain) DNP

Referee - G Annesley (NSW)

Crowd - 57,034   Gate - £1,107,423

Scoring - 2-0 6-0 6-4 8-4

Great Britain went into this test as rank outsiders and played almost three-quarters of the game a man short but contrived to win one of test history's greatest victories. Shades of Rorke's Drift and Prescott's Test of '58, without doubt. Moreover, a record British test crowd was there to witness the heroics and the first million pound test gate must have delighted the accountants.

Rain lashed Wembley as a minute's silence was observed in remembrance of Ashes giant Gus Risman who passed away a few weeks before. He would have relished this momentous occasion. The Kangaroo captain, Mal Meninga was creating another niche in history by playing his fifteenth Ashes test and so passing Keith Holman's Australian record.

Britain applied considerable pressure for the first fifteen minutes with Harrison, Jackson and Betts taking the game to a heavier Australian pack. Edwards was held on the line and Davies missed a relatively simple penalty before Australia made their first serious attacks as the first quarter ended. Then in the 25th minute beautiful Australian passing towards the right wing found Bradley Clyde out wide. Twenty yards from the British goal-line Clyde veered inside to be pole-axed by the flailing right arm of Shaun Edwards. Clyde lost the ball and his senses. Britain lost their captain, immediately red-carded by the referee. Edwards became the first man to be dismissed in an Ashes test in ten years. More disappointingly he was the first Great Britain captain ever sent off in a test. At this point Australia should have taken control but the British were men possessed. On 32 minutes Davies landed a simple penalty after Sironen had obstructed him as he chased his own kick. Four minutes later Davies effectively won the match with a try out of the blue. Britain moved the ball from left to right as they crossed half-way where Betts served Davies. The full-back gave the merest hint of a pass to Connolly but held on completely flumoxing Renouf and Fittler. As the defence fell away only Mullins was left in the race as Davies arced to the touch-line. His tackle was too late and Davies sailed over at the corner for a truly astonishing score. Although Davies missed the conversion and Goulding's attempted drop goal in injury time flopped under the bar, the home team had clearly taken the whip hand.

The first 20 minutes of the second half was all Australia. Play-makers Langer, Fittler and Daley tried all they knew. Fittler was over the line only to be ejected backwards by Connolly and Offiah. However, Britain held fast, came back and Offiah was just held on the Australian line. Meninga strode through but comically fell over his own feet. There was a final reward for Australia eight minutes from time when Meninga supplied Renouf with his only chance of the game. The centre turned Robinson inside out ten yards from the line and crashed through Connolly's tackle to score near the flag. Furner's conversion flew across the face of the posts and Australia still trailed.

In the last minute Harragon held down McDermott in a tackle and Goulding stroked over a 30 yard penalty goal to seal a stupendous triumph for Great Britain.

TEST MATCH 110

OLD TRAFFORD, MANCHESTER – 5 November, 1994
GREAT BRITAIN 8 AUSTRALIA 38 (HT 4-18)

G Steadman (Castleford)	BW Mullins (Canberra) 2T
JT Robinson (Wigan)	A Ettingshausen (Cronulla) T
GJ Connolly (Wigan)	MN Meninga (Canberra) capt
A Hunte (St. Helens)	S Renouf (Brisbane B) T
MN Offiah (Wigan)	RJ Wishart (Illawarra) 7G
DA Powell (Sheffield E)	LW Daley (Canberra) T
R Goulding (St. Helens) 2G	R Stuart (Canberra)
K Harrison (Halifax)	GP Lazarus (Brisbane B)
L Jackson (Sheffield E)	S Walters (Canberra)
CM Joynt (St. Helens)	I Roberts (Manly)
DC Betts (Wigan)	D Pay (Canterbury)
A Farrell (Wigan)	B Clyde (Canberra) T
P Clarke (Wigan) capt	B Fittler (Penrith)
SUB: P Newlove (Bradford N) T for Hunte	†SUB: G Florimo (Norths) for Roberts
SUB: GE Schofield (Leeds) for Powell	SUB: AJ Langer (Brisbane B) for Florimo
SUB: B McDermott (Wigan) for Betts	SUB: PI Sironen (Balmain) for Daley
SUB: M Cassidy (Wigan) for Joynt	SUB: T Brasher (Balmain) DNP

Referee - G Annesley (NSW)   Crowd - 43,930   Gate - £634,467
Scoring - 2-0 2-2 4-2 4-6 4-12 4-18 4-24 4-26 8-26 8-32 8-38

Australia threw off the apathy of their Wembley performance to completely overwhelm Great Britain, whose own performance was woeful in comparison to the heroics of the first test.

Whereas Edwards' dismissal had been the sole discordant note at Wembley, this second test was much more spiteful. As early as the second minute a high challenge by Goulding on Pay sparked a rumpus and it was Britain who displayed most of the indiscipline throughout. Although the Kangaroos looked the more threatening force throughout the opening 25 minutes Britain established a 4-2 lead with penalty goals kicked by Goulding (5 and 12 minutes) against one landed by Wishart after eight minutes.

Britain were pressing hard when the game was ripped away from them in ten catastophic minutes. In the 26th minute Goulding slung a long pass to Farrell fifteen yards from the Australian line only for Meninga to intercept before rumbling 70 yards down the right touch-line before Offiah nailed him. Meninga took the tackle but lobbed a lovely pass to Ettingshausen who ran the last ten yards to the corner for a stunning try. Six minutes later a Stuart bomb was allowed to bounce and five eager Kangaroos handled before Clyde dashed through a double tackle to score wide out. Wishart's well-struck conversion took Australia clear at 12-4 and on 36 minutes Wishart broke 50 yards straight up the middle. From the resultant play-the-ball Mullins skipped through weak tackling to the posts and Wishart's third goal put Australia out of sight at 18-4.

Two minutes into the second half Laurie Daley scored a delightful 25 yards solo try under the bar, duly converted by Wishart. Seven minutes later Harrison retired to the blood bin to be replaced by Barrie McDermott and the ground erupted. Displaying the ferocity of a wolverine and about as much intelligence, McDermott immediately launched a head tackle on the unfortunate Clyde. Walters waded into McDermott and a brawl ensued. McDermott and Walters were sin-binned and Wishart kicked the resultant penalty.

The next ten minutes proved Britain's best of the game. Connolly had a try ruled out for putting a foot in touch and Schofield was penalised having shot into the clear with an interception before Newlove crashed over for a try on the hour.

It was far too little, much too late, however, as the Kangaroos flexed their muscles again. In the 65th minute Florimo broke through 30 yards out and flipped an inside pass to Renouf who sliced through for a splendid try. Four minutes later Meninga burst through a ruck deep in his own half and conjured up an over the shoulder pass to Mullins who sprinted 70 yards to the British posts. Wishart converted both tries as the British challenge entirely disintegrated. Fittler sent a drop at goal wide in injury time. It was about the only thing Meninga's men missed all afternoon. Australia's third consecutive victory at Old Trafford had been as comprehensive a lesson to the Brits as any they had given in the last two decades. Would the nightmare ever end?

Elland Road, third test, 1994. Australia's captain Mal Meninga prepares for Great Britain prop Barrie McDermott's hand-off whilst two other tacklers move in.

TEST MATCH 111

ELLAND ROAD, LEEDS – 20 November, 1994
GREAT BRITAIN 4 AUSTRALIA 23 (HT 2-7)

GJ Connolly (Wigan)	BW Mullins (Canberra)
JT Robinson (Wigan)	A Ettingshausen (Cronulla)
A Hunte (St. Helens)	MN Meninga (Canberra) capt
P Newlove (Bradford N)	S Renouf (Brisbane B)
MN Offiah (Wigan)	RJ Wishart (Illawarra) T,3G
P Clarke (Wigan)	LW Daley (Canberra) T
S Edwards (Wigan) capt	R Stuart (Canberra) DG
K Harrison (Halifax)	GP Lazarus (Brisbane B)
L Jackson (Sheffield E)	S Walters (Canberra) T
B McDermott (Wigan)	I Roberts (Manly)
DC Betts (Wigan)	D Pay (Canterbury) T
A Farrell (Wigan) 2G	B Clyde (Canberra)
CM Joynt (St. Helens)	B Fittler (Penrith)
SUB: GE Schofield (Leeds) for Clarke	SUB: T Brasher (Balmain) for Ettingshausen
SUB: R Goulding (St. Helens) for Joynt	SUB: G Florimo (Norths) for Roberts
SUB: S Nickle (St. Helens) for McDermott	SUB: AJ Langer (Brisbane B) for Walters
SUB: DA Powell (Sheffield E) for Hunte	SUB: D Fairleigh (Norths) for Lazarus

Referee - W Harrigan (NSW)   Crowd - 39,468   Gate - £584,264
Scoring - 2-0 2-6 2-7 2-11 4-11 4-17 4-23

A thoroughly entertaining test teetered in the balance right until the last ten minutes when Australia's resilience in the face of enormous British persistence finally proved too much for their opponents. The Kangaroos, calmer, superbly disciplined and superior in the art of taking their chances, certainly deserved to maintain their hold on the Ashes but the score-line bore no relation to the nature of a gripping game.

During a first quarter which brought a crop of injuries but no real threat of a try, the only score was a fourth minute 35 yard straight penalty goal kicked by Farrell after Pay had made a late tackle on Edwards. Australia took the lead they would not relinquish on 20 minutes when Daley tried a chip kick 20 yards out and had the good fortune to gobble up a richochet off Newlove. The stand-off then stepped inside the hapless Connolly to touch down for a try converted by Wishart. For the remainder of the first half Britain were compelled to defend - dramatically, heroically, stoically, relentlessly. A minute into injury time Stuart dropped a goal from 12 yards to extend Australia's lead to five points.

For the first fifteen minutes of the second half it was the Australians who had to defend desperately. Two gilt-edged opportunities evaporated when Meninga intercepted Joynt's pass on the Kangaroos' line and Wishart scrambled away a wicked kick to the line from Farrell. Completely against the run of play Australia struck the killer blow after 57 minutes. Walters scuttled 40 yards on the fifth tackle and from the play-the-ball Stuart's and Daley's precision passes sent Wishart over at the flag. Even at 2-11 Britain were not out of the hunt. Offiah was forced into kicking high to the shadow of the Australian posts where Wishart and Daley contrived to concede an off-side penalty which Farrell made into two points.

Meninga's men were to finish the stronger of two totally committed teams, however. Daley was stopped on the goal-line and Renouf dropped a scoring pass two yards out before Walters scored a seemingly impossible try. The hooker shot away from a ruck ten yards out and held off the attentions of four opponents to force the ball down at the side of the posts. Wishart's conversion took Australia to a 17-4 lead.

Six minutes from time Stuart conjured an exquisite score. A dummy 35 yards from the home line followed by a short burst into the clear and Walters was stepping out of Edwards' tackle. Connolly blocked his way but could do nothing to stop the scrum-half from back-flicking out a delicious scoring ball to Pay. Wishart's conversion finished the scoring.

Two of the all-time great players, Mal Meninga and Garry Schofield, ended their test careers on a record note. Meninga's seventeenth Ashes appearance set him apart from all others whilst Schofield equalled Jim Sullivan's British mark of fifteen Ashes tests and Mick Sullivan's all-time record of 46 test matches.

STATISTICS

THE ASHES - SERIES BY SERIES

There have been 37 Ashes series. All but two have consisted of three matches. The exceptions occurred in the 1910 series in Australia when two matches were contested and in the 1929-30 series in Britain when four matches took place.

YEAR	VENUE	VICTORIES			POINTS	ASHES
		A	GB	D	A-GB	
1908-09	GB	-	2	1	32-43	GB
1910	A	-	2	-	37-49	GB
1911-12	GB	2	-	1	63-29	A
1914	A	1	2	-	23-44	GB
1920	A	2	1	-	42-35	A
1921-22	GB	1	2	-	21-14	GB
1924	A	1	2	-	27-38	GB
1928	A	1	2	-	33-37	GB
1929-30	GB	1	2	1	34-20	GB
1932	A	1	2	-	34-32	GB
1933	GB	-	3	-	21-30	GB
1936	A	1	2	-	38-32	GB
1937	GB	1	2	-	20-21	GB
1946	A	-	2	1	20-42	GB
1948-49	GB	-	3	-	37-62	GB
1950	A	2	1	-	24-11	A
1952	GB	1	2	-	38-47	GB
1954	A	2	1	-	78-66	A
1956	GB	1	2	-	32-49	GB
1958	A	1	2	-	60-73	GB
1959	GB	1	2	-	44-43	GB
1962	A	1	2	-	40-65	GB
1963	GB	2	1	-	83-30	A
1966	A	2	1	-	38-35	A
1967	GB	2	1	-	39-30	A
1970	A	1	2	-	61-64	GB
1973	GB	2	1	-	41-32	A
1974	A	2	1	-	45-40	A
1978	GB	2	1	-	52-33	A
1979	A	3	-	-	87-18	A
1982	GB	3	-	-	99-18	A
1984	A	3	-	-	63-21	A
1986	GB	3	-	-	96-35	A
1988	A	2	1	-	63-46	A
1990	GB	2	1	-	40-29	A
1992	A	2	1	-	48-49	A
1994	GB	2	1	-	65-20	A
		54	53	4	1,718-1,382	

ASHES VICTORIES

	A	GB
In Australia	9	10
In Great Britain	9	9
Totals	18	19

	Australia	Great Britain
Most points in a series	99 in 1982	73 in 1958
Fewest points in a series	20 in 1937 and 1946	11 in 1950

Highest points aggregate in a series   144 in 1954
Lowest points aggregate in a series   35 in 1921-22

Although Australia have won one fewer series than Great Britain (18 to 19) they have scored more points in 22 of the rubbers.

Dave Brown was arguably Australia's greatest player of the 1930s. A free-scoring centre, Brown captained Australia in the 1936 series.

Billy Jukes is the only forward to score three tries in an Ashes test (1910, Sydney).

SUMMARY OF TESTS IN AUSTRALIA

Until the Melbourne test of 1992 Ashes tests in Australia had been confined to the cities of Sydney and Brisbane. Thirty-seven tests have been staged in Sydney - 31 at the Cricket Ground - whilst eighteen have taken place at three Brisbane venues.

SYDNEY CRICKET GROUND

Year	Test	Victor	AUSTRALIA T	G	P	GREAT BRITAIN T	G	P	CROWD
1914	2	A	2	3	12	1	2	7	55,000
1914	3	GB	2	-	6	2	4	14	34,420
1920	2	A	5	3	21	2	1	8	40,000
1924	1	GB	1	-	3	4	5	22	50,005
1924	2	GB	1	-	3	1	1	5	33,842
1928	2	GB	-	-	0	2	1	8	44,548
1928	3	A	3	6	21	2	4	14	37,380
1932	1	GB	-	3	6	2	1	8	70,204
1932	3	GB	1	5	13	4	3	18	50,053
1936	1	A	4	6	24	2	1	8	63,920
1936	3	GB	1	2	7	2	3	12	53,546
1946	1	DRAW	2	1	8	2	1	8	64,527
1946	3	GB	1	2	7	4	4	20	35,294
1950	1	GB	-	2	4	2	-	6	47,275
1950	3	A	1	1	5	-	1	2	47,178
1954	1	A	7	8	37	2	3	12	65,884
1954	3	A	4	4	20	4	2	16	67,577
1958	1	A	5	5	25	2	1	8	68,777
1958	3	GB	3	4	17	8	8	40	68,720
1962	1	GB	2	3	12	7	5	31	69,990
1962	3	A	4	3	18	3	4	17	42,104
1966	1	GB	1	5	13	3	4	17	57,962
1966	3	A	5	2	19	2	4	14	63,503
1970	2	GB	1	2	7	4	8	28	60,962
1970	3	GB	1	7	17	5	3	21	61,258
1974	2	GB	3	1	11	3	4†	16	48,006
1974	3	A	4	5	22	2	6	18	55,505
1979	2	A	4	6	24	2	5	16	26,387
1979	3	A	4	8	28	-	1	2	16,854
1984	1	A	4	5†	25	1	2	8	30,190
1984	3	A	3	4	20	1	2†	7	18,756
			79	106	455	81	94	431	1,549,627

ROYAL AGRICULTURAL SHOWGROUND, SYDNEY

Year	Test	Victor	AUSTRALIA T	G	P	GREAT BRITAIN T	G	P	CROWD
1910	1	GB	4	4	20	7	3	27	42,000
1914	1	GB	1	1	5	5	4	23	40,000
1920	3	GB	3	2	13	5	4	23	32,000
			8	7	38	17	11	73	114,000

SYDNEY FOOTBALL STADIUM

Year	Test	Victor	AUSTRALIA T	G	P	GREAT BRITAIN T	G	P	CROWD
1988	1	A	3	3†	17	1	1	6	24,202
1988	3	GB	2	2	12	5	3	26	15,994
1992	1	A	4	3	22	1	1	6	40,141
			9	8	51	7	5	38	80,337

BRISBANE EXHIBITION GROUND

Year	Test	Victor	AUSTRALIA T	G	P	GREAT BRITAIN T	G	P	CROWD
1910	2	GB	5	1	17	6	2	22	18,000
1920	1	A	2	1	8	-	2	4	28,000
1924	3	A	3	6	21	3	1	11	36,000
1928	1	GB	2	3	12	3	3	15	39,200
1946	2	GB	1	1	5	4	1	14	40,500
1958	2	GB	4	3	18	5	5	25	32,965
			17	15	81	21	14	91	194,665

BRISBANE CRICKET GROUND

Year	Test	Victor	AUSTRALIA			GREAT BRITAIN			CROWD
			T	G	P	T	G	P	
1932	2	A	3	3	15	2	-	6	26,574
1936	2	GB	1	2	7	2	3	12	29,486
1950	2	A	3	3	15	1	-	3	35,000
1954	2	GB	5	3	21	6	10	38	46,355
			12	11	58	11	13	59	137,415

LANG PARK, BRISBANE

Year	Test	Victor	AUSTRALIA			GREAT BRITAIN			CROWD
			T	G	P	T	G	P	
1962	2	GB	2	2	10	3	4	17	34,760
1966	2	A	-	3	6	-	2	4	45,057
1970	1	A	5	11	37	3	3	15	42,807
1974	1	A	1	5†	12	-	3	6	30,280
1979	1	A	5	10	35	-	-	0	23,051
1984	2	A	3	3	18	1	1	6	26,534
1988	2	A	6	5	34	2	3	14	27,103
1992	3	A	2	4	16	1	3	10	32,313
			24	43	168	10	19	72	261,905

PRINCES PARK, MELBOURNE

Year	Test	Victor	AUSTRALIA			GREAT BRITAIN			CROWD
			T	G	P	T	G	P	
1992	2	GB	2	1	10	5	7†	33	30,257

† Includes a one-point drop goal.
Tries scored before 1984 were worth three points. Since 1984 they have been worth four points.

ANALYSIS OF TESTS PLAYED IN AUSTRALIA

	WINS			AUSTRALIA			GREAT BRITAIN			CROWDS
	A	GB	D	T	G	P	T	G	P	
Sydney CG	15	15	1	79	106	455	81	94	431	1,549,627
RAS, Sydney	-	3	-	8	7	38	17	11	73	114,000
Sydney FS	2	1	-	9	8	51	7	5	38	80,337
Brisbane EG	2	4	-	17	15	81	21	14	91	194,665
Brisbane CG	2	2	-	12	11	58	11	13	59	137,415
Lang Park	7	1	-	24	43	168	10	19	72	261,905
Princes Park	-	1	-	2	1	10	5	7	33	30,257
TOTALS	28	27	1	151	191	861	152	163	797	2,368,206

SUMMARY OF TESTS IN GREAT BRITAIN

In contrast to the virtual monopoly of Brisbane and Sydney in staging tests in Australia, no fewer than twenty venues in a dozen towns and cities have housed tests in England and Scotland.

HEADINGLEY, LEEDS

Year	Test	Victor	GREAT BRITAIN			AUSTRALIA			CROWD
			T	G	P	T	G	P	
1921	1	GB	2	-	6	1	1	5	32,000
1929	2	GB	1	3	9	1	-	3	31,402
1933	2	GB	1	2	7	1	1	5	29,618
1937	1	GB	1	1	5	-	2	4	31,949
1948	1	GB	7	1	23	5	3	21	36,529
1952	1	GB	3	5	19	-	3	6	34,505
1959	2	GB	3	1	11	2	2	10	30,184
1963	3	GB	4	2	16	1	1	5	20,497
1967	1	GB	2	5	16	1	4	11	22,293
1973	2	A	-	3	6	1	6+	14	16,674
1978	3	A	2	-	6	4	6+	23	29,627
1982	3	A	1	3+	8	6	7	32	17,318
			27	26	132	23	36	139	332,596

STATION ROAD, SWINTON

Year	Test	Victor	GREAT BRITAIN			AUSTRALIA			CROWD
			T	G	P	T	G	P	
1930	3	DRAW	-	-	0	-	-	0	34,709
1933	3	GB	3	5	19	2	5	16	10,990
1937	2	GB	3	1	13	1	-	3	31,724
1948	2	GB	4	2	16	1	2	7	36,354
1952	2	GB	5	3	21	1	1	5	32,421
1956	3	GB	5	2	19	-	-	0	17,542
1959	1	A	2	4	14	4	5	22	35,224
1963	2	A	2	3	12	12	7	50	30,843
1967	3	A	1	-	3	3	1	11	13,615
			25	21	117	24	21	114	243,422

ODSAL STADIUM, BRADFORD

Year	Test	Victor	GREAT BRITAIN			AUSTRALIA			CROWD
			T	G	P	T	G	P	
1949	3	GB	5	4	23	3	-	9	43,500*
1952	3	A	1	2	7	5	6	27	30,509
1956	2	A	1	3	9	4	5	22	23,634
1978	2	GB	2	6	18	2	4	14	26,447
			9	15	57	14	15	72	124,090

* Some sources give this crowd as 42,000

CENTRAL PARK, WIGAN

Year	Test	Victor	GREAT BRITAIN			AUSTRALIA			CROWD
			T	G	P	T	G	P	
1956	1	GB	5	3	21	2	2	10	22,473
1959	3	GB	2	6	18	2	3	12	26,089
1978	1	A	1	3	9	2	5†	15	17,644
1982	2	A	-	3	6	5	6	27	23,216
1986	3	A	2	4†	15	4	4	24	20,169
			10	19	69	15	20	88	109,591

WEMBLEY STADIUM, LONDON

Year	Test	Victor	GREAT BRITAIN			AUSTRALIA			CROWD
			T	G	P	T	G	P	
1963	1	A	-	1	2	6	5	28	13,946
1973	1	GB	4	5†	21	2	3	12	9,874
1990	1	GB	3	4†	19	2	2	12	54,569
1994	1	GB	1	2	8	1	-	4	57,034
			8	12	50	11	10	56	135,423

OLD TRAFFORD, MANCHESTER

Year	Test	Victor	GREAT BRITAIN			AUSTRALIA			CROWD
			T	G	P	T	G	P	
1986	1	A	3	2	16	7	5	38	50,583
1990	2	A	2	1	10	3	1	14	46,615
1994	2	A	1	2	8	6	7	38	43,930
			6	5	34	16	13	90	141,128

ELLAND ROAD, LEEDS

Year	Test	Victor	GREAT BRITAIN			AUSTRALIA			CROWD
			T	G	P	T	G	P	
1986	2	A	1	-	4	6	5	34	30,808
1990	3	A	-	-	0	3	1	14	32,500
1994	3	A	-	2	4	4	4†	23	39,468
			1	2	8	13	10	71	102,776

Headingley, second test, 1959. Neil Fox scores a try. Fox amassed 61 points in only eight Ashes tests (1959-67).
Only Jim Sullivan scored more Ashes points than Fox.

No other British ground has hosted more than two tests, the remaining fifteen being divided amongst the following thirteen venues:

	Year	Test	Victor	GREAT BRITAIN			AUSTRALIA			CROWD
				T	G	P	T	G	P	
PARK ROYAL, LONDON	1908	1	DRAW	6	2	22	4	5	22	2,000
ST. JAMES' PARK, NEWCASTLE	1909	2	GB	3	3	15	1	1	5	22,000
	1911	1	A	2	2	10	5	2	19	6,500
VILLA PARK, BIRMINGHAM	1909	3	GB	2	-	6	1	1	5	9,000
	1912	3	A	2	1	8	9	3	33	4,000
TYNECASTLE PARK, EDINBURGH	1911	2	DRAW	3	1	11	3	1	11	6,000
THE BOULEVARD, HULL	1921	2	A	-	1	2	4	2	16	21,504
THE WILLOWS, SALFORD	1922	3	GB	2	-	6	-	-	0	21,000
CRAVEN PARK, HULL	1929	1	A	2	1	8	7	5	31	20,000
ATHLETIC GROUNDS, ROCHDALE	1930	4	GB	1	-	3	-	-	0	16,743
BELLE VUE, MANCHESTER	1933	1	GB	-	2	4	-	-	0	34,000
FARTOWN, HUDDERSFIELD	1937	3	A	1	-	3	3	2	13	9,093
WHITE CITY, LONDON	1967	2	A	1	4	11	3	4	17	17,445
WILDERSPOOL, WARRINGTON	1973	3	A	1	1	5	5	-	15	10,019
BOOTHFERRY PARK, HULL	1982	1	A	-	2	4	8	8	40	26,771

† Includes a one-point drop goal.

ANALYSIS OF TESTS PLAYED IN GREAT BRITAIN

	WINS			GREAT BRITAIN			AUSTRALIA			CROWDS
	GB	A	D	T	G	P	T	G	P	
Headingley	9	3	-	27	26	132	23	36	139	332,596
Swinton	5	3	1	25	21	117	24	21	114	243,422
Odsal	2	2	-	9	15	57	14	15	72	124,090
Wigan	2	3	-	10	19	69	15	20	88	109,591
Wembley	3	1	-	8	12	50	11	10	56	135,423
Old Trafford	-	3	-	6	5	34	16	13	90	141,128
Elland Road	-	3	-	1	2	8	13	10	71	102,776
Other venues	5	8	2	26	20	118	53	34	227	226,075
TOTALS	26	26	3	112	120	585	169	159	857	1,415,103

ANALYSIS OF ALL ASHES TESTS 1908-1994

	WINS			GREAT BRITAIN			AUSTRALIA			CROWDS
	GB	A	D	T	G	P	T	G	P	
In Australia	27	28	1	152	163	797	151	191	861	2,368,206
In Great Britain	26	26	3	112	120	585	169	159	857	1,415,103
TOTALS	53	54	4	264	283	1382	320	350	1718	3,783,309

CROWD AVERAGES

In Australia	42,289	(56 tests)
In Great Britain	25,729	(55 tests)
Overall	34,084	(111 tests)

BIGGEST CROWDS

In Australia	70,204	1st test, 1932, Sydney
In Great Britain	57,034	1st test, 1994, Wembley

BIGGEST AGGREGATE

In Australia	179,816	1954 series
In Great Britain	140,432	1994 series

HIGHEST SCORES

AUSTRALIA		GREAT BRITAIN	
50-12	1963 at Swinton (2nd)	40-17	1958 at Sydney (3rd)
40- 4	1982 at Hull City (1st)	38-21	1954 at Brisbane (2nd)
38- 8	1994 at Old Trafford (2nd)	33-10	1992 at Melbourne (2nd)
37-12	1954 at Sydney (1st)	31-12	1962 at Sydney (1st)
37-15	1970 at Brisbane (1st)	28- 7	1970 at Sydney (2nd)
35- 0	1979 at Brisbane (1st)	27-20	1910 at Sydney (1st)
34- 4	1986 at Elland Road (2nd)	26-12	1988 at Sydney (3rd)
34-14	1988 at Brisbane (2nd)	25-18	1958 at Brisbane (2nd)
33- 8	1912 at Birmingham (3rd)		
32- 8	1982 at Headingley (3rd)		
31- 8	1929 at Hull KR (1st)		

Note - Britain's highest score in a home test is 23 points (1st and 3rd tests 1948-49)

LOWEST TEST AGGREGATE SCORES

0	Australia 0	Great Britain 0	1930 at Swinton (3rd)
3	Australia 0	Great Britain 3	1930 at Rochdale (4th)
4	Australia 0	Great Britain 4	1933 at Belle Vue (1st)
6	Australia 0	Great Britain 6	1922 at Salford (3rd)
7	Australia 5	Great Britain 2	1950 at Sydney (3rd)

Note - Great Britain have been "nilled" three times, Australia five times.

TRY-LESS TESTS

Only three Ashes tests have ended try-less:

Australia 0	Great Britain 0	1930 at Swinton (3rd)
Australia 0	Great Britain 4	1933 at Belle Vue (1st)
Australia 6	Great Britain 4	1966 at Brisbane (2nd)

GOAL-LESS TESTS

Only three Ashes tests have not produced a goal:

Australia 0	Great Britain 6	1922 at Salford (3rd)
Australia 0	Great Britain 0	1930 at Swinton (3rd)
Australia 0	Great Britain 3	1930 at Rochdale (4th)

Note - Every Ashes test played in Australia has yielded at least one goal.

THE ENGLISH RUGBY LEAGUE FOOTBALL TEAM.
AUSTRALIAN TOUR, 1932.

L. ADAMS, B. EVANS, J. T. WOODS, G. ROBINSON, A. J. RISMAN, J. F. THOMPSON, W. A. WILLIAMS, L. L. WHITE, J. LOWE, J. FEETHAM, B. HUDSON, W. HORTON, F. A. BUTTERS, M. HODGSON, A. ATKINSON, N. SILCOCK, A. ELLABY, A. FILDES, J. WRIGHT, W. DINGSDALE, N. FENDER, S. SMITH, S. BROGDEN, I. DAVIES, J. SULLIVAN (Capt.)

WEARING "GRIPU" SHORTS
PAT. No. 320698.

PLAYERS WITH EIGHT OR MORE APPEARANCES IN ASHES TESTS
AUSTRALIA

16†	Mal Meninga	1982-94
14	Keith Holman	1950-58
13	Clive Churchill	1948-56
12	Andrew Ettingshausen	1988-94
12	Graeme Langlands	1963-74
12	Wally Prigg	1929-37
12	Tommy Raudonikis	1973-79
12	Ian Walsh	1959-66
12††	Bob Lindner	1986-92
11	Kerry Boustead	1978-84
11	Sandy Pearce	1908-21
11††	Wally Lewis	1982-88
10	Arthur Beetson	1966-74
10	Brian Carlson	1952-59
10	Bob Fulton	1970-78
10	Tom Gorman	1924-30
10	Duncan Hall	1948-54
10	Ken Kearney	1952-58
10	Ray Price	1978-84
9	Frank Burge	1914-22
9	Tedda Courtney	1908-14
9	Mick Cronin	1974-79
9	Brian Davies	1952-58
9	Graham Eadie	1973-79
9	Chook Fraser	1911-22
9	Reg Gasnier	1959-67
9	Harold Horder	1914-24
9	Ken Irvine	1962-66
9	Garry Jack	1984-88
9	Johnny King	1966-70
9	Frank McMillan	1929-33
9	Mick Madsen	1929-36
9	Kel O'Shea	1954-58
9	Johnny Raper	1959-67
9	Steve Rogers	1978-82
9	Herb Steinohrt	1928-32
9	Peter Sterling	1982-88
9†	Craig Young	1978-84
8	Vic Armbruster	1924-30
8	Les Boyd	1978-82
8	Ron Coote	1967-74
8	Laurie Daley	1990-94
8	Noel Kelly	1963-67
8	Joe Pearce	1932-36
8	Wayne Pearce	1982-88
8	Rod Reddy	1978-82
8	Kevin Schubert	1948-52
8	Eric Weissel	1928-32
8†	Brett Kenny	1982-86
8†	Paul Sironen	1990-94
8††	Glenn Lazarus	1990-94

GREAT BRITAIN

15	Jim Sullivan	1924-33
15††	Garry Schofield	1984-94
13	Mick Sullivan	1956-63
12	Martin Hodgson	1929-37
12	Martin Offiah	1988-94
12	Gus Risman	1932-46
12	Ernest Ward	1946-52
12†	Roger Millward	1967-78
11	Stan Brogden	1930-37
11	George Nicholls	1973-79
11	Alan Prescott	1952-58
11	Cliff Watson	1963-70
10	Eric Ashton	1958-63
10	Ellery Hanley	1984-90
10	Bill Horton	1928-33
10	Jonty Parkin	1920-30
10	Nat Silcock	1932-37
10†	Andy Gregory	1982-92
9	Denis Betts	1990-94
9	Billy Boston	1954-62
9	Joe Egan	1946-50
9	Alf Ellaby	1928-33
9	Ken Gee	1946-50
9	Tommy Harris	1956-59
9	Alex Murphy	1958-63
9	Steve Nash	1973-82
9	Harold Wagstaff	1911-22
9†	Daryl Powell	1990-94
8	Arthur Atkinson	1929-36
8	Billy Batten	1908-21
8	Dave Bolton	1958-63
8	Bill Burgess, Sen.	1924-30
8	Douglas Clark	1911-20
8	Lee Crooks	1982-92
8	Neil Fox	1959-67
8	Phil Jackson	1954-58
8	Brian McTigue	1958-62
8	Stan Smith	1929-33
8	Dave Valentine	1948-54
8†	Andy Platt	1986-92
8††	Karl Harrison	1990-94
8††	Kevin Ward	1986-90

† Includes one appearance as substitute †† Includes 2 appearances as substitute

TEST MATCH LONGEVITY
The longest span for playing Ashes tests is held by Great Britain's Gus Risman who played for fourteen years (1932-46). Risman appeared at full-back, centre and stand-off, skippering his country in Ashes tests in 1936, 1937 and 1946.

Players with an Ashes test span of ten years:

14	Gus Risman (GB)	1932-46
13	Billy Batten (GB)	1908-21
13	Sandy Pearce (A)	1908-21
12	Mal Meninga (A)	1982-94
11	Chook Fraser (A)	1911-22
11	Graeme Langlands (A)	1963-74
11	Roger Millward (GB)	1967-78
11	Harold Wagstaff (GB)	1911-22
10	Lee Crooks (GB)	1982-92
10	Andy Gregory (GB)	1982-92
10	Harold Horder (A)	1914-24
10	Jonty Parkin (GB)	1920-30
10	Garry Schofield (GB)	1984-94

MOST TEST MATCH SERIES
Four players have figured in six Ashes series:

Graeme Langlands (A)	1963, 1966, 1967, 1970, 1973, 1974
Mal Meninga (A)	1982, 1984, 1986, 1990, 1992, 1994
Andy Gregory (GB)	1982, 1984, 1986, 1988, 1990, 1992
Garry Schofield (GB)	1984, 1986, 1988, 1990, 1992, 1994

Five Ashes series:	Australia -	Clive Churchill
		Keith Holman
		Wally Prigg
		Johnny Raper
	Britain -	Stan Brogden
		Martin Hodgson
		Roger Millward
		Jonty Parkin
		Gus Risman
		Jim Sullivan
		Mick Sullivan

Mal Meninga played in 16 Ashes tests and scored 108 points - both are all-time records.

OLDEST PLAYERS
Syd "Sandy" Pearce (born 31 May, 1883) was 38 years 158 days old when he hooked for Australia in the second test at Hull on 5 November, 1921.
Gus Risman (born 21 March, 1911) was Great Britain's oldest Ashes player. He was 35 years 119 days old when he captained the Lions in the third test at Sydney on 20 July, 1946.

YOUNGEST PLAYERS
Great Britain centre Garry Schofield (born 1 July, 1965) is the youngest Ashes test player. He was 18 years 344 days old when he played in the first test at Sydney on 9 June, 1984.
The youngest Australian to figure in an Ashes test is believed to be winger Kerry Boustead (born 12 August 1959) who was aged 19 years 70 days when he played in the first test at Wigan on 21 October, 1978.
Lee Crooks (born 18 September, 1963) is believed to be the youngest forward to have played Ashes rugby. He was 19 years 42 days old when he played for Great Britain in the first test at Boothferry Park, Hull on 30 October, 1982.

NOTABLE SCORING FEATS
TRIES
The only man to have scored four tries in an Ashes test has been the British winger Jim Leytham who performed the feat in the second test of 1910 at Brisbane Exhibition ground.
The following players have scored three tries in an Ashes test:

AUSTRALIA		GREAT BRITAIN	
Jim Devereux	1908 (1st)	Billy Jukes	1910 (1st)
Reg Gasnier	1959 (1st)	Stan Smith	1932 (3rd)
Reg Gasnier	1963 (1st)	Arthur Bassett	1946 (2nd)
Ken Irvine	1963 (2nd)	Mick Sullivan	1958 (3rd)
Ken Irvine	1966 (3rd)		
Gene Miles	1986 (1st)		
Michael O'Connor	1986 (1st)		

** Only Ken Irvine has scored three tries on home territory (1966, Sydney).
** All the British hat-tricks have been scored in Australia and vice versa with the exception of Irvine's.
** Billy Jukes is the only forward to have scored three tries.
** Arthur Bassett scored three tries on his test debut.
** Jim Devereux and Reg Gasnier scored hat-tricks in their first Ashes tests but both had already played in test rugby against New Zealand.

MOST ASHES TRIES IN AGGREGATE

AUSTRALIA		GREAT BRITAIN	
12 Ken Irvine	1962-66	9 Billy Boston	1954-62
9 Reg Gasnier	1959-67	8 Mick Sullivan	1956-63
9 Mal Meninga	1982-94	8 Garry Schofield	1984-94
8 Brian Carlson	1952-59	6 Jim Leytham	1910
7 Ray Price	1978-84	6 Roger Millward	1967-78
6 Kerry Boustead	1978-84	6 Stan Smith	1929-33
6 Keith Holman	1950-58		
6 Johnny King	1966-70		
6 Graeme Langlands	1963-74		

MOST TRIES IN AN ASHES SERIES

6 Jim Leytham (GB)	1910 in Australia	
5 Arthur Bassett (GB)	1946 in Australia	
5 Ken Irvine (A)	1963 in Britain	
5 Reg Gasnier (A)	1963 in Britain	
5 Garry Schofield (GB)	1986 in Britain	

TRIES IN EACH TEST OF A THREE-MATCH SERIES

1908-09	Johnny Thomas (GB)	in Britain
1908-09	George Tyson (GB)	in Britain
1924	Jonty Parkin (GB)	in Australia
1958	Ike Southward (GB)	in Australia
1962	Ken Irvine (A)	in Australia
1963	Ken Irvine (A)	in Britain
1986	Garry Schofield (GB)	in Britain
1988	Sam Backo (A)	in Australia
1990	Mal Meninga (A)	in Britain

Johnny Raper is widely regarded as Australia's finest loose-forward. He played in nine Ashes tests. Here he is the "middle-man" in a tackle on Britain's captain, Bill Holliday, at Leeds in 1967.

** Irvine scored in six successive Ashes tests for Australia (1962-63).
** Thomas scored in five successive Ashes tests for Britain (1908-10).
** Backo is the only forward to have scored in each test in a series.
** Meninga is the only player to have scored a try and a goal in each match of an Ashes series, a feat he achieved in 1990.

GOALS

Only two players have kicked ten goals in an Ashes test, both feats being performed in tests in Brisbane. The first man to accomplish the deed was Great Britain full-back Lewis Jones, who landed six conversions, two penalty goals and two drop goals in the second test of 1954 at Brisbane Cricket Ground. Quarter of a century later Australian centre Mick Cronin emulated Jones in the first test of 1979 at Lang Park. Cronin bagged six penalties and four conversions.
The most goals in an Ashes test in Britain is the eight kicked by Australia's centre Mal Meninga at Boothferry Park, Hull in the first test of 1982. No British player has landed more than six goals in a home test. Only Neil Fox (at Wigan, 3rd test, 1959) and George Fairbairn (at Odsal, second test, 1978) have achieved the latter feat.

The following are the most prolific kicking performances in Ashes tests:

AUSTRALIA			GREAT BRITAIN		
10	Mick Cronin	1979 (1st)	10 Lewis Jones	1954 (2nd)	
9	Graeme Langlands	1970 (1st)	8 Eric Fraser	1958 (3rd)	
8	Noel Pidding	1954 (1st)	7 Roger Millward	1970 (2nd)	
8	Mick Cronin	1979 (3rd)	6 Neil Fox	1959 (3rd)	
8	Mal Meninga	1982 (1st)	6 John Gray	1974 (3rd)	
7	Graeme Langlands	1963 (2nd)	6 George Fairbairn	1978 (2nd)	
7	Allan McKean	1970 (3rd)	6 Paul Eastwood	1992 (2nd)	
7	Mal Meninga	1982 (3rd)	5 Jim Sullivan	1924 (1st)	
7	Rod Wishart	1994 (2nd)	5 Jim Sullivan	1933 (3rd)	
6	Noel Pidding	1952 (3rd)	5 Willie Horne	1952 (1st)	
6	Mick Cronin	1979 (2nd)	5 Eric Fraser	1958 (2nd)	
6	Mal Meninga	1982 (2nd)	5 Neil Fox	1962 (1st)	
5	Dally Messenger	1908 (1st)	5 John Woods	1979 (2nd)	
5	Eric Weissel	1929 (1st)			
5	Eric Weissel	1932 (3rd)			
5	Dave Brown	1933 (3rd)			
5	Gordon Clifford	1956 (2nd)			
5	Gordon Clifford	1958 (1st)			
5	Keith Barnes	1959 (1st)			
5	Graeme Langlands	1963 (1st)			
5	Keith Barnes	1966 (1st)			
5	Graham Eadie	1973 (2nd)			
5	Graeme Langlands	1974 (3rd)			
5	Mick Cronin	1978 (3rd)			
5	Michael O'Connor	1986 (1st)			
5	Michael O'Connor	1986 (2nd)			
5	Michael O'Connor	1988 (2nd)			

MOST ASHES GOALS IN AGGREGATE

AUSTRALIA			GREAT BRITAIN	
43 Graeme Langlands	1963-74		31 Jim Sullivan	1924-33
37 Mal Meninga	1982-94		26 Neil Fox	1959-67
36 Mick Cronin	1974-79		17 Eric Fraser	1958-59
26 Noel Pidding	1950-54		15 Lewis Jones	1954
23 Michael O'Connor	1986-88		13 Paul Eastwood	1990-92
19 Keith Barnes	1959-66		12 Roger Millward	1967-78
17 Gordon Clifford	1956-58		11 Ernest Ward	1946-52
15 Eric Weissel	1928-32		10 John Gray	1974
13 Dave Brown	1933-36		10 George Fairbairn	1978-82
13 Rod Wishart	1992-94			
10 Dally Messenger	1908-10			

MOST GOALS IN AN ASHES SERIES

24 Mick Cronin (A)	1979 in Australia
21 Mal Meninga (A)	1982 in Britain
15 Lewis Jones (GB)	1954 in Australia
15 Noel Pidding (A)	1954 in Australia
14 Michael O'Connor (A)	1986 in Britain
13 Eric Fraser (GB)	1958 in Australia
13 Graeme Langlands (A)	1963 in Britain
12 Gordon Clifford (A)	1958 in Australia
12 Neil Fox (GB)	1962 in Australia
11 Mick Cronin (A)	1978 in Britain
10 Eric Weissel (A)	1932 in Australia
10 Roger Millward (GB)	1970 in Australia
10 John Gray (GB)	1974 in Australia
10 Rod Wishart (A)	1994 in Britain

POINTS

The following are the best returns by individual players in Ashes tests:

G	T	P		
5	3	22	Michael O'Connor (A)	1986 (1st)
10	-	20	Lewis Jones (GB)	1954 (2nd)
7	2	20	Graeme Langlands (A)	1963 (2nd)
7	2	20	Roger Millward (GB)	1970 (2nd)
10	-	20	Mick Cronin (A)	1979 (1st)
8	1	19	Noel Pidding (A)	1954 (1st)
8	1	19	Mal Meninga (A)	1982 (1st)
9	-	18	Graeme Langlands (A)	1970 (1st)
6	2	18	Mick Cronin (A)	1979 (2nd)
8	-	16	Eric Fraser (GB)	1958 (3rd)
8	-	16	Mick Cronin (A)	1979 (3rd)
6	1	15	Noel Pidding (A)	1952 (3rd)
6	1	15	Neil Fox (GB)	1959 (3rd)
6	1	15	Mal Meninga (A)	1982 (2nd)

MOST ASHES POINTS IN AGGREGATE

AUSTRALIA			GREAT BRITAIN	
108 Mal Meninga	1982-94		62 Jim Sullivan	1924-33
104 Graeme Langlands	1963-74		61 Neil Fox	1959-67
78 Mick Cronin	1974-79		42 Roger Millward	1967-78
66 Michael O'Connor	1986-88		35 Garry Schofield	1984-94
61 Noel Pidding	1950-54		34 Eric Fraser	1958-59
42 Ken Irvine	1962-66		34 Paul Eastwood	1990-92
38 Keith Barnes	1959-66		30 Lewis Jones	1954
35 Dave Brown	1933-36			
34 Gordon Clifford	1956-58			
33 Eric Weissel	1928-32			
30 Brian Carlson	1952-59			
30 Rod Wishart	1992-94			

MOST POINTS IN AN ASHES SERIES

54 Mick Cronin (A)	1979 in Australia
48 Mal Meninga (A)	1982 in Britain
44 Michael O'Connor (A)	1986 in Britain
36 Noel Pidding (A)	1954 in Australia
35 Graeme Langlands (A)	1963 in Britain
30 Lewis Jones (GB)	1954 in Australia
29 Roger Millward (GB)	1970 in Australia
27 Neil Fox (GB)	1962 in Australia
26 Eric Fraser (GB)	1958 in Australia

Note - the highest haul of points by a British player in a home series is the 21 (5 tries, 1 drop goal) claimed by Garry Schofield in 1986.

DISTRIBUTION OF TRIES IN ASHES TESTS

	AUSTRALIA	GREAT BRITAIN	OVERALL
Full-backs	10 (3.1%)	4 (1.5%)	14 (2.4%)
Wingers	99 (30.9%)	105 (39.8%)	204 (34.9%)
Centres	74 (23.1%)	50 (18.9%)	124 (21.2%)
Half-backs	47 (14.7%)	41 (15.5%)	88 (15.1%)
Forwards	90 (28.1%)	64 (24.2%)	154 (26.3%)
TOTALS	320	264	584

ASHES TEST CAPTAINS

	AUSTRALIA	GREAT BRITAIN
1908-09	HH Messenger (1,2), A Burdon (3)†	TB Jenkins (1), J Lomas (2,3)
1910	HH Messenger (1), WG Heidke (2)	J Lomas (1,2)
1911-12	CH McKivat (1,2,3)	J Thomas (1), J Lomas (2,3)
1914	SP Deane (1,2,3)	H Wagstaff (1,2,3)
1920	A Johnston (1), H Gilbert (2,3)	H Wagstaff (1,2), WG Thomas (3)
1921-22	C Fraser (1,2,3)	H Wagstaff (1,3), J Parkin (2)
1924	JH Craig (1,2,3)	J Parkin (1,2,3)
1928	T Gorman (1,2,3)	J Sullivan (1,3), J Parkin (2)
1929-30	T Gorman (1,2,3,4)	LS Fairclough (1), J Parkin (2,3), J Sullivan (4)
1932	H Steinohrt (1,2,3)	J Sullivan (1,2,3)
1933	F McMillan (1,3), P Madsen (2)	J Sullivan (1,2,3)
1936	DM Brown (1,2,3)	A Atkinson (1), JW Brough (2), AJ Risman (3)
1937	WJ Prigg (1,2,3)	AJ Risman (1,2,3)
1946	J Jorgenson (1,3), R Bailey (2)	AJ Risman (1,2,3)
1948-49	WP O'Connell (1), CM Maxwell (2), IW Tyquin (3)	E Ward (1,2,3)
1950	CB Churchill (1,2,3)	E Ward (1,2,3)
1952	CB Churchill (1,2,3)	W Horne (1,2,3)
1954	CB Churchill (1,2,3)	EJ Ashcroft (1), RL Williams (2,3)
1956	KH Kearney (1,2,3)	GA Prescott (1,2,3)
1958	B Davies (1,2,3)	GA Prescott (1,2), PB Jackson (3)
1959	WK Barnes (1,2,3)	E Ashton (1), JM Stevenson (2,3)
1962	RW Gasnier (1), WK Barnes (2), AJ Summons (3)	E Ashton (1,2,3)
1963	IJ Walsh (1,2,3)	E Ashton (1,2), T Smales (3)
1966	IJ Walsh (1,2,3)	JB Edgar (1,2,3)
1967	RW Gasnier (1), PM Gallagher (2), JW Raper (3)	W Holliday (1,2,3)
1970	GF Langlands (1), JW Sattler (2), PF Hawthorne (3)	F Myler (1,2,3)
1973	GF Langlands (1), R McCarthy (2), T Raudonikis (3)	CA Sullivan (1,2,3)
1974	GF Langlands (1,3), AH Beetson (2)	C Hesketh (1,2,3)
1978	R Fulton (1,2,3)	R Millward (1,2,3)
1979	GC Peponis (1,2,3)	CD Laughton (1), G Nicholls (2,3)
1982	M Krilich (1,2,3)	S Nash (1), J Grayshon (2), D Topliss (3)
1984	WJ Lewis (1,2,3)	BD Noble (1,2,3)
1986	WJ Lewis (1,2,3)	D Watkinson (1,2,3)
1988	WJ Lewis (1,2,3)	EC Hanley (1,2,3)
1990	MN Meninga (1,2,3)	EC Hanley (1,2,3)
1992	MN Meninga (1,2,3)	GE Schofield (1,2,3)
1994	MN Meninga (1,2,3)	S Edwards (1,3), P Clarke (2)

† Some British sources indicate that SP Deane captained Australia in the third test of the 1908-09 series.

** Thirty-nine men have captained Australia whilst Great Britain's captains number 37.

** Four players share the record for Ashes captaincies (9 tests) in Jim Sullivan (Great Britain), Clive Churchill, Wally Lewis and Mal Meninga (Australia).

** Fourteen forwards have captained Australia and ten have captained Great Britain.

** Ellery Hanley (Great Britain) is the only man to have captained Ashes test teams as both a back and a forward.

** Herb Steinohrt was the first Australian forward to lead an Ashes test team (1932) whilst Alan Prescott (1956) was the first Briton.

SENDINGS OFF

A total of 37 players have been dismissed from the field during 111 Ashes tests - 22 Britons and 15 Australians. In chronological order they were:

Year	Test	Year		Test	
1910	2	George Ruddick (GB)	1963	3	Cliff Watson (GB)
1920	3	Bill Richards (A)	1963	3	Brian Hambly (A)
1924	1	Norm Potter (A)	1963	3	Barry Muir (A)
1924	3	Jim Bennett (A)	1966	2	Bill Ramsey (GB)
1924	3	Frank Gallagher (GB)	1966	3	Cliff Watson (GB)
1928	3	Bill Horton (GB)	1967	1	Dennis Manteit (A)
1936	1	Ray Stehr (A)	1967	3	Noel Kelly (A)
1936	1	Nat Silcock (GB)	1970	2	Syd Hynes (GB)
1936	3	Ray Stehr (A)	1970	3	Arthur Beetson (A)
1936	3	Jack Arkwright (GB)	1973	2	Brian Lockwood (GB)
1946	1	Jack Kitching (GB)	1978	1	Steve Nash (GB)
1946	2	Joe Egan (GB)	1978	1	Tommy Raudonikis (A)
1946	3	Arthur Clues (A)	1979	1	Trevor Skerrett (GB)
1950	2	Ken Gee (GB)	1979	3	Steve Norton (GB)
1950	2	Tommy Bradshaw (GB)	1982	2	Les Boyd (A)
1952	3	"Duncan" Hall (A)	1982	3	Lee Crooks (GB)
1962	3	Mick Sullivan (GB)	1984	1	David Hobbs (GB)
1962	3	Derek Turner (GB)	1994	1	Shaun Edwards (GB)
1962	3	Dud Beattie (A)			

** 1st test dismissals	10 (4A, 6GB)	
** 2nd test dismissals	8 (1A, 7GB)	
** 3rd test dismissals	19 (10 A, 9GB)	

** Dismissals in Australia	25 (8A, 17GB)	
** Dismissals in Britain	12 (7A, 5GB)	

** Most dismissals in a series 4 (1936)
** Most dismissals in a test   3 (3rd test, 1962 and 3rd test, 1963)

** Only eight dismissals have been backs - Kitching, Bradshaw, Sullivan, Muir, Hynes, Nash, Raudonikis and Edwards.

** Ray Stehr is the only man to have been sent off twice in a series (1936). Cliff Watson is the only other man to have marched twice but his sendings off occurred in separate series (1963 and 1966).

** Fifteen players had been dismissed in Ashes tests in Australia before the first sending off occurred in Britain when "Duncan" Hall, the Kangaroo prop, incurred the ultimate sanction in the notorious "Battle of Odsal" third test of 1952.

** First Briton to be sent off on home soil was Cliff Watson (1963).

** The only captain to be sent off in an Ashes test is Shaun Edwards.

REFEREES

** Tom McMahon (NSW) refereed in most Ashes tests. He controlled eight tests over four series (1910, 1914, 1920, 1924). His son, Tom McMahon, Jun., also refereed three Ashes tests (1946,1950).

** Darcy Lawler (NSW) refereed seven tests (1954, 1958, 1962) whilst Bob Robinson (Bradford) holds the British record with six tests in a record eighteen year span (1912-30).

** Lal Deane (NSW) sent off a record six players in five tests (1928-36).

** The only man to have played and refereed in Ashes tests is the remarkable George Bishop, the Balmain hooker, who figured in the first and second tests of 1929. In 1950 he refereed the first test at Sydney. In his debut as a test player Bishop became the first hooker to score in an Ashes test and to complete his rugby education he eventually became an Australian test selector.

** The first neutral Ashes referee was Julien Rascagneres (France) who controlled all three tests in 1982. He also controlled the three tests of 1986.

** The first neutral referee to officiate in an Ashes test in Australia was the New Zealander, Ray Shrimpton, who took the first and second tests of 1984.

** The first Australian referee to control an Ashes test in Britain was Graham Annesley who had charge of the first and second tests of 1994 at Wembley and Old Trafford. As yet no British referee has officiated in an Ashes test in Australia.

STILL AVAILABLE FROM THE AUTHOR OF "THE STRUGGLE FOR THE ASHES II"

"GONE NORTH: WELSHMEN IN RUGBY LEAGUE" (Volume 1)
184 pages, fully illustrated. Price £6.50 - The story of Wales' greatest Rugby League players. This volume features, amongst others, Billy Boston, Wattie Davies, Trevor Foster, Roy Francis, Jim Sullivan, Jim Mills, Tommy Harris, Emlyn Jenkins, John Mantle, Colin Dixon, Kel Coslett
An unusual and compelling history - Paul Fitzpatrick, *The Guardian*
A thoroughly readable book - John Kennedy, *South Wales Echo*
Compelling reading for followers of both codes - Raymond Fletcher, *Yorkshire Post*

"GONE NORTH: WELSHMEN IN RUGBY LEAGUE" (Volume 2)
182 pages, fully illustrated. Price £9.99 - More great Welsh Rugby League players including Gus Risman, Johnny Freeman, Garfield Owen, Lewis Jones, Clive Sullivan, Johnny Ring, Ben Gronow, David Watkins, Maurice Richards, Alan Edwards, Joe Thompson, Danny Hurcombe, Johnny Rogers
Scrupulously researched, incisively perceptive and admirably readable - Huw Richards, *City Limits*
Once taken up I could not put it down - Ray French, *Rugby Leaguer*
Overflowing with superlatives - Trevor Delaney, *Code 13*

NOTE: Both volumes of *Gone North* may be obtained for £13.50 the pair (post free)

"THE STRUGGLE FOR THE ASHES"
208 pages, fully illustrated. Price £8.00 - The first edition of the book you are reading now.
Published in 1986, *The Struggle For The Ashes* covers Anglo-Australian test matches from 1908 to 1984. The illustrative material is completely different to *The Struggle For The Ashes II*.
Not only a statistician's dream but a darned good read - Brian Smith, *Telegraph & Argus*
Quite simply the best book on Rugby League, ever - Louis Kasatkin, *Leeds Other Paper*
One of the game's most ambitious writing projects has turned out a winner - David Middleton, *Rugby League Week*
If points are awarded for this book, Mr. Gate scores ten out of ten - John Billot, *The Western Mail*

"CHAMPIONS: A CELEBRATION OF THE RUGBY LEAGUE CHAMPIONSHIP 1895-1987"
192 pages, fully illustrated. Price £12.00 - A pictorial and statistical record of Rugby League's most important competition featuring all Rugby League's champion teams.
Nostalgia drips from the pages - Harry Edgar, *Open Rugby*
The photographs alone were worth the price - Ray French, *Rugby Leaguer*
Deserves a place on the bookshelf of anyone with an eye for the history of the game - Phil Lyon, *Halifax Evening Courier*

"THERE WERE A LOT MORE THAN THAT: ODSAL 1954"
120 pages, fully illustrated. Price £11.95 - The story of Rugby League's most epic occasion - the 1954 Challenge Cup Final Replay between Halifax and Warrington which attracted the largest ever crowd for a Rugby League match. Over 100 eye-witness accounts bring a never-to-be-forgotten sporting landmark vividly to life.
A great story waiting to be told - Dave Hadfield, *The Independent*
A vital compilation of previously unearthed material - Harry Edgar, *Open Rugby*
The author's passion for Rugby League shines through brightly as does his writing talent - Mike Gardner, *North-West Evening Mail*

ALSO BY THE AUTHOR IN ASSOCIATION WITH MICHAEL LATHAM

"THEY PLAYED FOR WIGAN"
78 pages, fully illustrated. Price £5.99 - a complete statistical record of all the players who have appeared in the cherry and white of Wigan between 1895 and 1992.

All the above books are available post free from
   Robert Gate,
   Mount Pleasant Cottage, Ripponden Bank, Ripponden, Sowerby Bridge, HX6 4JL
   Please make cheques payable to RE Gate

SUPER VALUE BOOKS FROM TREVOR DELANEY

"THE INTERNATIONAL GROUNDS OF RUGBY LEAGUE" (published 1995) Price £12.95
Covers every stadium in the world where international matches have been staged. A superb book.

"RUGBY DISUNION - BROKEN TIME" (published 1993) Price £3.95
The first of a two part work on the background to Rugby's Great Schism of 1895. A scholarly insight into the conflict between amateurism and professionalism in late Victorian Rugby.

"CODE 13" - a quarterly magazine covering all aspects of Rugby League heritage which ran to 17 issues. All except numbers 4, 5 and 10 are still available at 75 pence each.

All the above can be obtained post free (United Kingdom only) from
    Trevor Delaney,
    6, Elmwood Terrace, Ingrow, Keighley BD22 7DP
Cheques should be made payable to TR Delaney.

BOOKS FROM MIKE RL PUBLICATIONS

"THEY PLAYED FOR LEIGH" (published 1991) Price £4.95
A statistical and pictorial study of the Leigh club's players' records and achievements (1895-1991)

"THE RUGBY LEAGUE MYTH" (published 1993) Price £8.99
The forgotten clubs of Lancashire, Cheshire and Furness. A different slant on the Great Rugby Schism of 1895. Histories of 19 Lancashire Second Competition clubs (1897-1901)

"LEIGH RUGBY LEAGUE CLUB: A COMPREHENSIVE RECORD 1895-1994" (published 1994)
Price £11.95
One of the most comprehensive club histories ever produced. A marvellous database and pictorial record of one of Rugby League's oldest clubs.

"BUFF BERRY AND THE MIGHTY BONGERS" (published 1995) Price £9.95
The story of John *Buff* Berry, one of the most celebrated players of the late Victorian era. Berry, a flawed genius, enjoyed a brilliant but controversial career with Kendal Hornets and Tyldesley.

Copies are available post free from
    Mike RL Publications, 28, Windermere Drive, Adlington, Chorley PR6 9PD
Cheques should be made payable to Mike RL Publications

BOOKS FROM LONDON LEAGUE PUBLICATIONS LTD

"THE SIN BIN" (published October, 1996) Price £5.00
A collection of Rugby League cartoons and humour. Caricatures of League personalities. The adventures of Mo. The flatcappers. Bath v Wigan. League life down South.

"I WOULDN'T START FROM HERE" (published April, 1996) Price £5.00
A travelling supporters' guide to British Rugby League grounds. Includes details of ground facilities, price discounts, road directions and public transport information.

"TOUCH AND GO" (published August, 1995) Price £9.00
A history of professional Rugby League in London. Wonderful value - 380 pages, profusely illustrated.

Postage: 1 book 50p, 2 books £1.00, all 3 post free.
Please make cheques payable to London League Publications Ltd and send to:
    London League Publications Ltd, PO Box 10441, London E14 0SB

Wigan, first test, 1956

KEY TO COVER ILLUSTRATIONS

Front Cover
Top (left to right): Dally Messenger, Garry Schofield, Roger Millward, Billy Batten.
Bottom (left to right): Reg Gasnier, Wally Lewis.

Back Cover
Top: Martin Hodgson and Wally Prigg, 1936.
Bottom: Ken Irvine and Billy Boston, 1962.

Illustrations by Stuart Smith